"Glen Gilmore sta   l   s the   th   edia law. *Social Media Law for Busin*   )   e a   ty   ne   ders and digital marketers."

— ..rk Schaefer, bestselling author of *Return on Influence*

"As an instructor of digital marketing at Rutgers Business School, Glen has crafted and presented instruction on a wide variety of topics for our executive education department, from modules on social media law, crisis communications, and even on the intricacies of compliance in the integration of emerging technologies and social platforms. As an attorney and marketer, Glen brings a unique perspective on the need to balance marketing and compliance for business success. He can be counted on to know the latest trends, issues, and strategies to help businesses leverage social media and technology for optimal success. Glen's book on social medial law should become not only required reading in the classroom, but also in the boardroom—and in any business where people care about getting social media marketing right."

—Peter Methot, managing director of executive education at Rutgers Business School

"*Social Media Law for Business* is a layperson's blueprint for minimizing the legal risks of social media marketing, while maximizing the opportunities for digital marketing success. In It, Glen Gilmore, a recognized problem-solver and leader in the social media marketing space, helps people understand that business success in digital marketing requires more than business and advertising sense—it requires knowing how to avoid the legal land mines that others have tripped on. In easy-to-understand language, Gilmore's book equips businesses and business leaders to step more confidently onto the social media stage, by tapping into techniques used by some of the best brands to excel in digital marketing while minimizing their legal and brand reputation risks."

—Amy Howell, founder of Howell Marketing Strategies and coauthor of *Women in High Gear*

"If you're going to sell through social media—and you should—you need to have a command of the do's and don'ts that'll get you in trouble if you get them wrong. *Social Media Law for Business* is written in layman's terms so that everyone can understand the basics of getting things right!"

—Ryan T. Sauers, founder of Sauers Consulting and author of
Everyone Is in SALES

"*Social Media Law for Business* should be a ready companion for anyone using social media for business, as compliance issues should be top of mind at all times."

—Ann Tran, a Forbes Top 20 Women Social Media Influencer,
social media consultant, and contributor to the Huffington Post

SOCIAL MEDIA LAW
FOR
BUSINESS

A Practical Guide for
Using Facebook, Twitter, Google +,
and Blogs Without Stepping on
Legal Land Mines

GLEN GILMORE, ESQ.

Mc
Graw
Hill
Education

New York   Chicago   San Francisco   Athens   London
Madrid   Mexico City   Milan   New Delhi
Singapore   Sydney   Toronto

To my wife, Rosa, who always gives me inspiration
and a reason to smile.
And to our Ariana, who brings us great joy!

1 2 3 4 5 6 7 8 9 0   DOC/DOC   1 2 0 9 8 7 6 5 4

ISBN   978-0-07-179960-7
MHID   0-07-179960-5

e-ISBN   978-0-07-179961-4
e-MHID   0-07-179961-3

This publication is designed to provide accurate and authoritative information in regard to the subject matter covered. It is sold with the understanding that neither the author nor the publisher is engaged in rendering legal, accounting, securities trading, or other professional services. If legal advice or other expert assistance is required, the services of a competent professional person should be sought.
    —*From a Declaration of Principles Jointly Adopted by a Committee of the*
    American Bar Association and a Committee of Publishers and Associations

Library of Congress Cataloging-in-Publication Data

Gilmore, Glen.
  Social media law for business : a practical guide for using Facebook, Twitter, Google+, and blogs without stepping on legal land mines / by Glen Gilmore.
    pages cm
  ISBN 978-0-07-179960-7 (alk. paper) — ISBN 0-07-179960-5 (alk. paper) 1. Social media—Law and legislation—United States. I. Title.
  KF390.5.C6G55 2014
  343.7309'944—dc23

                                                                    2014027211

Contents

CONTENTS

Acknowledgments

To:

My dear friend Mark W. Schaefer, who was kind enough to suggest the idea for this book after hearing me speak on the topic in New York. He connected me with his publisher at McGraw-Hill to make it happen.

McGraw-Hill. Thank you for your patience and trust! Casey Ebro, my editor, and her predecessors, Casie Vogel and Stephanie Frerich, for allowing me the time to wade through these waters. Dannalie Diaz for helping me across the finish line. And additional McGraw-Hill team member Peter McCurdy, and Harleen Chopra (Cenveo Publisher Services).

Amy Howell, from Memphis, and Anne Deeter Gallagher, from Harrisburg, two women in high gear. Both founded their own marketing firms, and both, independently, invited me to be their special social media consultant. They helped make my transition from law and government to marketing and social media an adventure with great rewards!

Rutgers University. Again, my friend from Twitter, Mark Schaefer, made the introduction for me to the staff of the Rutgers University Center for Business Development. As a result, for the last several years, I have had the great privilege and pleasure of teaching there. The support I have received there, beginning with that from Eric Greenburg and Jackie Scott, and now from Peter Methot and Emily Rodriguez, has truly made teaching there a dream come true. (Rutgers is my undergraduate alma mater!)

My old law firm of Stark and Stark, where friendships run deep. The Honorable Judge Thomas Dilts, Judge of the New Jersey Superior Court (Rtd.), for having taught me much as his law clerk. The Honorable New Jersey Assemblyman Joseph D. Patero (Rtd.), who taught me that the law is always about people.

ACKNOWLEDGMENTS

Mom and Dad, who always encouraged and helped me in my love of learning. A special thanks, too, to my older brother, Brian, who gave me some lasting lessons in writing while I was a kid.

And, to the many, many people who contributed to this book through their time and insights. Due to the expansiveness of the subject and the length constraints of the book, some contributions could not be included, but I deeply appreciate the time and courtesies given by all:

Richard Cleland, Assistant Director, Advertising Practices, Bureau of Consumer Protection at the FTC

Price Floyd, @PriceFloyd, previously with DoD and BAE Systems, now with Blue Engine Media

Devon Eyer, @DevonEyer, Social Media Director at Johnson & Johnson

Ryan M. Garcia, @SoMeDellLawyer, Social Media Lawyer for Dell and Professor of Law & Social Media at University of Texas School of Law

Jessica Giglio, @savvybostonian, Social Media Manager at Dunkin' Brands

Scott Monty, @ScottMonty, former head of Ford Social Media

Marc Monseau, @MDMonseau, Managing Partner at Mint Collective, LLC, and former Director of Corporate Communications, Social Media, Johnson & Johnson

Esta H. Singer, @sheconsulting, virtual assistant

Meg Towner, @MegTowner, Community Manager at 1000heads and former Social Media Manager at the Waldorf Astoria

Ann Tran, @AnnTran_, travel expert and social media consultant

My apologies to anyone I may have missed. Please tweet me, @GlenGilmore or e-mail me, GlenGilmore@GlenGilmore.com, or message me at LinkedIn with the oversight, and I will be glad to make amends!
Thank you!

Introduction

WHAT IS SOCIAL MEDIA LAW, AND WHY DOES IT MATTER TO MY BUSINESS, MY MARKETING, AND MY CAREER?

Why read a book about social media law if you're not a lawyer? Survival. Personal and business success.

Social media is pervasive. You and your business are part of the social media conversation even if you personally are not. What does that mean? It means that you and your business are being talked about somewhere by someone on a social network. Count on it. Social media is a business imperative: it must be used to keep up with the competition, whether it's others in your industry or others vying for the same job you're aspiring to achieve. You will be using social media constantly in your personal and professional life, as it has become the place where most online conversations, networking, and marketing take place. It's much more than LinkedIn. Knowing how to spot legal land mines in social media will help keep you from derailing your own career and business goals; it will also help keep you ahead of your competition.

Social media missteps are not just the province of college students posting ill-advised pictures to their Facebook wall. Social media missteps have ensnared some of the world's leading brands, savvy marketers, the biggest nonprofits, small businesses, and smart individuals, caught by a misunderstanding or lack of awareness of some legal principles governing the social media sphere. Investing a little time in learning some key social media law principles should pay a life-long dividend.

Importantly, this book is not a substitute for legal counsel and it is not legal advice: it is, instead, an overview of social media legal and regulatory issues that business leaders, marketers, and individuals must understand to avoid some of the legal land mines that have already damaged careers and businesses.

The case studies discussed here are real. The lessons learned the hard way by others should prevent you and your business or organization from repeating them. If you're a small business, you won't have the luxury of tapping into a legal department to answer your questions or to brief you on the subject. If you work for a larger enterprise, having a grasp of key legal and regulatory issues relating to social media marketing will help you to lead your business in a more effective and efficient way and to know better when to tap your attorneys for additional advice.

Celebrities may help us understand the impact of social media senselessness quickly. Unfortunately, for marketers and business leaders, there is usually just one chance to get it right. A single mistweet (yes, a misdirected or misspoken message on Twitter) or misposting on LinkedIn can, in fact, get you or your organization in serious trouble with the FTC (Federal Trade Commission), or the FDA (Food and Drug Administration), or the SEC (Securities and Exchange Commission), or your state attorney general, or even the EU (European Union). (Though this book will focus primarily on social media law from a U.S. perspective, it will also share significant insights relating to international law, given the unavoidability of such issues when sharing content globally on the Internet.) Or it may simply get you in trouble with your boss.

"But I'm not using Twitter or Facebook or LinkedIn for anything crazy, just some business development."

Well, that's all it takes to make a social media law–related misstep that could cost you your career or damage a business you've worked very hard to set up.

Thanks to the advent of smartphones, most of us are connected to the web nearly all the time. The flow of conversation is in real time and is usually broadcast to thousands. More than a third of smartphone users begin their day by grabbing their smartphone and checking into a social network. They do the same at night.

Whether we are attending a meeting, enjoying a sporting event, or watching our favorite television show, there is a good chance we are still on the web, still messaging in social networks, on our tablets or on our smartphones. When we check into our favorite restaurant or watering hole, we are just as likely to check into Foursquare or Yelp at the same time. The consequence of all this is that we are creating a vast database about what we do and what we think. Are you ready for your social media background check? It's likely already under way.

You as an individual have a personal brand, and prospective employers, college recruiters, your current employer, your competition, regulators, and many others are listening both to what you are saying and sharing today and to the echoes of what you have said and posted long ago. Now is the time for you to figure out what you can do to leave a good digital imprint and stay on the right side of the law when you are working to advance your business and career.

Although I am an attorney by profession, I'm going to do my best to share some important best practices and insights without the usual lawyer legalese. I want the small businessperson, the Madison Avenue ad agent, and the HR director to be able to read this book and come away with new knowledge on how to spot social media legal and compliance issues that others would stumble over.

The advice I will be sharing in this book comes not only from constantly studying the subject of social media and the law, as an attorney and social media strategist, but from working in the trenches with small businesses, large organizations, and individuals determined to tap into the power of social media. Not only do I teach digital marketing and social media law at a leading university, Rutgers, I also work in a hands-on capacity with companies and individuals struggling to understand how to use social media for marketing in powerful, yet legally compliant, ways. That work has included establishing and managing social media accounts, creating and curating content, connecting with influencers, and, most importantly, building engaged communities.

The work I do in social media has brought me to different parts of the world and into the boardrooms and offices of some of the most dynamic businesses and organizations anywhere. The good news? There's plenty of opportunity for us all to do better. By making the commitment to come to grips with some of the core legal principles affecting the limits and language of social media, you will be able to do much better for your career and your business through your social media participation and leadership.

Knowing the basics of social media law is no longer something that only attorneys need to worry about: it is a personal and business essential. Knowing your social media rights and responsibilities is crucial to you and your business's success over the long haul. This book will explore some of the best practices that should help you navigate new media with greater confidence.

Finally, even with the best social media practices in place, social media crises will occur. Some will be small. Others may be big and threaten your career or your very business or organization. This book will also explore how to prepare for the social media crisis that will invariably arrive when you least expect it, and we will examine how to respond to it when it does.

Before we begin our journey into the jungles of social media law, however, may I suggest you pause for a moment; grab a cup of coffee or tea; check your e-mails, Facebook, and Twitter; and connect with me on:

- **My Blogs.** SocialMediaVoice.com and SocialMediaLawToday.com

- **Twitter.** @GlenGilmore, @GlenGilmoreEsq, @SocialMediaLaw1, @HealthcareSMM, @FinancialSM, @CrisisSocMedia, @NYSocialMedia, @EUSocialMedia, @UKSocialMedia

- **Facebook.** https://www.facebook.com/SocialMediaLaw

- **G+.** https://plus.google.com/+GlenGilmore

- **Instagram.** http://instagram.com/glengilmore

- **LinkedIn.** http://www.linkedin.com/in/glendgilmore

- **Pinterest.** http://www.pinterest.com/glengilmore

- **YouTube.** https://www.youtube.com/user/GlenGilmoreEsq

And yes, I do have a website: SocialMediaLawForBusiness.com. Thanks! Happy reading!

1

How to Write a Social Media Policy . . . Without Stepping on Legal Land Mines

Consider the legal land mines below:

- You don't have a social media policy. As a consequence, when your employees do something ill-advised online, it is unlikely that you are going to be able to convince anyone that your enterprise exercised a duty of reasonable care that should insulate it from the social misdeeds of wayward employees. The legal liabilities may also well pale in comparison to the damage done to your brand.

- You do have a social media policy, but it is one, like most, that violates the law, as it ignores the parameters set by the National Labor Relations Board (NLRB or Board).

- Your policy tells your employees: "Be respectful." "Don't release confidential information."

- You do have a social media policy, but it is does not include the FTC guidance concerning "material connections."

- The attorney who drafted your social media policy doesn't realize that a body of law has emerged along with social media, so the preceding regulatory issues were still missed.

- You have two versions of your social media policy: one, short and sweet, in "plain language"; the other longer and in "legalese"—and you don't mention in your plain-language version that there are details in your longer version that must also be read.

- You neglected to include any reference to your existing company policies and guidelines.

- You have some really bright, social media–savvy employees who have done a splendid job building a big, engaged community for your social media accounts . . . but you have never established who actually owns your branded accounts.

- You've put together the perfect social media policy, but you forgot to brief your temps, interns, or volunteers about the policy, and they decide to share a "funny" patient or client story online.

SOME OF THE BIGGEST BRANDS BLOW IT WHEN IT COMES TO WRITING SOCIAL MEDIA POLICIES

Target. General Motors. DISH Network. They are big brands with bright attorneys. Yet they have all managed to run afoul of federal law in the construction of their social media policies, at least by the assessment of one federal regulatory authority, the NLRB, which is tasked with policing the National Labor Relations Act (NLRA or Act) and unlawful labor practices. (We'll be learning more about the NLRB and NLRA later in the chapter.)

How could the big shots have messed up in writing a social media policy?

Well, let's say for a moment that we decided to play it safe and come up with a really simple, "safe" social media policy. For example:

Social Media Policy

1. Be respectful.

2. Don't release confidential information.

3. Don't pick fights.

4. Communicate in a professional tone.

5. Be fair and courteous.

Now that looks harmless enough. Might not be the most elaborate policy, but it should do the job.

Do we need to go any further?

Well, believe it or not, under NLRB guidance, all five provisions, as written, would likely be ruled unlawful in a legal dispute.

REGULATORY REVIEWS SHOULD PROMPT SOCIAL MEDIA POLICY REVIEWS

An important point to understand is that before the NLRB reviewed and found unlawful various social media policies, providing its reasoning in applying the law to invalidate various policy provisions, what had previously appeared to be perfectly reasonable provisions are now no longer reasonable as they are no longer lawful—and we now *know* this to be the case, having the benefit of the Board's decision.

Even among some larger businesses and nonprofits that have become pretty adept at using the tools and platforms of social media marketing, there is still a reluctance to include social media within the customary budgetary and compliance business plan. They believe that if they haven't had any problems yet, they won't have any in the future. This is a mistake.

THE NATIONAL LABOR RELATIONS ACT SMASHES ASIDE MOST SOCIAL MEDIA POLICIES

I'd say that most businesses' social media policies, as written, would not withstand NLRA scrutiny. To help you understand why I believe this to be the case, we'll take a close look at some of the findings of the Board in its review of social media policy provisions that it has found to be "unlawful" in real-world policies.

Before we do this, however, we will touch on some social media policy issues from a broader perspective.

SOCIAL MEDIA POLICIES: ONE SIZE DOES *NOT* FIT ALL

When it comes to social media policies, please keep in mind that one size does not fit all. Not surprisingly, when the time comes that an enterprise finally gets around to deciding to write a social media policy, there is generally a scramble to locate one online.

A second word of caution: While there are certainly plenty of good social media policy examples online, there are also many that are bad. By "bad," I mean social media policies that get the law wrong. Some of these policies that stray from the law belong to companies with familiar names. These policies are ticking bombs.

Writing a social media policy is not something that can come from a cookie cutter. You need to consider your business, your business model, your industry, your employees, and any regulatory guidance that may be specific to your field of business. You can venture forward once you've considered these factors.

MORE THAN 50 PERCENT OF BUSINESSES DO NOT HAVE A SOCIAL MEDIA POLICY—AND NEARLY HALF REPORT EMPLOYEE MISUSE OF SOCIAL MEDIA

A 2011 survey of public and private companies conducted by Grant Thornton and the Financial Executives Research Foundation, Inc., found that 76 percent of respondent companies did not have a clearly defined social media policy.

An additional 2011 study by the Proskauer International Labor & Employment Group, a study of 120 multinational employers, found that nearly half of all the companies surveyed that were using social media did not have social networking policies in place, despite the fact that 43 percent of the respondents reported employee misuse of social networks. According to this survey, a staggering one-third of the businesses had also taken disciplinary action against employees in connection with their misuse of social networks.

BEWARE THE "SOCIAL MEDIA LAWYER" WHO ISN'T "SOCIAL"

"Your social media policy should prohibit any disparagement of the company," an attorney from a prominent law firm wrote in an article appearing in a regional business magazine on the subject of how to write a social media policy.

"Splendid! That's exactly how I'd like our social media policy to start," I could hear scores of business executives shout. The only problem? That recommendation, if adopted, would be a violation of the law.

"Wait. I thought you said it was an attorney who wrote the article?"

I did—and he got the law dead wrong.

The issue he missed is not a subtle point. It has been the subject of over a hundred regulatory reviews in a single year.

So how could an attorney have missed an issue that has played out so prominently within the social media space? Well, a few minutes of online sleuthing showed that he had very little personal experience with social media.

Don't get me wrong. The lawyer had been on Twitter for about year . . . and had tweeted . . . a handful of times. A blog? Nope. LinkedIn? Yes, but only partially completed.

"Are you suggesting that an attorney must tweet and blog to understand social media law?"

No, but both would help. This goes, by the way, to the question of how someone who is not an attorney and who does not have access to a legal department can possibly stay on top of the law regarding social media. Fortunately, the social media community itself is pretty good at sharing information on developments regarding the law and social media, leaving some nonlawyers better versed on the subject than some lawyers.

I am not suggesting for a moment that you should forgo legal advice when questions of law arise. I am, however, recognizing that many small businesses have very limited resources and should understand that by being "social" and listening in "social," many of the biggest law-related social media land mines will be flagged with frequency by the social media community itself. One will learn much about the state of social media law simply by being social, just as even a lawyer will miss much by not.

NLRB SPOTLIGHTS SIX MAJOR BRANDS FOR GETTING THEIR SOCIAL MEDIA POLICIES WRONG—AND *ONE* FOR GETTING ITS RIGHT!

In May 2012, the acting general counsel for the NLRB, Lafe E. Solomon, issued the Board's third report on social media cases involving the agency. This report, for the first time, focused entirely on the legality and illegality of social media policy provisions governing the use of social media by employees. Reviewing seven policies, the Board's acting general counsel concluded that six of them contained unlawful provisions, while the seventh policy, belonging to mega-retailer Walmart, was attached to the report with a statement that "the entire policy was found to be lawful."

In announcing the report, the Board noted that social media policies "are found to be unlawful when they interfere with the rights of employees under the National Labor Relations Act, such as the right to discuss wages and working conditions with co-workers."

With this general proposition in mind, we will look at the process of putting together a social media policy and then the task of choosing the right words and provisions, using the Board's social media policy report as a guidepost.

SEVEN STEPS TO ESTABLISHING A SOCIAL MEDIA POLICY

STEP 1: Establish a Social Media Team

Establishing a social media policy should be a team effort, even if one person, preferably an attorney, is initially tasked with putting a draft document together. The goal of a social media policy should be to empower employees to be social in an efficient and compliant manner, aligned with your organization's strategic objectives.

Who Should Be on Your Social Media Team?
The structure of your social media team will depend on the size and structure of your organization. The team, however, should be a cross section of your enterprise, bringing together as many stakeholders as possible. Assuming a medium-sized business, members of your team should include representatives from:

- C-suite
- Legal/Compliance
- Marketing
- Customer Service
- HR
- IT
- Research and Development
- Other stakeholders

When you think "social," you should consider all aspects of your enterprise, from recruitment and retention, to customer service and product development. Your social media team should reflect this broad perspective. It is also beneficial to overcome the "silo" mentality that often impedes organizations from having a vibrant social media presence due to territorial battles that drag every initiative in the social space. Bringing everyone together from the beginning will help your enterprise craft a social media policy that best reflects the realities of your organization's resources and objectives.

Embedding Social

Your social media team should strive to embed "social" within your organization's corporate culture. It is a commitment to creating a compliance and guidance framework that is user-friendly, empowers employees to be social, and fosters a sense that "social" will truly be a collaborative effort within your organization. It means embracing a sense of collective and continuing education and shared responsibility about social media best practices.

Allocation of Resources

As you begin to hammer out a policy, you should also be considering how the tasks that are being defined are going to be managed. Successful social media engagement is labor intensive and comes with a serious learning curve. The drafting of a social media policy should get your organization to consider resource and budgetary planning. This is about time, talent, and training.

STEP 2: Define Your Social Media Objectives, Aligning Business and Social

Social media for business is ultimately about business. There are obvious benefits from being social that go far beyond the balance books, such as creating an engaged online community and converting customers to brand advocates, but business development, brand promotion, and customer retention should certainly be part of the equation. As you identify the business objectives to being social, you should also consider how your social media policy should address and forward these objectives.

For example, if improving customer service is one of your goals, as it should be, then somewhere in your policy you will need to address how you will monitor and respond to brand mentions. This might include identifying the people who will do the listening and the time parameters for responding to inquiries.

If crisis prevention, preparedness, and management constitute another incentive for your venturing into social, you should flesh out this objective by identifying the framework within your policy.

STEP 3: Write Your Plan

It is a rare thing to have a regulatory agency provide a framework for a key business document. In this case, however, the NLRB, which has proactively reviewed and found scores of social media policies to be unlawful, has examined a social media policy from a major retailer and declared "the entire social media policy" to be "lawful under the (National Labor Relations) Act." Since the NLRB is the regulatory authority most likely to deem your social media *policy* unlawful, the policy it has hailed as a model of correctness might be a good place to start the process of writing your plan. We'll talk shortly about the additional provisions your enterprise might need to add to the sample policy in order to lessen your social media legal risks.

STEP 4: Invite Employees, Stakeholders, and Customers to Comment on Your Policy

Letting your employees and customers comment on your social media policy may seem daunting to some, but if there is a problem with your policy, best to get it addressed early on. As transparency is a core principle of being social, you should begin with having the guts to let others review and comment on your social media policy. It does raise the stakes a bit for the launch of your policy, but share it with a recognition that it does need to be a "living" document and that it will need to be refined on a regular basis as best practices, social networks, and technologies continue to evolve.

STEP 5: Hone Your Policy

You wrote your policy. You invited comment. Hone your policy with the comments and suggestions you have received, and also as you learn of better "best practices," developments in the law, or changes in social media platforms.

STEP 6: Provide In-House Training with Your Policy

If one of your goals is to "embed social" within your corporate culture, providing in-house social media training is a must. Effective compliance also calls for training to accompany your social media policy creation. The training is an excellent opportunity to consider what you may have missed in your policy, learn about employee concerns, and even identify some social media stars, in-house resources you'll need as your enterprise becomes more social.

STEP 7: Monitor and Engage

A 2012 study of 1,180 businesses worldwide, published by Satmetrix, a leading provider of cloud-based customer experience software, found that 39 percent of businesses have no social media tracking in place and 55 percent of companies "ignore customers who provide feedback via social media—by having no process in place to respond."

Your social media policy is meaningless if you do not monitor your brand and engage your community. Platforms such as Hootsuite.com (free and paid), make tracking of social mentions much easier. Other software exists to provide tons of data to help measure the impact of your social media activity as well as the sentiment within the social space concerning your brand.

In monitoring your brand, don't overlook the usefulness of Google alerts. It doesn't matter if you use Gmail for your e-mail, Google will send alerts you customize to whatever e-mail address you use. To sign up, simply visit http://www.Google.com/alerts.

While you're at the task of establishing alerts, you should include whatever products are yours, your name (i.e., your personal brand), your primary competition, and some industry keywords.

To further monitor your brand, pay a visit to SocialMention.com and do a search of your brand and other keywords related to your enterprise. You will find that this free service often comes up with social mentions not included in your Google alerts.

LEGAL ISSUES SHOULD BE ANSWERED BY AN ATTORNEY FROM YOUR JURISDICTION

Now before you rush forward and slap your business name to that sample policy and slap yourself on the back for having found it, let's talk about some provisions your enterprise might need to add to its sample policy to lessen legal risks.

Please note, as well, that drafting a social media policy yourself is a major legal land mine. If your organization can afford to bring an attorney on board to draft one, it should.

Additionally, please note that because a social media policy has been found to be "lawful," does not necessarily mean that it is one that will protect your organization or even be "lawful" for your organization, depending on the type of enterprise you are. This is especially true if you are in the medical or financial field. Only an attorney familiar with the laws of your jurisdiction and enterprise can properly ask and address the questions that need to be explored in putting together a proper social media policy. While this review of ours should assist you in spotting the issues that will help you better participate in the process of drafting a compliant social media policy, it should not in any way be considered a replacement for legal advice.

UNDERSTANDING THE NATIONAL LABOR RELATIONS ACT AND ITS PROMINENT CONNECTION TO SOCIAL MEDIA GOVERNANCE AND POLICIES

Section 7 of the NLRA provides a powerful protection of employee communications relating to the terms and conditions of employment when such communications are undertaken in a "concerted fashion." We will be exploring this provision at some length, as it is a particularly important principle of protected speech for employees that many employers have gotten wrong—and as a consequence, difficult personnel issues have only gotten much more complicated and costly. Understand that the protection of employee communications under this Act is vigorously defended against even the slightest intrusion.

THE NATIONAL LABOR RELATIONS BOARD

The NLRB is the federal authority tasked with enforcing the NLRA. It has taken a notably proactive approach to identifying and correcting employers whose social media policies and actions infringe upon the employees' rights to communicate about the terms and conditions of their employment "and conditions of their employment in a concerted fashion."

To determine if a social media policy provision "would reasonably tend to chill employees in the exercise of their Section 7 rights" (most commonly understood in the context of social media policy disputes as the right of workers to tweet about or post on Facebook about wages and working conditions with coworkers), the Board uses a two-step inquiry.

STEP 1: The Board First Examines If Any Social Media Policy Provision "Explicitly Restricts Section 7 Protected Activities"

If a social media policy provision "explicitly restricts" the right of employees to use social media to communicate about the terms or conditions of employment with other workers or third parties, it will be deemed unlawful as a violation of the NLRA.

If, however, a social media policy provision does not expressly restrict a Section 7 protected activity, the Board will move to the second prong of its inquiry.

STEP 2: An Unlawful Restriction on Section 7 Rights Will Still Be Found Upon a Showing of Any One of Three Criteria

1. Employees would reasonably construe the language to prohibit Section 7 activity.

2. The rule was promulgated in response to union activity.

3. The rule has been applied to restrict the exercise of Section 7 rights.

AMBIGUITY IN REGARD TO APPLICATION AND THE ABSENCE OF LIMITING LANGUAGE IS FATAL TO THE LEGALITY OF A SOCIAL MEDIA POLICY PROVISION

In citing its two-prong test in its 2012 report on social media policies, the Board provided a restatement of law that is the standard by which every social media policy provision should be examined for compliance with the NLRA Section 7 protections:

> Rules that are ambiguous as to their application to Section 7 activity, and contain no limiting language or context that would clarify to employees that the rule does not restrict Section 7 rights, are unlawful. See University Medical Center, 335 NLRB 1318, 1320-1322 (2001), enf. Denied in pertinent part 335 F.3d 1079 (D.C. Cir. 2003).

> In contrast, rules that clarify and restrict their scope by including examples of clearly illegal or unprotected conduct, such that they would not

reasonably be construed to cover protected activity, are not unlawful. See Tradesmen International, 338 NLRB 460, 460-462 (2002).

So just how broadly does the NLRB construe its mandate and the protections of the NLRA?

HOW A RESTRICTION ON THE RELEASE OF CONFIDENTIAL INFORMATION CAN VIOLATE THE LAW

A prohibition on the release of confidential information is one of the most common provisions in social media policies.

"How could someone possibly muck up such a provision so badly that it would be ruled unlawful?!"

Fair question. Here's how. Let's take a look at a confidentiality provision from a major retailer that the NLRB reviewed and found to be unlawful:

Don't release confidential guest, team member or company information . . .

"Ah, that's it?! That sounds a lot like our confidentiality provision . . ."
Yep. Yours and a lot of others.

Car Manufacturer General Motors Steers Off Course with Confidentiality Provision

Car giant General Motors (GM) ran afoul of the Board's policing with a policy provision that instructed employees not to "reveal non-public company information on any public site." GM's policy went on to explain that "non-public information" includes:

[a]ny topic related to the financial performance of the company; [i]nformation that has not already been disclosed by authorized persons in a public forum; and [p]ersonal information about another [Employer] employee, such as . . . performance, compensation or status in the company.

If your social media policy attempts to color Section 7–protected activities (e.g., discussion of wages) as confidential information, it will violate the NLRA.

In the case of GM, it was the policy's examples of confidential information that cinched the provision being found unlawful by the Board:

Because this explanation specifically encompasses topics related to Section 7 activities, employees would reasonably construe the policy as precluding them from discussing terms and conditions of employment among themselves or with non-employees.

"When in Doubt... DO NOT POST. Check with Communications or Legal"—Unlawful

When I said that writing a social media policy is a legal land mine and that it "ain't easy," I meant it. It has become a bit complicated.

Case in point: GM's social media policy also included a provision for employees who had questions about whether a topic concerned nonpublic information and was therefore prohibited by the company from being discussed by employees online. The policy stated:

> When in doubt about whether the information you are considering sharing falls into one of the above categories, DO NOT POST. Check with [Employer] Communications or [Employer] Legal to see if it's a good idea.

"That seems like a reasonable enough provision."

Actually, the NLRB ruled it to be an unlawful provision as well:

> The section of the policy that cautions employees that "[w]hen in doubt about whether the information you are considering sharing falls into one of the [prohibited]categories, DO NOT POST. Check with [Employer] Communications or [Employer] Legal to see if it's a good idea[,]" is also unlawful. The Board has long held that any rule that requires employees to secure permission from an employer as a precondition to engaging in Section 7 activities violates the Act. See Brunswick Corp.,282 NLRB794, 794-795 (1987).

There remains the question of whether such a provision would be lawful if it specifically excluded Section 7 activities. Ambiguity, as discussed, is fatal on this point.

DISH Network was also found to run afoul of the NLRA prohibition against any requirement of prior authorization for communication of protected speech due to the company's policy requirement that employees obtain prior authorization from the Corporate Communications Department before participating in a wide variety of public communications. *DISH Network, Case 16-CA-066142*

"We Don't Need Your Permission to Use Your Logo!"

> Do not incorporate [Employer] logos, trademarks, or other assets in your posts.

"Seems simple enough."

It is. And it's also unlawful.

Striking this provision, as well, in GM's policy, the NLRB reasoned:

The Employer's policy also unlawfully prohibits employees from posting photos, music, videos, and the quotes and personal information of others without obtaining the owner's permission and ensuring that the content can be legally shared, and from using the Employer's logos and trademarks. Thus, in the absence of any further explanation, employees would reasonably interpret these provisions as proscribing the use of photos and videos of employees engaging in Section 7 activities, including photos of picket signs containing the Employer's logo. Although the Employer has a proprietary interest in its trademarks, including its logo if trademarked, we found that employees' non-commercial use of the Employer's logo or trademarks while engaging in Section 7 activities would not infringe on that interest.

Prohibiting "Inappropriate Remarks" . . . You Guessed It—Unlawful

What other egregious provision did GM dare to include in its social media policy?

TREAT EVERYONE WITH RESPECT

Offensive, demeaning, abusive or inappropriate remarks are as out of place online as they are offline, even if they are unintentional. We expect you to abide by the same standards of behavior both in the workplace and in your social media communications.

Here's how the NLRB came to the conclusion that this very even-tempered-sounding provision got it wrong:

[W]e found unlawful the instruction that "[o]ffensive, demeaning, abusive or inappropriate remarks are as out of place online as they are offline." Like the provisions discussed above, this provision proscribes a broad spectrum of communications that would include protected criticisms of the Employer's labor policies or treatment of employees. Similarly, the instruction to be aware that "[c]ommunications with coworkers . . . that would be inappropriate in the workplace are also inappropriate online" does not specify which communications the Employer would deem inappropriate at work and, thus, is ambiguous as to its application to Section 7.

There are two points to be made here: (1) Protected employee communications about the terms and conditions of employment do not need to be couched in polite terms: courts have considered profane speech to still be protected speech in this arena. And (2) ambiguity about whether a provision is restricting protected rights is fatal to the lawfulness of any such provision.

"You May Not Make Disparaging or Defamatory Comments About [Employer], Its Employees, Officers, Directors . . ."—Unlawful

If you recall from the beginning of this chapter, I had mentioned how an attorney from a prominent law firm offered similar advice on wording to begin a social media policy. DISH Network included this language in its social media policy. The Board didn't hesitate in finding the provision to be unlawful:

> First, the prohibition on making "disparaging or defamatory" comments is unlawful. Employees would reasonably construe this prohibition to apply to protected criticism of the Employer's labor policies or treatment of employees. Second, we concluded that the prohibition on participating in these activities on Company time is unlawfully overbroad because employees have the right to engage in Section 7 activities on the Employer's premises during non-work time and in non-work areas. See Republic Aviation Corp. v. NLRB, 324 U.S. 793, 803 n.10 (1945). DISH Network, Case 16-CA-066142

Telling Employees to "Think Carefully About Friending Co-Workers" . . . Unlawful

GM's policy also had this provision: "Think carefully about 'friending' co-workers . . . on external social media sites."

"Where's the problem here?"

According to the NLRB:

> The provision of the Employer's social media policy instructing employees to "[t]hink carefully about 'friending' co-workers" is unlawfully overbroad because it would discourage communications among co-workers, and thus it necessarily interferes with Section 7 activity. Moreover, there is no limiting language clarifying for employees that it does not restrict Section 7 activity. General Motors, Case 07-CA-053570

"Don't Pick Fights . . . Communicate in a 'Professional Tone'"—Unlawful

McKesson Corp., an international healthcare services company, prides itself on goodwill and professionalism. How could it have strayed so far as to incur the wrath of the NLRB?

Here's what McKesson dared to include in its social media policy:

> *Don't pick fights. . . . Remember to communicate in a professional tone.*

Here's what the NLRB said in finding the provision unlawful:

> We found this rule unlawful for several reasons. First, in warning employees not to "pick fights" and to avoid topics that might be considered objectionable or inflammatory—such as politics and religion, and reminding employees to communicate in a "professional tone," the overall thrust of this rule is to caution employees against online discussions that could become heated or controversial. Discussions about working conditions or unionism have the potential to become just as heated or controversial as discussions about politics and religion. Without further clarification of what is "objectionable or inflammatory," employees would reasonably construe this rule to prohibit robust but protected discussions about working conditions or unionism.

In NLRB rulings, ambiguity is always construed against the employer and in favor of protecting Section 7 protected speech.

NLRA Disclaimer Provision in Social Media Policy . . . Works No Magic

Mindful of the strictures of the NLRA, McKesson sought to inoculate itself against any claims that its policy might infringe upon protected Section 7 rights by including what the NLRB referred to as a "savings clause." This NLRA disclaimer provided:

> **National Labor Relations Act.** This Policy will not be construed or applied in a manner that improperly interferes with employees' rights under the National Labor Relations Act.

Duly unimpressed with the provision, the NLRB wrote:

> We found that this clause does not cure the otherwise unlawful provisions of the Employer's social media policy *because employees would not*

understand from this disclaimer that protected activities are in fact per-mitted. McKesson Corp., Case 06-CA-066504 (Emphasis added)

Interestingly, the Board's reasoning in rejecting the effectiveness of this provision turns on the assertion that "employees would not understand from this disclaimer that protected activities are in fact permitted." This leaves open the possibility that a more detailed explanation in such a "savings clause," one that outlines Section 7 protected rights, might well be found to clear ambiguities elsewhere in favor of an employer. Ambiguities, however, as we have seen, are a powder keg of liability for employers and should not be left to be remedied by a savings clause that itself might be deemed ineffective.

SOCIAL MEDIA POLICY DEEMED LAWFUL BY THE NLRB

In showcasing the policy that follows, the NLRB noted that it is a "revised" policy, leaving one to wonder whether the earlier edition of the policy would have passed regulatory scrutiny and perhaps highlighting the importance of regularly reviewing one's policy. The Board did note that because it found the employer's new policy to be lawful, it was "unnecessary to rule on the Employer's social media policy that was initially alleged to be unlawful."

Importantly, in declaring the policy to be "lawful," the NLRB specifically noted that social media policy provisions that are "ambiguous as to their application to Section 7 activity (again, the right of employees to speak in a concerted manner about the terms and conditions of their employment) and that contain no limiting language or context to clarify that rules do not restrict Section 7 rights are unlawful." The NLRB applied this standard to its review of Walmart's social media policy and concluded that the policy provided the context and clarity to make it clear that it was not limiting the employees' "protected communications" about "terms and conditions of employment."

"BE RESPECTFUL" REVISITED—A POLICY PROVISION WITH EXAMPLES MAY BE LAWFUL

In its examination of the Walmart social media policy, the Board looked at a provision that elsewhere it had deemed to be unlawful, a provision entitled "Be Respectful." Here the Board found the provision to be lawful, but it noted that the employer had provided clear examples so that employees would not confuse an exhortation to "be respectful" as an overly broad provision that would encompass employee complaints about the terms and conditions of employment.

Reviewing the provision's examples of prohibited conduct, under the exhortation "Be Respectful," the Board explained that Walmart's version:

> provides sufficient examples of plainly egregious conduct so that employees would not reasonably construe the rule to prohibit Section 7 conduct. For instance, the rule counsels employees to avoid posts that "could be viewed as malicious, obscene, threatening or intimidating." It further explains that prohibited "harassment or bullying" would include "offensive posts meant to intentionally harm someone's reputation" or "posts that could contribute to a hostile work environment on the basis of race, sex, disability, religion or any other status protected by law or company policy." The Employer has a legitimate basis to prohibit such workplace communications, and has done so without burdening protected communications about terms and conditions of employment.

Elaborating on its determination that the sample policy's confidentiality provision was lawful, the Board noted:

> We also found that the Employer's rule requiring employees to maintain the confidentiality of the Employer's trade secrets and private and confidential information is not unlawful. Employees have no protected right to disclose trade secrets. Moreover, the Employer's rule provides sufficient examples of prohibited disclosures (i.e., information regarding the development of systems, processes, products, know-how, technology, internal reports, procedures, or other internal business-related communications) for employees to understand that it does not reach protected communications about working conditions. [Walmart, Case 11-CA-067171]

Here the NLRB noted that this provision is lawful, as it "prohibits plainly egregious conduct, such as discrimination and threats of violence or other similar inappropriate or unlawful conduct." In this instance, the examples clarify the scope of the limitation, "inappropriate postings."

In other words, a prohibition of "inappropriate postings," without examples or clarification, would likely have led to a finding of unlawfulness as being too broad in scope and having a chilling effect on the protected communication rights of employees.

HOW THE STATEMENTS "BE RESPECTFUL" AND "BE FAIR AND COURTEOUS" COULD BE A VIOLATION OF THE LAW IN A SOCIAL MEDIA POLICY

"'Be respectful,' a violation of the law?! 'Be fair and courteous' an unlawful provision in a social media policy?! Under what farfetched theory could such sensible and reasonable social media policy provisions violate the law?!"

The NLRB's report on social media policies, reviewing the Walmart policy, explains how:

> In certain contexts, the rule's exhortation to be respectful and 'fair and courteous' in the posting of comments, complaints, photographs, or videos, could be overly broad.

The Board, in its review of social media policies, is constantly concerned about seemingly innocuous-sounding provisions that really have at their core either an intentional or unintentional chilling effect on the right of employees to speak out about the terms and conditions of their employment with others.

Whether an employer intended to limit an employee's Section 7 rights (broad freedom to communicate about the terms and conditions of employment) is unimportant to the Board's inquiry and determination of whether a social media policy rule provision violates the law. The question comes down to whether a social media policy provision would have a "chilling effect," i.e., limitation on an employee's right to speak out about the terms and conditions of employment. That's it. The right and the protection are that broad.

IN DRAFTING YOUR SOCIAL MEDIA POLICY, BEWARE THE "WARM AND FUZZY" PROVISIONS

Be mindful in putting together your social media policy of the NLRB's warning against ambiguity: broad, even flowery, friendly sounding provisions within a social media policy may be unlawful if they don't come with examples or clarifications that limit their scope. In the eyes of the NLRB, even a warm and fuzzy "Be respectful" can easily become a thinly disguised and unlawful "Don't say anything negative about your supervisors or working conditions."

As an employer, it may seem that the cards are stacked against you when it comes to writing a social media policy, but the reality is that the NLRB has provided clarity for its own part on what it does and does not want to see in a social media policy.

As you craft your social media policy, carefully consider every provision as a "stand-alone" item and be sure that you have put enough flesh on the bones so that there is no confusion or uncertainty about the scope of any limitations or restrictions included in your policy.

AUDIT COMPLIANCE WITH YOUR POLICY AND BEST PRACTICES

Affirmatively look at how you, your organization, and your employees are using social media. If your budget allows, bring in someone from the outside as well to audit your presence so that you get a perspective untainted by any "groupthink." It's important that you periodically assess how you are doing in social as compared with your competition and your alignment to your business objectives.

ADDITIONAL SOCIAL MEDIA POLICY ISSUES

Fair Labor Standards Act Compliance

You may wish to include a provision that managers review social media–related assignments from a time management and hourly compliance perspective. Careful consideration should be given to the assignment of social media monitoring or community management tasks to hourly employees to ensure adherence with the Fair Labor Standards Act (FLSA), which requires overtime pay for covered employees who work in excess of 40 hours a week. It is extremely easy for a diligent social media manager to chalk up numerous hours quickly, especially when the social media assignment is an additional work assignment. Time management and FLSA compliance may be something to address in your policy or elsewhere, depending on the nature of your workforce. *Fair Labor Standards Act (FLSA), 29 U.S. Code Chapter 8, Sec. 207*

Keep Employees Informed of Changes to the Social Media Policy

Employees should be informed any time there is a change to the social media policy so that they are not left guessing if there have been any changes. A "Social Media Policy/Best Practices Update" should become a regular enterprise communication. It reminds employees of the enterprise's expectations about their online behavior and will help make them more conversant in social media best practices.

A notation in your social media policy document about when it was last modified should be helpful in flagging changes for employees as well.

Acknowledgment of Receipt and Understanding of the Social Media Policy

As with other important enterprise documents, employees should be asked to provide an acknowledgment of their receipt and understanding of the social media policy. A record of this acknowledgment should be maintained by the enterprise.

Substantial Changes to a Social Media Policy Should Come with Updated Training

Where there are any substantial changes in the social media policy, a best practice would be to provide in-house training on the revision or addition and require employees to sign an acknowledgment of understanding regarding the updated policy.

Social Media Policy Format: Plain-Language Version, Followed by "Legal"

Many leading organizations present their social media policy and community moderation policy in a two-step approach:

1. Short, plain-language version

2. Longer, "legal" language version

A common mistake in this approach is to make no reference in the "simple" version of the necessity of still reading the longer, second version. This is a mistake when the second version contains important information that is not readily apparent in the plain-language version. It becomes very easy for a person to say—and a court to be persuaded that the statement is reasonable—that "I thought everything I needed to know was presented in the 'plain-language' version!"

I know that it may seem disheartening or defeat the purpose of having a "plain-language" version, but unless you are absolutely confident that you have covered everything significant in your plain-language version, let readers know that they must still read the longer version if there are significant details that are only covered in the "legal" version.

"Now that you have a general sense of our guidelines, please read the full text of our guidelines for some additional details that are also important for you to understand and affect your rights and responsibilities. Thanks!"

Some may choose not to go on and read the longer version, but at least you have provided your enterprise with a little extra protection.

DO WE NEED BOTH A BLOG MODERATION POLICY AND A SOCIAL MEDIA POLICY?

In a word, *yes*. Some businesses do attempt to create just a single guide, but clarity and efficiency tend to make having two separate documents the better choice.

The social media policy should focus on providing employees with guidance about the enterprise's expectations regarding their online "social" behavior, both when they are on the job and during their personal time. The blog moderation policy, on the other hand, presupposes that the enterprise has a blog and speaks to the community expectations regarding those who choose to post content there.

Although there is typically an overlap in the guidance offered by both a social media policy and blog moderation policy, there are distinctions as well that benefit the user and the business separating the two guides, as discussed in Chapter 10.

SOCIAL MEDIA MARKETING: INCLUDE THE FTC'S SOCIAL MEDIA DISCLOSURE GUIDELINES

It is the duty of a sponsor to inform a sponsored blogger of the blogger's duty to disclose the material connection between the blogger and the company when blogging about the company or its products or services. In the case of Anne Taylor Loft, the FTC, in its closing letter to the Loft, said that it had decided not to pursue an enforcement action against the retailer, in part, because:

> LOFT adopted a written policy in February 2010 stating that LOFT will not issue any gift to any blogger without first telling the blogger that the blogger must disclose the gift in his or her blog.

For companies that sponsor bloggers, a similar provision would be a smart addition to their social media policy.

SOCIAL MEDIA POLICIES REQUIRE TRAINING, UPDATING, AND AUDITING

As we've seen, social media compliance can be a bit complicated, especially when it comes to writing a social media policy. Understanding some core regulatory principles, however, should make the task of social media compliance much easier for everyone. Do your business and employees a favor: when you write your social media policy, invite input from across your company and welcome suggestions for updates. Know, too, that guidelines, without ongoing employee training, simply become another legal land mine. Make social media compliance and training part of your business plan, and regularly audit your policy and company compliance.

2

Social (and Mobile) Recruiting, Hiring, and Firing: Legal Issues You Need to Know

Acording to Jobvite's 2012 Social Recruiting Survey, 92 percent of recruiters use or plan to use social recruiting, and a whopping 73 percent have already successfully hired a candidate through social media.

Social Business News reports that "one third of employers have disciplined employees for something posted on social media" and that only a quarter of those businesses that reported disciplining an employee for his or her social media conduct had a social media policy. This is a recipe for disaster.

In 2012, the FTC brought its first action against a company using social networking for consumer reports being used for employment screening. It resulted in an $800,000 settlement.

More regulatory actions and lawsuits can be expected in the area of social media recruiting, hiring, and firing.

TWEET THIS: YOU ARE, MOST LIKELY, AN "EMPLOYEE AT WILL"

Before you lecture me on how you have a constitutional right to say what you want, where you want (wrong, wrong), it's probably best that we get our arms around a legal concept that likely affects you very personally and profoundly: the status of being "an employee at will." Unless you are a star athlete, a Hollywood celebrity, or perhaps a union employee, it's unlikely that you have a written contract of employment. This is something very different from a document simply telling you your start date and what your group insurance number is.

Being an "employee at will" means you serve at the will or whim of your employer. As such, you may be fired for causes such as inappropriate posting on Twitter, Facebook, Google+, so on.

SOME EXCEPTIONS TO THE EMPLOYEE-AT-WILL ("FIRE-AT-WILL") STATUS

When dealing with the law, one realizes that there are often exceptions to laws or legal doctrines, regardless of however rock-solid the laws or doctrines may seem. Depending on where you live in the United States, there may be limited exceptions to the employee-at-will (fire-at-will) doctrine or circumstances surrounding your employment, which may provide you with a defense from firing that would not otherwise ordinarily exist. In some instances, spoken assurances from persons with authority or promises conveyed in an employee handbook have been found to trump the otherwise harsh realities of the employee-at-will, or fire-at-will, status.

In a handful of states, an implied covenant of "good faith and fair dealing" arises to defeat terminations based solely on the will or whim of an employer against a presumed employee at will. In those states, courts have looked to find "good cause" for an employee's termination, a far cry from the broad freedom to fire allowed under the employee-at-will (fire-at-will) doctrine.

Word to the wise: Whether or not you have an employment contract or do or don't live in a state that provides exceptions to the employee-at-will doctrine, be judicious in your social media networking—because it may still get you fired. Even where an employer must demonstrate "just cause" in order to terminate an employee, your social media antics may be just enough to satisfy "just cause."

IF YOUR COMPANY HAS A SOCIAL MEDIA POLICY, STUDY IT BEFORE YOU BLOG YOURSELF INTO UNEMPLOYMENT

Word of advice: If your company has a social media policy, study it very carefully. Unsure of something it says? Ask someone with the authority to explain it.

If your company does *not* have a social media policy, still ask about what is permitted and what is not.

By following your company's social media policy very carefully, or by following the advice you are given on what to do or not to do with social media in the absence of a formal policy, you will be arming yourself to stay on the right side of your company when it comes to social networking—and in the event you were to be fired for your social media activity, you will perhaps have secured some basis for retaining your post, even if it is "at-will" employment.

Conversely, employers should be mindful of any assurances they give to employees regarding acceptable social media conduct; they may be creating a binding policy unwittingly.

EMPLOYEE AT-WILL STATUS MAY BE CHANGED BY EMPLOYER COMMUNICATIONS

To elaborate further on an "employee at will," though such a status ordinarily means you can be fired at will, should your employer have a social media policy or have given you some guidance about what to do or not to do on social media in the absence of a formal policy, you may well have additional rights to retain your employment should a termination be based on your social media activity. If such a termination were to occur, protections against your termination and in favor of your reinstatement, or a claim for damages, might arise based on your reliance on the guidance you were given and your adherence to that guidance.

HOW TO TWEET YOURSELF OUT OF A NEW JOB ON YOUR WAY HOME FROM THE INTERVIEW

The #CiscoFatty Incident

In the social network, Twitter hashtags (words or abbreviations with the pound symbol in front of them) become links and a way people quickly identify a certain subject. For this subject, which is a seminal example of "how to use social media to limit your job prospects," the hashtag #CiscoFatty is used to refer to the incident and example. It is a hashtag that became viral when the incident first arose, and then picked up volume and speed when the job prospect suddenly decided that it was best to remove her tweet from the public stream . . . with little success.

A potential employee interviewed with Cisco, and shortly after she got the job, she tweeted out a rather unfortunate statement: "Cisco just offered me a job! Now I have to weigh the utility of a fatty paycheck against the daily commute to San Jose and hating the work."

Cisco responded to the ungracious tweet: "Who is the hiring manager. I'm sure they would love to know that you will hate the work. We here at Cisco are versed in the web."

Needless to say, the job offer was rescinded.

"Hey, they can't do that!!! . . .The Constitution says . . ."

Stop. They can. The Constitution does not say what you think it says. (Please refer to our earlier discussion of employee at will–fire at will.)

Turning Your Twitter Account to Private *After* You've Made an Ill-Advised Tweet Won't Clean Up the Mess

In the case above, the new hire quickly made her Twitter account private after receiving the response from Cisco, hiding any new tweets from the public stream. However, the tweet about how she would hate to actually work at the company went viral, being shared across the web (and written about years later!) as an example of how not to start your first day with the new company!

Mistweet? Thoughtless photo upload? You can delete it, but you can't erase it.

UNWISE TWEETS OR SOCIAL MEDIA POSTINGS ARE NOT PROTECTED SPEECH

In case you are still wondering if there aren't any legal issues posed by an employer using something posted to the public stream as a basis for pulling a job offer or firing someone . . . there really aren't. Unwise tweets or posts are not protected speech under the law.

Now that well-cited incident happened way back in 2009, when we were all just babes in the social media woods. Old news. We've all learned from the hard lessons of the early days . . .

"WE 'LIKE' YOUR RÉSUMÉ. DO YOU MIND GIVING US YOUR SOCIAL MEDIA PASSWORDS?"

You have got nothing to worry about. You're social media savvy. You've gone through the trouble of cleaning up your social media public profiles. You've tightened up your privacy settings and cleaned up your Facebook wall. Removed a few photos; deleted a few posts. You're all set your interview. Nicely done.

So what are you going to do when they ask for your Facebook password?

"They can't do that!"

Sure they can, and some of them do ask. Depends, though, on where you live, as some states have already begun enacting legislation to prevent employers from asking job candidates for their social network passwords.

According to the National Conference of State Legislatures, an organization that serves legislators of the nation's 50 states, at least 13 states, as of the writing of this book, had "introduced legislation that would restrict employers from requesting access to social networking usernames and passwords of applicants, students or employees."

Maryland: First State to Ban Employers from Demanding Passwords from Employees and Job Applicants

Maryland legislators faced opposition from the state chamber of commerce in signing this ban on employers requesting passwords. The legislation was the culmination of a battle begun by Robert Collins, a former corrections officer in Maryland, who said that he was asked by a supervisor to provide the password to his Facebook account when he was being recertified for his job following a leave of absence. Although he was informed that consent to the request was purely voluntary, Collins later reported that he felt that the request was coercive and that the procedure was embarrassing as he watched his supervisor pore through his private pictures and messages.

In a letter to the Maryland Corrections Department, the Maryland ACLU, which was enlisted by Officer Collins in his battle against the "voluntary" policy, questioned whether any "governmental requests for access to an applicant's social media accounts can ever be perceived as truly voluntary. The situation is inherently a coercive one, placing pressure on the applicant to accede to this privacy violation or risk being viewed as someone with something to hide."

The ACLU also argued that the "friends" of applicants would have their privacy violated as well, with no opportunity to object to the government scrutiny of what they had believed was private communication, a view shared by Facebook.

WHY FACEBOOK DOESN'T LIKE THE EMPLOYER PASSWORD REQUEST POLICY

As the practice of some employers asking employees and job applicants for the password to their Facebook account attracted some buzz, it also attracted the attention, not surprisingly, of Facebook itself. In a tightly crafted missive on the subject, Erin Egan, Facebook's chief privacy officer, warned that the employer practice "undermines the privacy expectations and the security of both the user and the user's friends. It also potentially exposes the employer who seeks this access to unanticipated legal liability."

Laying out its position to its users, Facebook, through Egan, said:

> As a user, you shouldn't be forced to share your private information and communications just to get a job. And as the friend of a user, you shouldn't have to worry that your private information or communications will be revealed to someone you don't know and didn't intend to share with just because that user is looking for a job. That's why we've made it a violation of Facebook's Statement of Rights and Responsibilities to share or solicit a Facebook password.

Facebook's position recognizes a fundamental threat posed by such a license to rummage through an employee's or job applicant's Facebook account: not only would it have a chilling effect on the freedom of information sharing by the job seeker on even the "private" portion of his or her Facebook account, but it would also intrude upon the privacy of the job seeker's family and friends who would begin to fear that their own privacy might be unknowingly compromised by a social connection's employer or would-be employer.

"UNANTICIPATED LEGAL LIABILITIES" FOR EMPLOYERS WHO SEEK SOCIAL ACCOUNT PASSWORDS

As to the "unanticipated legal liability" an employer might expose itself to in requesting a job seeker's or employee's social networking account passwords, Egan warned of three general categories of liability:

1. **Discrimination claims.** If an employer were to see on Facebook that someone is a member of a protected group (e.g., over a certain age), the employer could expose itself to claims of discrimination if it doesn't hire that person.

2. **Liability for mishandling of private information.** Employers also may not have the proper policies and training for reviewers to handle private information.

3. **Liability for exposure to information that may trigger additional responsibilities.** The employer may assume liability for protecting the information it has seen or for knowing what responsibilities may arise based on different types of information (e.g., if the information suggests the commission of a crime).

"Facebook takes your privacy seriously," Egan assured Facebook users. More to the point, she promised, "We'll take action to protect the privacy and security of our users, whether by engaging policymakers or, where appropriate, by initiating legal action, including by shutting down applications that abuse their privileges."

"I believe privacy should not be an alternative in lieu of securing employment, but a fundamental right," Officer Robert Collins said in a statement following Maryland's adoption of the ban on demanding people's social media passwords. "Moving forward, our children will have one less hurdle to overcome in their quest to secure gainful employment and become contributing members to our great society," he said, echoing a sentiment that was clearly shared by a majority of the Maryland legislature. Collins also called on other states to follow Maryland's lead.

Maryland's ban became effective October 2012.

H.R. 5050: SOCIAL NETWORKING ONLINE PROTECTION ACT

New York Congressman Eliot Engel has introduced the Social Networking Online Protection Act, federal legislation that would:

> prohibit employers and certain other entities from requiring or requesting that employees and certain other individuals provide a user name, password, or other means for accessing a personal account on any social networking website.

A violation of the Act would expose an employer to a fine of up to $10,000 per violation. Under the Act, an "employer" means "any person acting directly or indirectly in the interest of an employer in relation to an employee or an applicant for employment." In other words, an employer could not skirt around the prohibition by outsourcing the hiring or screening process to a third party that would then seek access to an applicant's social media account.

The prohibition would also apply to colleges.

As of this writing, the legislation has been referred to a congressional committee for review and recommendation to the House of Representatives.

IF YOU DON'T ASK WHAT YOUR COMPANY'S SOCIAL MEDIA POLICY IS, YOU MAY FIND OUT THE HARD WAY: A CAUTIONARY TALE

According to a story reported in the *LA Times*, Francesca's, an apparel and accessory retailer, made a simple announcement that it had terminated its chief financial officer's employment "after finding 'that he improperly communicated

Company information through social media.'" The *LA Times* reported that the company did not explain how the violation occurred or on which social network the information was posted. The *LA Times* did note, however, that the CFO did have a Facebook page with more than 100 friends, a LinkedIn account with about 400 connections, and a blog. The actual cause of the firing, however, remained a mystery, other than the company's intriguing statement that the firing was related to the executive's social media usage.

Even *Forbes* reported on the story, trying to discern a meaning from the company's announcement, observing that:

> Morphis (the CFO) seemed to mostly use Facebook as a travel log, noting which airport he flew from and to, and also to muse about the music he enjoyed. Still, he often posted about his duties as Francesca's finance chief—a position he held since October 2010—flirting with today's blurry line about what is appropriate to share in public forums like Facebook and other social media.

Traditional media was intrigued by this curious tale and seemed desperately to want to turn it into a cautionary tale. Mystery though it remains, it does seem to provide enough information to serve as a cautionary tale: a high-level employee, just as easily as someone just offered a job, can find himself out of one because of the blurring between personal and professional life, or a very subtle or not-so-subtle misstep in social media.

WHAT IS THE FAIR CREDIT REPORTING ACT, AND HOW DOES IT RELATE TO SOCIAL RECRUITING?

The Fair Credit Reporting Act (FCRA) "promotes the accuracy, fairness, and privacy of information in the files of consumer reporting agencies (CRAs)." If you use an outside agency to assist you in your social media recruiting, those agencies are likely considered CRAs for the purpose of FCRA, which means that they have specific obligations under FCRA, as do you, the employer using their services.

RESPONSIBILITIES OF AGENCIES COLLECTING SOCIAL DATA FOR EMPLOYMENT SCREENING

Social recruiting or screening agencies (considered CRAs under FCRA) must:

- Carry out the duty of "maximum possible accuracy" by exercising reasonable care to ensure the "maximum possible accuracy" of what's in their reports. (Employers should inquire how a social media screening firm will meet its obligation of maximum possible accuracy. Software analytics absent human analysis would seem unlikely to meet such an obligation.)

- Inform the employers that they must provide an employee or job applicant with notice of any adverse action taken on the basis of the social media analysis report.

- Inform the employer of its duty to notify the job candidate of his or her right to get a copy of the report and to request a free reinvestigation of information the person thinks is in error. *FTC.gov*

RESPONSIBILITIES OF EMPLOYERS USING SOCIAL DATA FROM CRAS FOR EMPLOYMENT SCREENING

Employers who use outside agencies to assist them in social recruiting by providing them with candidate social media reports must provide candidates with:

- Notice of adverse action. This step is taken on the basis of the social media analysis report.

- Notice of the right of candidates to get a free copy of the report.

- Notice of the right of candidates to get a free reinvestigation. Job candidates who are the subject of an adverse action have a right to a free reinvestigation of information the person thinks is in error and must be informed of that right. (Employers should look to the vendor contract to see if it imposes any additional fees in the event of a candidate request for a "free" reinvestigation.) *FTC.gov*

SOCIAL MEDIA AND THE FIRST AMENDMENT (FREEDOM OF SPEECH)

First Amendment of the Bill of Rights

Congress shall make no law respecting an establishment of religion, or prohibiting the free exercise thereof; or abridging the freedom of speech, or of the press; or the right of the people peaceably to assemble, and to petition the Government for a redress of grievances.

The First Amendment to the U.S. Constitution, cited in its glorious entirety above, enshrines freedom of speech and is perhaps the most referenced amendment of the 27 ratified amendments to the U.S. Constitution. It is just as well possibly the most misunderstood and misquoted of the amendments.

"Congress shall make no law. . . ." Congress. It is talking about the U.S. Congress not making any laws concerning the establishment or exercise of religion, limiting free speech or press, or prohibiting the right of people to peaceably assemble and petition government. Do you see any mention of your employer? Neither do I.

Although the due process clause of the Fourteenth Amendment has been used to apply most of the rights and privileges of the Bill of Rights to state and local governments, "freedom of speech," as it is usually bandied about, is unlikely to give an employee little comfort or assistance in an employee-employer social media quarrel.

NO, GOVERNMENT EMPLOYEES DO *NOT* GET A FREE PASS WHEN IT COMES TO "FREE SPEECH"

In *Waters v. Churchill, 511 U.S. 661 (1994),* the U.S. Supreme Court examined the free speech rights of public employees in the workplace. To the point, the Court in Waters noted that "even many of the most fundamental maxims of our First Amendment jurisprudence cannot reasonably be applied to speech by government employees." *Id. at 672.* In other words, even if you work for the government, don't think you get a free pass when it comes to talking about your employer. Some restrictions do apply.

Driving home the point, *Waters*, citing, *Branti v. Finkel, 445 U.S. 507, 518 (1980),* observed that "though a private person is perfectly free to uninhibitedly and robustly criticize a state governor's legislative program, we have never suggested that the Constitution bars the governor from firing a high-ranking deputy for doing the same thing." *Id.*

The First Amendment speaks to governmental action, not private. If your employer does not like your "speech" on Twitter or Facebook—or your picture boards on Pinterest—you may just be fired, without the right of being reinstated.

FACEBOOK POST: "MY SUPERVISOR IS A BLEEPING IDIOT!"— CAUSE FOR TERMINATION OR PROTECTED SPEECH? SECTION 8(A)(1) OF THE NATIONAL LABOR RELATIONS ACT

Despite what we've just covered about the First Amendment not providing employees with much protection in their social media messaging, a powerful protection does exist where certain circumstances are met. In the previous chapter on how to draft a social media policy, we reviewed at length the implications of the National Labor Relations Act. Here's the overall message: if an employee tweets, blogs, or posts on Facebook something relating to that person's working conditions and it is deemed to have been done in a "concerted fashion" (i.e., it was not simply one employee ranting, but more than one employee posting about the conditions of their employment in some concerted manner), the speech may well be protected speech under the Act and given great freedom.

Under the application of the NLRA, even the use of profanity in such social media speech to lambaste a supervisor is likely to be deemed protected speech by the NLRB if it falls within the NLRA's narrow exception. If a company's social media policy happens to say that an employee can't make negative tweets about his or her work or supervisors . . . the employee is likely going to have the freedom to return to work, and the business will likely be directed to narrow its overly broad social media policy.

Oh, in case you're wondering, this has nothing to do, really, with the First Amendment. It has everything to do with the NLRA.

MONITOR AND MANAGE YOUR "SOCIAL" REPUTATION

The reality is that a person's "social" presence and digital footprint are primary considerations in the hiring of new employees. Sophisticated employers, to insulate themselves from charges of unlawful discrimination in hiring—i.e., that they may have considered improper factors, such as age, ethnicity, sexual orientation, or religious affiliation, in their review of a job candidate's social media accounts—turn to third-party vendors to assist in the task. The role of the third-party vendor is to provide impartiality in the vetting process and to identify "red flags," such as issues of anger, substance abuse, or the sharing of "inappropriate content," such as the use of profanity.

HOW DO SOCIAL SCREENING SERVICES WORK?

One free service that aims to assist users in identifying potential problems within their own social media accounts, NetworkClean.com, provides an excellent, albeit troubling, example of just how such a review might be accomplished and viewed from the employer's perspective.

Let's assume that I am a big company. I have a lot of openings and a lot of applicants for those openings. It's a good company that pays well.

What happens when you give your employer your Facebook password?

Enter a service like NetworkClean, hypothetically speaking. (NetworkClean, however, at this time, is only being offered as an individual reputation management tool and not as a third-party app for employers.) Your employer might simply enter your user name and password into the NetworkClean app. (Please review the sidebar in this chapter covering the FTC's settlement with Spokeo, Inc., to recognize the implications that the use of such an app for such a purpose would have.)

After a few minutes, your employer would get an e-mail with a pretty impressive analysis of the account. The report would include an easy-to-read pie chart divided into various red-flag issues, with an opportunity to review each and every post that made up the compilation of red flags represented within the colored pie chart.

"Want to work for me?"

"Sure do."

"OK, good. I think you'll fit right in, and I already have a nice office with a big window picked out for you."

"Wow, that's great."

"One small thing . . . Our HR department needs the password to your Facebook account."

"I beg your pardon?"

"Oh, and your Twitter account, too. It's routine. Not to worry. We'll keep everything confidential. We're just going to make sure that there aren't any red flags we need to address. You know that we'll be trusting you with a lot of confidential information of our own, not to mention letting you make some important decisions for us."

"Oh, OK."

For the individual social media account holder, NetworkClean does a really nice job of helping to flag potential problems from the prospective employer's perspective. Unfortunately for the would-be job candidate who hasn't taken any steps to monitor and tidy up his or her own social media footprint, the results of a NetworkClean–like review could have devastating consequences. In a world where resources are strained and job openings are comparatively few, there is little doubt that apps such as NetworkClean will be used to help employers sift through mountains of applicants, despite FTC and FCRA prohibitions. Too many red flags? Next candidate please.

SOCIAL RECRUITING? THERE'S AN APP FOR THAT

After reading these rules, you might be wondering if there isn't an app for social recruiting and employment screening that would sidestep the FCRA and FTC's reporting rules. Well, there do appear to be several apps out there that collect data about the social networking habits of users and could be used by employers for social screening.

"Perfect!"

Not so fast. The FTC has already looked at several apps that appear to provide background screening reports but claim not to be for that purpose.

THE FTC'S THOUGHTS ON APPS THAT COME WITH EMPLOYMENT SCREENING DISCLAIMERS

If it walks like employment screening, talks like employment screening, and looks like employment screening, it probably is and would trigger FCRA reporting obligations for both the developer of the app and an employer using it. The FTC examines such applications in a fact-specific way, and a disclaimer would be ineffective in sidestepping the FCRA obligations.

The FTC's Lesley Fair, whose report on the topic served as the basis for much of this review, said it best: "'App law' may be a developing area, but savvy businesses take it as a given that well-settled consumer protection principles carry forward as transactions go mobile."

(continued)

$800,000—THE PRICE OF GETTING SOCIAL RECRUITING AND SCREENING WRONG

In June 2012, the FTC announced a settlement of its first case to address the sale of social media data in the employment screening context. It was a settlement of $800,000 with Spokeo, Inc., a data broker that collects and sells information profiles on millions of consumers, gleaning some of its information from social media sites.

Broadly speaking, the FTC said that Spokeo marketed profiles to companies "without taking steps to protect consumers required under the Fair Credit Reporting Act."

FTC ALLEGED SPOKEO FAILED TO FOLLOW THREE "KEY REQUIREMENTS" OF THE FCRA

According to the FTC's settlement announcement, Spokeo failed to follow three key requirements of the FCRA:

1. Maintain reasonable procedures to verify who its users are and that the consumer report information would be used for a permissible purpose;

2. Ensure accuracy of consumer reports; and

3. Provide a user notice to any person that purchased its consumer reports (i.e., inform employers or users of the reports of their notification requirements).

In 2010, Spokeo had changed its terms of service to state that it was "not a consumer reporting agency and that consumers may not use the company's website or information for FCRA-covered purposes." The FTC looked beyond Spokeo's disclaimer to assess the type of report the company was providing to its clients. It concluded that the reports fit the definition of "consumer reports, as defined in section 603(d)" of the FCRA, *15 U.S.C.§ 1681a(d)*:

any written, oral, or other communication of any information by a consumer reporting agency bearing on a consumer's credit worthiness, credit standing, credit capacity, character, general reputation, personal characteristics, or mode of living which is used or expected to be used or collected in whole or in part for the purpose of serving as a factor in establishing the consumer's eligibility for. . . (B) employment. . . .

The FTC reached its determination based on its conclusion that Spokeo's reports:

bear on a consumer's character, general reputation, personal characteristics, or mode of living and/or other attributes listed in section 603(d), and are "used or expected to be used in whole or in part" as a factor in determining the consumer's eligibility for employment or other purposes specified in section 604.

So What Happened When I Ran My Own Facebook Account Through NetworkClean.com?

Now don't fault the application. The application is doing exactly what it should. Like most social media monitoring tools, however, NetworkClean does an impartial analysis and gives potentially troubling data based on various keywords. The result can be dangerously misleading if not, in turn, analyzed by an individual. (Without this analysis, it would seem that the use of the app from an employment screening perspective would be problematic under the FTC's "maximum possible accuracy" standard.)

So in the case of my Facebook page, it flagged "anger" as an issue. I then did something that someone looking at a pile of reports on prospective job candidates is unlikely to do: I looked for the "why," what triggered the detection of an anger issue. I found the careless post. It seems that I was flagged for having an anger issue because I had had the foolish lapse of "liking" the Academy Award–nominated movie *12 Angry Men*.

NetworkClean is an impressive app. It spotted that I had "liked" something angry. It is proposed as a reputation management tool, and it serves the task well. It would be a particularly helpful tool integrated with human analysis: it flags potential issues and allows another to decipher the true meaning of issues that were flagged. In my case, one would hope that an analysis would remove any notation of a potential "anger" issue and replace it with something like "Enjoys classic movies." A larger issue of concern, however, is whether, realistically, anyone would ever go beyond simply creating two piles: those with red flags and those without.

This seems to be part of why the FTC is attempting to carefully monitor the use of social reports as they become far more prevalent in usage and reliance.

What Advice Does NetworkClean COO Doug Haustein Offer Job Candidates?

Job seekers should not take for granted that just because they have various parts of their Facebook profiles set to private that this information will not be accessible for anyone to see. For instance, an inappropriate photo, video, note or event you may be tagged in may be public since another person may have uploaded or created it. Employers could also gain access through a friend of a friend to view your Facebook content. In this day and age, it is critical to keep your social image clean.

By the way, Doug, who was kind enough to answer questions about his service, volunteered that, personally, he is not in favor of employers asking for employee passwords to Facebook—an impressive position given his app.

So What's the Benefit of a Service Like NetworkClean?

According to Doug:

NetworkClean solves a critical need for social media members by placing the control back into the users' hands, enabling them to monitor and protect their own social image around the clock. In today's world, people cannot risk being tarnished because of something that they posted or someone else posted about them on their Facebook. NetworkClean offers a simple self-service solution where users will constantly be alerted to this type of content.

For this purpose, one of individual reputation management, it certainly seems to do its job well.

AN INTERVIEW WITH @TWEETMYJOBS

Yair Riemer, Vice President of Global Marketing

TweetMyJobs, as its name suggests, literally tweets information about job openings to job seekers who have signed up for the company's services. It's

---

able to bring a steady stream of job openings to job seekers thanks to collaborations with companies such as Citi, Sears, and Starbucks. It has even partnered with some major U.S. city governments to help better target the job opportunities shared.

Job seekers can receive an e-mail, text, or tweet about any job opportunities meeting their specifications. Employers, in turn, are given the opportunity to share their job openings with TweetMyJobs to keep the job opportunities coming. The company receives between 3 million and 4 million monthly online visits.

According to a 2012 TweetMyJobs survey, 45 percent of companies will have increased their budget on social recruiting in 2012, and 57 percent of companies say social recruiting improves company branding.

Q. What social media advice do you have for job seekers?

A. For job seekers, the key to leveraging social media for the job search process is using the vast amount of information now available at their fingertips, that didn't exist even 5–10 years ago. Companies, more and more, are supplementing their corporate career websites by creating Twitter accounts related to careers as well as Facebook pages dedicated to corporate culture and jobs. Seekers can now communicate with decision makers and recruiters in HR via Facebook and Twitter and get a real sense of what a corporate culture is like—through photos, videos, and narrative being spread through social media. That provides the candidate with a true competitive advantage over the applicant who isn't taking advantage of social media and thus, isn't as hooked in to a company's culture or recent news items.

Q. What common mistakes do job seekers make in social media?

A. It really depends on what social media platform—for LinkedIn, the common mistake is not keeping your profile up to date. When applying for a job, more often than not, recruiters or HR professionals will Google the applicant to learn about their past business experiences. If your LinkedIn

(continued)

profile is out of date, or even worse, does not line up with the résumé you have submitted to HR, your chances of landing that job will be significantly reduced.

Q. What positive attributes do employers tend to look for in a candidate's social media presence?

A. This varies industry by industry, and position by position. But first and foremost, employers are looking for basic judgment and an overall fit with the culture of the firm. If a candidate is applying for a customer care position, or sales position, or outwardly facing position like PR or corporate communications where interpersonal skills are a must-have, then a social media presence that includes positive conversational style, or experience attending or interacting around industries, conferences, and relevant events, shows that a candidate is passionate about what they do, and passionate about connecting with others in the industry, and thus, will more likely be passionate about the organization they may join.

Q. How important is a person's social media presence to finding a job?

A. It's extremely important. More than half of employers research potential candidates on social networks, according to a survey from Career-Builder. In fact, if a candidate doesn't have any social media presence (no LinkedIn, no Twitter, no Facebook, etc.) it often raises more alarm bells than not, as employers may (wrongly or rightly) assume that the candidate is not tech savvy.

Q. What do you attribute the success of social media recruiting to?

A. The power of social recruiting is in the power of the passive candidate. Two in five adults in the U.S. are either open to or seeking a new job. That's a massive pool of job seekers, and prior to social media, these passive seekers (those not submitting their résumés week in and week out) were difficult to communicate with, or even identify. Now, through Twitter lists and chats, LinkedIn groups, and Facebook pages, companies can create talent communities and interact with these social job seekers in real time.

Q. What advice do you have to HR departments/recruiters when it comes to using social media for recruiting?

A. Since job seekers are actively mining social networks for opportunity, it's imperative that employers don't miss out. Employers need to have a branded careers presence on Facebook, Twitter, and LinkedIn. Would a company try to recruit without having a corporate website? A storefront? Having a presence on social media is no different. It's no longer a "nice to have," but it's now a "must-have," to have a presence to interact with job seekers via social media and create the talent communities and branding for your company that will lead to successful long term hires.

Q. Anything else that you would care to share?

A. Social recruiting is all about distribution in real time. Job seekers not only want highly relevant job matches, which we provide, but they want them wherever they are (on any device—be it email, text message, or on social networks like Twitter) and whenever they please—instantaneously, daily, weekly, etc. That's the power of social recruiting. Great job matches. Where you want them, when you want them.

TAKEAWAYS

- A business' social media policy, either written or verbal, may modify the rights of employees when it comes to employee social media conduct; it may limit or expand the ability of an employer to discipline or terminate an employee for social media conduct.

- Requiring an employee to surrender passwords to personal social media accounts may violate state law (varies state to state), is likely to violate the terms of service imposed by social networks (possibly triggering litigation by a social network against an employer demanding passwords), and is likely to expose the employer to a host of other civil liabilities (e.g., invasion of privacy against social network "friends" of the employee, discrimination from adverse actions due to awareness of protected-class status, etc.)

- An employer's use of social media, generally (i.e., from the public stream), to vet a candidate for employment or an employee for promotion, may expose the employer to claims of discriminatory conduct (e.g., denial of rights due to improper consideration of protected-class status, such as disability, religious affiliation or sexual orientation).

- An employer's use of a third party to vet a candidate for employment or an employee for promotion is likely to trigger responsibilities (such as notice of adverse use and the right to exam the report used) to employees under the Fair Credit Reporting Act.

- The Constitutional right of "Freedom of Speech," enshrined in the First Amendment to the U.S. Constitution, which prohibits Congress from making any law "abridging the freedom of speech," is unlikely to bar an employer's firing of an employee for social media misconduct, even when the misconduct occurs on an employee's own social media account and is posted on the employee's free time.

- The National Labor Relations Act provides employees with broad speech protections, even in social media, when the speech is made in a "concerted fashion" and relates to the "terms and conditions of employment."

- Social media policies that have a "chilling effect" on the broad right of employees to speak "in a concerted fashion about the terms and conditions of their employment" are likely to trigger scrutiny by the National Labor Relations Board, and are likely to expose an employer to liability under the National Labor Relations Act.

Copyright, Trademark, and Fair Use: How to Share Content on Social Networks Without Getting Sued . . . or Losing Your Social Media Accounts

L et's start with the basics.

WHAT IS A COPYRIGHT?

YouTube, now owned by Google, offers one of the best definitions of *copyright* at its users' copyright center ("Copyright on YouTube"):

> Copyright is a form of (legal) protection provided for original works of authorship, including literary, dramatic, musical, graphic and audiovisual creations. "Copyright" literally means the right to copy, but has come to mean that body of exclusive rights granted by law to copyright owners for protection of their work.

WHAT IS A TRADEMARK?

According to the U.S. Patent and Trademark Office:

> A trademark is a word, phrase, symbol, and/or design that identifies and distinguishes the source of the goods of one party from those of others.

In everyday terms, a trademark is typically thought of as the logo or design or catch-phrase that identifies a business or a brand.

HOW IS A COPYRIGHT DIFFERENT FROM A PATENT OR A TRADEMARK?

Copyrights, trademarks, and patents are three legal protections that are often mentioned together. For the sake of clarity, it should help to note how each is distinguished from the other. The U.S. Copyright Office has explained the differences as follows:

1. **Copyright** protects original works of authorship.

2. **Patent** protects inventions or discoveries.

3. **Trademark** protects words, phrases, symbols, or designs identifying the source of the goods or services of one party and distinguishing them from those of others.

The Problem with Trademarks

When you post a photo or a video or an article of your own creation, or even shared from another, be careful not to include commonplace brand logos or catch tunes, as they may cause your entire work to be banned from being shared on social networks. There are exceptions to this rule, but it is a general principle that should guide your review of social sharing.

"WHAT DO I HAVE TO DO TO COPYRIGHT MY WORK?"

By simply creating an original work, such as an essay on your tablet, a photo, or a video recording of a song, your work, by virtue of being "fixed" in a "tangible" form, has copyright protection under U.S. law.

BE CAREFUL WITH "WORKS MADE FOR HIRE"

A word of caution about "works made for hire"—for our purposes, this is the creative content that you may direct an employee or contractor to create on your behalf. If you're paying the bill, you would assume that the copyright would belong to you. Under U.S. copyright law, the right of exclusive control of a work, i.e., the right of copyright protection, of "a work made for hire"—that is, a work made by an employee or contractor while acting as an employee or contractor—may belong to the employer, whether that employer is a firm, organization, or individual. But as the U.S. Copyright Office warns, "The concept of a 'work made for hire' can be complicated." If you are going to use a contractor to create a work on behalf of your business, be sure to spell out in a written agreement the issue of copyright ownership and discuss with a lawyer the criteria established under the law that also needs to be met. As the Copyright Office warns, it "can be complicated." *See Circular 9, U.S. Copyright Office, Work-Made-for-Hire Under the 1976 Copyright Act. 17 U.S.C. 101.*

WHAT IS COPYRIGHT INFRINGEMENT?

According to the U.S. Copyright Office:

> As a general matter, copyright infringement occurs when a copyrighted work is reproduced, distributed, performed, publicly displayed, or made into a derivative work without the permission of the copyright owner.

"What If Someone Has Infringed on My Copyright and I Want to Sue?"

If you have been unable to resolve a copyright infringement on one of your works and you wish to file a lawsuit, you will need to register your work with the U.S. Copyright Office. Although you do not need to file anything with the U.S. Copyright Office to have your work protected as a copyrighted work, you will need to file a formal preregistration or registration if you wish to enforce your rights by filing a lawsuit. *17 U.S.C. § 411(a)*

THE MUDDY WATERS OF COPYRIGHT LAW AND FAIR USE

Now I must confess that I have cited Google's definition of a copyright without obtaining Google's permission. So have I just infringed on Google's copyright? It would seem that I have, given the definition of "copyright infringement" that we just reviewed. However, should Google decide to seek a remedy (sue me) for my citation of its work without its permission, I would argue that my use of Google's definition is a "fair use," which is an express exception (some object to the use of the term "exception," seeing fair use not as an exception to the copyright laws, but as part and parcel to the copyright laws, something strenuously argued in such disputes) to the necessity, in certain instances, of obtaining a copyright owner's permission to use a portion of the copyrighted work.

Google, should it still wish to object to my use of its copyrighted definitions without express permission, would no doubt argue that my defense of the term "fair use" is weak, given the commercial nature of this book, not to mention its immense readership (OK, we're hypothesizing here!). Who would be right? Who would win? One can never presume a court's judgment, though I suspect that for a variety of factors, too lengthy to be discussed here, I would prevail. Welcome to the muddy waters of copyright. (We will review the doctrine of fair use in greater detail very shortly.) A trump card might be that Google's definition of "copyright" also very closely resembles the one provided by the U.S. Copyright Office, and information from government publications, generally speaking, is not subject to any copyright restrictions.

The waters of copyright law become even muddier in the realm of social media, where social share buttons are often placed right next to copyrighted works by the creators of the works, who then sometimes go on to include, often buried at the bottom of their post, a draconian warning of the need to obtain their permission before sharing their work!

Go Ahead, Tweet or Pin My Work—I Dare Ya!

What is one to do when a creator of a work places a social share button next to his or her work, only to include, usually buried at the bottom of the post, a boilerplate copyright warning about obtaining the permission of the author of the work before sharing the work? It is a not-so-uncommon scenario in the social space.

The "official" response? Get the copyright owner's permission.

If, however, I see a social share button next to a work that I believe has been posted by the creator and copyright owner of that work, I'll go ahead and retweet it or pin it because I am prepared to argue that the placement of such a social share button next to a work is an implied, limited license from the copyright owner that I am permitted to retweet or pin, as the case might be. Now this is an approach I would take for myself and not one that I would recommend to a risk-averse client, as it does not reflect the current state of the law, as of the writing of this book. It is an argument waiting to be made and decided by a court of law. It is one of the many open questions in the evolving area of social media law.

To be clear, though I feel strongly about this point, i.e., that the placement of a social share button next to a work by the copyright owner of the work creates a limited license to share the work via the social share button placed next to the work, understand that this is not, yet, and may never become the law of the land (though you can say you heard it here first, as I am predicting that it will eventually become the law of the land, should a court of law be confronted by such an issue).

"OK, So What Exactly Is the Fair Use "Exception or Privilege" to the U.S. Copyright Laws?"

"Fair use" is an exception or privilege included in the copyright law that outlines various criteria that must be used in assessing whether or not a given use of a copyrighted work would be deemed a "fair use," which is a use of a copyrighted work that does not require the consent of the copyright owner.

The Distinction Between Fair Use and Infringement—Is Not Always Clear

Going back to the theme of "muddy waters" in copyright law, the U.S. Copyright Office warns:

> The distinction between what is fair use and what is infringement in a particular case will not always be clear or easily defined. There is no specific number of words, lines, or notes that may safely be taken without permission. Acknowledging the source of the copyrighted material does not substitute for obtaining permission.

FOUR FACTORS ARE WEIGHED TO DETERMINE WHETHER A USE IS A "FAIR USE"

Under the copyright law, 17 USC § 107, the fair use of a copyrighted work "for purposes such as criticism, comment, news reporting, teaching (including multiple copies for classroom use), scholarship, or research" is not an infringement of the copyright.

To determine whether a use of a copyrighted work is a fair use of that work, the copyright law outlines four factors that a court must consider to make the determination:

1. Purpose
2. Nature

3. Amount

4. Effect

To be clear, however, before arriving at the four-point "fair use" assessment required by the law, the use must be for a purpose "such as" (i.e., the examples listed are *not* exhaustive, but simply exemplary, meaning that they are only illustrative of the types of purposes that would be permitted under the fair use provision, requiring the four-point assessment to be made):

- Criticism

- Comment

- News reporting

- Teaching (including multiple copies for classroom use)

- Scholarship

- Research

The law outlines four factors that must be considered by a court when assessing whether a use of a copyrighted work without the copyright owner's permission is a fair use:

1. Purpose and character of the use, including whether such use is of a commercial nature or is for nonprofit educational purposes;

2. Nature of the copyrighted work;

3. Amount and substantiality of the portion used in relation to the copyrighted work as a whole; and

4. Effect of the use upon the potential market for or value of the copyrighted work 17 USC § 107

Parody: A Common Defense to Copyright and Trademark Infringement Claims

Humor is often used to comment on and criticize the actions or inactions of others. Parody, an imitative work for comical and critical effect, raises a number of legal privileges that can, under certain circumstances, be used to overcome both copyright and trademark limitations on usage. During the worst of BP's oil spill in the Gulf of Mexico, for example, a parody Twitter account, calling itself @BPGobalPR, emblazoned with a slight variation of BP's official trademarked logo, tweeted comical and not-so-comical messages to an audience that dwarfed that of BP's official Twitter account. The biting humor of the account's messages and what appeared to be a leaking version of the trademarked logo provided the account with sufficient leeway not to run afoul of Twitter's rules against trademark infringement, as it was an obvious parody of the official brand account.

Be warned that "being funny" in imitative works is by no means an automatic or easy defense to claims of copyright or trademark infringement—though it could help, depending on the circumstances!

WHAT IS THE "PUBLIC DOMAIN," AND WHAT DOES IT REALLY MEAN?

The U.S. Copyright Office explains that a work is in the "public domain" if it is "no longer under copyright protection or if it failed to meet the requirements for copyright protection. Works in the public domain may be used freely without the permission of the former copyright owner." Copyright does not protect "facts, ideas, systems, or methods of operation, although it may protect the way these things are expressed."

The Life of the Work's Creator plus 70 Years (or plus 50 Years or for a Term of 95 Years)

As with all other aspects of the law, copyright periods of protection are subject to revision and may vary from nation to nation. *The following is provided to give readers a general overview of the subject but should not be relied upon to assess whether or not a given work from a given jurisdiction might or might not have copyright protection, as the rules are subject to change and limitations or expansions.*

In General, in the United States, the Period of Copyright Protection Lasts the Life of the Work's Creator plus 70 Years

Under U.S. law, generally speaking, a work created on or after January 1, 1978, enjoys the protection of copyright for the life of the creator plus 70 years, after which the work, absent some other consideration or exception to the law, would enter the "public domain," meaning that it could be used by others without the necessity of obtaining permission. *17 U.S.C. § 302(a)*

- **Joint works.** Where a work was jointly created by two or more individuals "who did not work for hire, the copyright endures for a term consisting of the life of the last surviving author and 70 years after such last surviving author's death." *17 U.S.C. § 302(b)*

- **Anonymous works, pseudonymous works, and works made for hire.** Where a copyrighted work was anonymously made, or was a pseudonymous work, or was a work made for hire, "the copyright endures for a term of 95 years from the year of its first publication, or a term of 120 years from the year of its creation, whichever expires first." *17 U.S.C. § 302(c)*

International Copyright Law: Other Countries Provide a Period of Copyright Protection for the Life of the Creator plus 50 Years or for Other Durations

The U.S. Copyright Office points out that "[t]here is no such thing as an 'international copyright' that will automatically protect an author's writings throughout the world. Protection against unauthorized use in a particular country depends on the national laws of that country."

Most countries, however, including the United States, have ratified international copyright agreements that require each to honor the other's copyright protections. In some countries, such as Canada, the People's Republic of China, and Saudi Arabia, the period of copyright protection is shorter than the U.S. period of the life of the creator plus 70 years, being, instead, for the duration of the life of the work's creator plus 50 years. Some nations provide for even shorter periods of copyright protection.

However, the life of the creator plus 70 years is the most common period of copyright protection among nations, with the life of the creator plus 50 years being the second most common duration of copyright protection.

"SO WHAT'S ALL THIS ABOUT 'CREATIVE COMMONS' COPYRIGHT LICENSING?"

Creative Commons (CC) licensing is a licensing system established by a nonprofit organization that goes by the same name, Creative Commons. The system is a do-it-yourself resource that is used by scores of artists to share their works that offers six types of licenses with varying degrees of permissions. A visit to the organization's website comes with a welcome for visitors to use their licenses and tools that walk users through a series of questions, helping them identify the type of license that might best suit their needs. Understand that the organization has no governmental affiliation but that the licenses offered do come with real legal consequences.

The Creative Commons organization can be found online at http://www .creativecommons.org.

What You Need to Know About CC Licenses

CC licenses can be useful to creators of works who wish to share their content while still retaining some rights to their work, without the expense of consulting a lawyer. Do-it-yourself licensing, however, comes with the same risks related to any do-it-yourself legal kits: the law is, generally speaking, complicated, and binding yourself without the benefit of legal advice can come with lasting consequences you might regret, especially should your work later prove be "the work," that photo or song everyone just can't get enough of!

Other Points You Should Consider When Using a CC License

The following points are offered to help provide additional clarification on the use of a CC license or work:

- CC licenses are likely to be deemed legally binding, which means that if you use them, you are, in fact, giving others the right to use your works as described by the specific license you chose to use.

- Do not think that because CC is a do-it-yourself site that you can simply change your mind if someone chooses to use your work consistent with the CC license you have used. This means that even if a *really* big company decides to use a work of yours where your only requirement under the CC license was that you receive attribution for your work—that's likely all you will be entitled to receive: credit for your work. You should, however, check to see if the user has followed the letter of the license you have given. If it has not, you may still have a claim. *And in all situations where you have a legal question, talk with a lawyer from your jurisdiction, as this discussion is for general, not fact-specific, informational purposes only.*

- As with any license to use the copyrighted work of another, you might want to take added precautions to ensure that the self-proclaimed owner of the work is, in fact, the owner of the work. (This means actually contacting the "owners" to be sure they are who they say they are.)

- Even if a work has a CC license, it isn't a guarantee that those people photographed in such a work, for example, have given their permission to have their image or likeness used, creating potential right-to-privacy or right-of-publicity claims. (The right to privacy, of course, is a right to be left alone. The right of publicity is a related claim recognized, in varying degrees, by the laws of about half the states of the United States, giving individuals a right to retain the commercial use of their image or likeness.)

- Do-it-yourself licensing comes with the same risks related to any do-it-yourself legal kits: the law is, generally, complicated, and binding yourself without the benefit of legal advice can come with lasting consequences you might regret, especially should your work prove at some point to become "the work."

DISPELLING SOME COMMON COPYRIGHT INFRINGEMENT MYTHS

"I'm not making money from the pictures I posted, so that's not a violation of copyright law, right?" Wrong.

"I put a notice on my page where everyone can see it that no 'copyright infringement is intended,' so I can't be sued if I use someone else's work, because they can just contact me if there's a problem." Nope.

Once again tipping my hat to YouTube's copyright center, there are several common copyright myths that should be dispelled:

It is important to note that your video can still be affected by a claim of copyright infringement, even if you have ...

1. **Given credit** to the copyright owner

2. **Refrained from monetizing** the infringing video

3. **Noticed similar videos** that appear on YouTube

4. **Purchased the content** on iTunes, a CD, or DVD

5. **Recorded the content yourself** from TV, a movie theater, or the radio

6. **Stated that "no copyright infringement is intended"**

Beware: Privacy and Publicity Rights May Trump Copyright Privileges

You did your homework. You tracked down the photographer who took the picture that you desperately wanted to share on your company's coolest Pinterest board. You even got the photographer to sign a written release so that you could pin the photo to your company board without paying any royalties!

Photo pinned to company's hottest board on Pinterest. Twenty minutes letter, phone buzzes. "Bet it's legal asking if I got a release from the photographer!"

"Jenny, Legal. Do we have a release from the person pictured in our newest photo?"

"Did I get a release from the person *pictured* in our newest photo?!"

"They're kidding, right?"

Nope. See, e.g Cal. Civ. Code *§ 3344: California Code*.

THE "SAFE HARBOR" OF THE DIGITAL MILLENNIUM COPYRIGHT ACT

As discussed in greater detail later in the chapter on blogging, Section 512 of the Digital Millennium Copyright Act (DMCA or the Act) creates a so-called safe harbor against copyright infringement claims against the provider of an Internet site that allows others to post content to the site. Such a site could be a social network, such as Facebook, or a corporate blog. A provider of a social sharing site will have a "safe harbor" against copyright infringement claims under the Act, as long as the provider of the site has a policy that "repeat infringers" will have their accounts terminated, does not receive a financial benefit from the infringing content, was not aware of the infringing content on its site or of facts that would have made the infringing nature of the content apparent, accommodates standard copyright protection measures, and had in place a procedure in which copyright owners or their agents could notify a designated contact for the site provider of infringing content so that it could be—and would be—quickly removed.

"Unclean Hands"—No Safe Harbor

It is important to understand that this "safe harbor" protection presupposes the innocence of the site provider in any copyright infringement case, meaning that the infringing content placed on the site was shared there by a third party and not shared by the provider of the site. Furthermore, it is equally important to understand that safe harbor protection demands that the site providers terminate the accounts of repeat infringers. *17 U.S.C. § 512*

As one might expect, immense social networking sites are particularly keen about not losing the immunity of the safe harbor protection, creating, for some, a terminate-now and answer-questions-later approach to suspected repeat infringers.

HOW *NOT* TO USE THE DMCA #CRISISCOMMUNICATIONS

In February 2013, a graphic video of a horrific NASCAR race car crash was uploaded by a fan in the stands. The video captured a large cloud of small debris scattering into the stadium as cars seemed to disintegrate in the crash (all the drivers were able to walk away from their cars). Capturing the confusion that followed, the video then caught spectators waving for help, after which the camera focused in on a tire eerily laid to rest in a spot on the crowded benches and then on a fan covering someone with his shirt.

The video was yanked from YouTube shortly after it appeared following a DMCA "take-down" complaint, commonly known as a copyright infringement complaint, by NASCAR.

Shortly after the video was taken down from YouTube, it reappeared on the site, along with an explanation, as reported by the *Washington Post,* that because there is no copyright-infringing content, YouTube's partners and users do not have the right to take down videos from YouTube.

NASCAR, according to the *Washington Post*, explained the incident with the following formal statement:

> The fan video of the wreck on the final lap of today's NASCAR Nationwide Series race was blocked on YouTube out of respect for those injured in today's accident. Information on the status of those fans was unclear and the decision was made to err on the side of caution with this very serious incident.—Steve Phelps, NASCAR Senior Vice President and Chief Marketing Officer

---

BOXING AGAINST SHADOWS WHEN IT COMES TO COPYRIGHT INFRINGEMENT TERMINATIONS

It apparently came as a complete surprise to Cool Hunter's founder, Bill Tikos, when, inexplicably, his brand's social network account with 788,000 fans and lots of content was gone. According to Tikos, "We have never intentionally broken any Facebook rules and we are willing to do whatever it takes to get our page back. But we do not have the answers and we do not know how to get them. We have tried everything in our power, and we are getting nowhere."

Tikos's frustration underscores an important point: a real or imagined violation of the network's copyright policies can leave a company at a deep business disadvantage, losing the privilege of an account on a social network most would consider indispensable for marketing in the age of social media. What might be the value of a social media account with nearly 1 million followers and significant engagement? And what would be not only the lost business opportunity of losing that account for a brief period of suspension, but also the consequences of that loss, over time, if the "suspension" were to become a permanent ban from using the leading social network?

"Infringement of What?"

Elaborating on this point, Tikos conceded something a majority of social media users would need to concede: "We sometimes use images even when we do not know who has taken the picture." Tikos quickly added, "We *want* to give credit always, but in many cases we cannot find that information."

As Cool Hunter attempted to balance its desire to share "cool" content even when the owner of that content was unknown, with a desire to not infringe on the copyright of others, Tikos noted that "[o]n our 'About Us' page and on our (now extinct) Facebook page we specifically state that if we have posted an image that belongs to you, we want to know, so that we can give you the appropriate credit."

In Tikos's answer lies part of the problem: unless a use of the work of another is a "fair use," as discussed earlier, crediting the work of another does not give one the right to use or share the work of another. Additionally, although the law also provides a safe harbor provision to those who "provide" online, interactive forums, that protective provision does not extend to protect the host of an interactive site when it is the host and not some third party that has shared the copyrighted content.

GIVING CREDIT TO A COPYRIGHT HOLDER OR HAVING A TAKE-DOWN PROVISION ON YOUR SITE DOES NOT GIVE YOU PERMISSION TO USE ANOTHER'S WORK WITHOUT CONSENT

A basic rule of copyright law is that only the owner of a copyright may give permission to another to use the owner's work. Crediting the author or a creator of a work, assuming the person to be the owner of the copyright (the person may have created the work but given or sold the ownership right to someone else), is not the same as getting the copyright holder's permission to share a work. This is a point of confusion for some. It can be a costly mistake.

AN EASY WAY TO CLOSE DOWN THE COMPETITION?

Unscrupulous businesses might be tempted to assert a copyright infringement claim, thinking that it might be an easy way of closing down the social media account of a competitor. On the flip side of that is the fact that any business victimized in such a way would certainly have good cause to seek legal action to uncover the "anonymous" copyright complainant, disprove the complaint, and pursue an action for "tortious interference with prospective business opportunities," among a slew of other causes of action (i.e., grounds for a lawsuit and recovery).

The downside to filing legal action to remedy such a situation, apart from the cost, is the time such a process would take, as it might be a challenge to persuade a court to treat such a matter as an emergent one. The process could drag on.

As of this writing, the brand's Facebook page had not been restored.

PINTEREST AND COPYRIGHTS

Pinterest warns that its policy, "in appropriate circumstances and at its discretion," is "to disable and/or terminate the accounts of users who repeatedly infringe or are repeatedly charged with infringing the copyrights or other intellectual property rights of others."

Pinterest has also put into place procedures in accordance with the Digital Millennium Copyright Act of 1998, as outlined in its section on copyright guidelines at http://pinterest.com/about/copyright/.

PINTEREST AND TRADEMARKS

On the topic of trademarks, Pinterest rules provide:

Pinterest respects the trademark rights of others. Accounts with usernames, Pin Board names, or any other content that misleads others or violates another's trademark may be updated, transferred or permanently suspended.

Anyone with a trademark-related concern is invited to contact http://about.pinterest.com/en/trademark. More information on the topic may be found at http://pinterest.com/about/trademark/.

TWITTER AND TRADEMARKS

Twitter rules specifically say that the network "reserves the right to reclaim user names on behalf of businesses or individuals that hold a legal claim or trademark on user names." Additionally, accounts "using business names and/or logos to mislead others will be permanently suspended."

SOME ADDITIONAL POINTS ON SOCIAL SHARING

Caution is always the best guide when it comes to social sharing.

- The fact that you are the second or third or twentieth person to repin or post a photograph, video, or other content does not immunize you in any way from a copyright claim.

- Want to avoid copyright infringement claims? Before you share, pin, or Google+ work you have been creating, make sure you didn't inadvertently include someone else's logo, song in the background, or smiling face, without that "someone's" consent.

SO WHY DID PINTEREST THROW EVERYONE INTO A COPYRIGHT PANIC?

If you share a blog post that you didn't write yourself, without the permission of the author, chances are that when you hit the retweet button, you've just committed a copyright infringement.

So what's the difference with a photo? Why is posting a cool photo on one of my social media accounts so darn dangerous? Why the panic?

A COTTAGE INDUSTRY OF DEMANDING PAYMENT FOR PHOTO INFRINGEMENTS

The difference between sharing a cool blog post you found on the web that doesn't belong to you and sharing a cool photo you also found on the web that doesn't belong to you is that a cottage industry has sprung up of unscrupulous companies that buy up every photo collection they can possibly get their hands on and then troll the web searching for those who had the misfortune and temerity to use one of their photos without their permission. Once a copyright troll finds its prey, it pounces, sending a steady barrage of scary-sounding letters, usually to a small business owner, demanding payment, usually thousands of dollars, for the unlicensed use of the photo. The letters persist in pouring in until the victim relents by sending the requested payment.

"Hey, What About the Rights of the Photographer?!"

To be very clear, what I am talking about here is not an instance where a legitimate photographer has been deprived of fair compensation for the use of a photograph or image or work that took hours or days to get right, using expensive equipment, after years of arduous training. Instead I am talking about a rampant abuse of the legal processes by unscrupulous businesses that profit by a collection of images they have amassed and by all the terror they can stuff into a series of envelopes addressed to whoever has posted something from their precious collection. I mention the issue because it is a legal land mine that a small business—or even a larger one—is most likely to step on. Understanding why it is such a prevalent issue should be helpful, too.

THE U.S. COPYRIGHT OFFICE ONLINE PROVIDES GREAT RESOURCES

When it comes to copyright issues, there are always a hundred questions. Fortunately, the U.S. Copyright Office does a notable job of providing a wealth of information online for most questions, at http://www.copyright.gov/.

4

Marketing in Social Media: What You Need to Know

THE FTC'S SOCIAL MEDIA GUIDELINES

In 2009, the Federal Trade Commission (FTC) came out with social media guidelines. They came by way of an update to the FTC's Guides Concerning the Use and Endorsements of Testimonials in Advertising. *16 CFR Part 255.* They were big news at the time they were announced. Somehow, like a story that goes viral and then disappears, news of the FTC's new guidelines seemed to stay around only long enough for people to say "wow!" and then forget about them. Unfortunately for marketers and businesses, ignorance of the law is not bliss. It will only get you in trouble, embarrass your brand, and, perhaps, ruin your career.

The FTC, for its part, insists that its new guidelines are really just the same old advertising rules it has always had, spiced up with some social media examples. The examples are helpful, but the practical application of existing advertising law in the medium of new media can, in fact, be a little complicated, as we are about to see.

As the FTC explained the revised guidelines in its update announcement:

The revised Guides also add new examples to illustrate the long standing principle that "material connections" (sometimes payments or free products) between advertisers and endorsers—connections that consumers would not expect—must be disclosed. These examples address what constitutes an endorsement when the message is conveyed by bloggers or other "word-of-mouth" marketers.

ANNTAYLOR STORES HOSTS A BLOGGING EVENT

Three months after the FTC came out with its updated guidelines, which provided some new examples of old rules using social media, the Loft division of Ann Taylor decided to host a blogging event for its summer 2010 collection. Blogging events in 2010 were pretty cutting edge. For many, they still are.

According to an *Advertising Age* article about the event and enforcement action, bloggers received an invitation "promising that those posting coverage from the event would be entered into a 'mystery gift-card drawing,' where they could win between $50 and $500."

FTC LETTER TO ANNTAYLOR STORES, CORP., LEGAL COUNSEL (OPENING PARAGRAPH)

As you know, the staff of the Federal Trade Commission's Division of Advertising Practices has conducted an investigation into whether your client, AnnTaylor Stores Corporation, violated Section 5 of the Federal Trade Commission Act, 15 U.S.C. § 45, in connection with providing gifts to bloggers who the company expected would post blog content about the company's LOFT division. . . . Our decision not to pursue enforcement action is not to be construed as a determination that a violation may not have occurred, just as the pendency of an investigation should not be construed as a determination that a violation has occurred. The Commission reserves the right to take such further action as the public interest may warrant.

Ouch. Not the sort of happy ending a brand or digital marketer would want—or expect—to see come from a blogging event. It was a shot heard around the blogosphere . . . back in April 2010.

I did ask Ann Taylor if it wanted to comment on the subject. The company declined, noting, "We consider the FTC matter closed and we don't believe it would be appropriate for us to comment at this time for the same reason we chose not to comment while the investigation was ongoing." Completely understandable.

Clearly mindful of the FTC social media endorsement guidelines, Ann Taylor took the precaution of posting a sign at the event. No one disputes this.

The sign told bloggers at the event that they should disclose the gifts if they posted comments about the preview.

Isn't a Sign at the Event Telling Bloggers of Their Duty to Disclose Gifts Enough?

"Did Ann Taylor comply with the FTC's obligations under the revised guidelines," I will ask my students at this point. There's generally a slight pause before a hand goes up. When it does, I'm not quite sure what the answer will be: sometimes it's yes; sometimes it's no.

"What if a blogger attending the event were blind," a student asked at a recent class, adding a new twist to the scenario. Fair point. He or she would likely miss the sign.

But even for bloggers without visual limitations, the FTC, in its letter closing its investigation of the Ann Taylor Loft blogging event, in a footnote, noted the presence of the sign and simply stated, "It is not clear, however, how many bloggers actually saw that sign."

TRYING TO GET IT RIGHT AND GETTING IT RIGHT ARE NOT THE SAME

I tell my students that it seems to me that Ann Taylor made a good-faith effort to host an innovative and compliant marketing event, but unfortunately for the company, it didn't get it quite right. In fact, it seems to me that the FTC used the event as an occasion to fire a warning shot about its updated guidelines for a new medium, choosing a juicy plum that it could easily reach for to make an example—and would get a lot of attention in the process.

Now I don't mean to cast aspersions on anyone, especially on the FTC, which seems to do a yeoman's job with limited resources. But it does seem to me that Ann Taylor was trying to get it right. Perhaps even the FTC thought so. But trying to get it right and getting it right is not the same.

HERE'S HOW THE FTC ANALYZED THE ANN TAYLOR BLOGGING EVENT

The FTC began its analysis of the Ann Taylor Loft blogging event by citing Section 5 of the FTC Act.

Statement of the Law: Section 5 of the FTC Act

As set forth in its investigatory closure letter to the retail giant, the Act requires:

> [T]he disclosure of a material connection between an advertiser and an endorser when such a relationship is not otherwise apparent from the context of the communication that contains the endorsement. Depending on the circumstances, an advertiser's provision of a gift to a blogger for posting blog content about an event could constitute a material connection that is not reasonably expected by readers of the blog.

BEST PRACTICE

If you give anything of value to a blogger, recognize that under the guidelines you have most likely created a "material connection" with that blogger, triggering a set of obligations, the first being to ensure that the blogger is informed of his or her duty to disclose the connection in a "clear and conspicuous" manner.

WHY THE FTC DECIDED NOT TO RECOMMEND AN ENFORCEMENT ACTION AGAINST ANN TAYLOR

In its letter to Ann Taylor Stores, Corp., the FTC gave a litany of reasons why it was not recommending an enforcement action:

- The January 26, 2010, preview was the first only such preview event.

- Only a very small number of bloggers posted content about the preview.

- Several of those bloggers disclosed that Loft had provided them gifts at the preview.

- Loft adopted a written policy in February 2010 stating that Loft will not issue any gift to any blogger without first telling the blogger that the blogger must disclose the gift in his or her blog.

- The FTC staff expects that Loft will both honor that written policy and take reasonable steps to monitor bloggers' compliance with the obligation to disclose gifts they receive from Loft. (You must actually monitor the bloggers you sponsor for compliance of their duty to disclose. The FTC has suggested that spot-checking bloggers for compliance may suffice.)

BEST PRACTICES BASED ON THE ANN TAYLOR CASE STUDY

If you are planning a blogging event, put these best practices high on your checklist:

- **Inform bloggers in their invitation to a blogging event of their duty to disclose.** This has the added bonus of letting bloggers know that you play by the rules. Bloggers who care about their reputations will feel better about attending such an event, as your invitation will make it clear that you care about the rules and your reputation. Influential bloggers care about compliance because they care about their reputation.

- **Inform bloggers of your duty and plans to audit bloggers for compliance.** The guidelines require those sponsoring the bloggers to monitor the bloggers for compliance with their duty to disclose. Letting bloggers know of this responsibility and your plans to keep this obligation should enhance blogger compliance, as well as make your event even tighter from a compliance and public perception perspective, as well as will help bloggers understand any communication you may need to make with them in the event that you see them failing to make a disclosure or otherwise providing inaccurate information about your goods or services.

- **Include a provision in your social media policy citing the FTC guidelines, specifically mentioning that your brand will not issue any gift to any blogger without first telling the blogger that the blogger must disclose the gift in his or her blog.** Including the FTC-sponsored blogger rules in your social media policy can help keep you out of hot water!

- **Take reasonable steps to monitor bloggers' compliance with the obligation to disclose gifts they receive from you.** The FTC does not say how those who are sponsoring bloggers should monitor bloggers for compliance with their duty to disclose—except to say that those sponsoring the bloggers must.

IF YOU ARE INVESTIGATED BY THE FTC, YOU DON'T WIN

One would think that from all the hoopla, Ann Taylor was found to have done something wrong. It was not. For purposes of transparency and instruction, however, FTC investigatory closure letters are made public. They are intended to be instructive to others. Unfortunately for the subject of them, they become fodder for many articles and posts, and sometimes case studies in a book. The investigatory closure letters tend to end with the same closing paragraph, like the one in the Ann Taylor Loft case:

> Our decision not to pursue enforcement action is not to be construed as a determination that a violation may not have occurred, just as the pendency of an investigation should not be construed as a determination that a violation has occurred. The Commission reserves the right to take such further action as the public interest may warrant.

Nobody gets to claim victory. The warning shot is left ringing in everybody's ears.

THE BIGGER YOU ARE, THE MORE LIKELY IT IS THAT COMPLIANCE RELATED TO YOUR ONLINE ACTIVITIES WILL BE SCRUTINIZED—AND TARGETED, IF NOT RIGHT

On the subject of disclosures, let me make one . . . or two. I like Ann Taylor. I like the store. I like the people who work there. My mom and sisters love the store, as does my wife. Do I think that Ann Taylor acted in good faith in putting together its blogging event? I sure do. Do I think that it was being picked on by the FTC? No. The company just happened to be the innovators who stepped forward when the issue of sponsored blogging was coming under the focus of everyone. Your brand now has the benefit of the bumps that Ann Taylor took.

And I'm going to let you in on a secret: it seems to me that the bigger you are, the more likely it is that compliance related to your online activities will be scrutinized by the nation's consumer protection agency, the FTC. Ask Sears, Facebook, Twitter, Google, MySpace. They have all been the subject of FTC investigations and settlements.

THE FTC'S REVISED ENDORSEMENT AND TESTIMONIAL GUIDES

"Wait a second, aren't these just 'guidelines'?"

Yes, but before you walk away, you might want to hear what the FTC has said about its "guidelines":

> The Guides are administrative interpretations of the law intended to help advertisers comply with the Federal Trade Commission Act; they are not binding law themselves. In any law enforcement action challenging the allegedly deceptive use of testimonials or endorsements, the Commission would have the burden of proving that the challenged conduct violates the FTC Act.

BEST PRACTICE

If you want to stay on the right side of the law in social media marketing, follow the FTC's guidelines. If you don't, chances are you will be violating the law. The guidelines give clear examples of how the law operates in the real world. They are instructive and predictive of what would happen to your business if it followed or strayed from the practices described. In any enforcement action, you would be cited for a violation of the FTC Act, not the guidelines—though if you had followed the guidelines, you would be unlikely to violate the Act.

NEW MEDIA OR OLD, THE FTC IS STILL "THE NATION'S CONSUMER PROTECTION AGENCY"

The FTC actually describes itself as "the nation's consumer protection agency," working for the consumer "to prevent fraud, deception, and unfair business practices in the marketplace." Although the FTC was created by Congress in 1914 to prevent unfair competition, its role has been greatly expanded through additional congressional mandates. In 1938, Congress passed a broad prohibition against "unfair and deceptive acts or practices," leaving the FTC to advance that prohibition of such practices through the development of policies, educational programs, and enforcement actions.

With the advent of social media, the FTC has continued its policing of the marketplace, recognizing that social networks have become the newest platform for biggest advertising. Though the medium has changed, the FTC's determination to ferret out and sanction "unfair or deceptive acts or practices" has not.

Unfair or Deceptive Blogging or Tweeting? The FTC Can Police and Enforce

According to the FTC:

> [T]he Commission may initiate an enforcement action if it has "reason to believe" that the law is being or has been violated. . . . The basic consumer protection statute enforced by the Commission is Section 5(a) of the FTC Act, which provides that 'unfair or deceptive acts or practices in or affecting commerce . . . are . . . declared unlawful. (15 U.S.C. Sec. 45(a)(1)). See FTC.gov.

UNDERSTANDING THE FTC'S ENDORSEMENT GUIDELINES

Properly known as Revised Testimonial and Endorsement Guides, the guidelines provide the "general principles" that the Commission uses in evaluating endorsements and testimonials for deceptiveness or fraud. The purpose of the Endorsement Guides, according to the FTC, is to "provide the basis for voluntary compliance with the law by advertisers and endorsers."

Businesses and bloggers should not confuse the FTC's description of its guidelines as "voluntary" to mean that the guidelines are purely optional: they establish, instead, a sound basis for best practices to lessen the likelihood of a business or blogger being sanctioned for a violation of the law.

FTC'S UPDATE OFFERS NEW SOCIAL MEDIA EXAMPLES, KEEPS SAME LEGAL PRINCIPLES

Importantly, although the FTC social media update of its Endorsement Guides includes new examples using social media scenarios, the FTC notes that "[t]he legal principles haven't changed."

Elaborating on the point, the FTC explained:

> The Guides aren't new, but they've recently been updated. It's always been the law that if an ad features an endorser who's a relative or employee of the marketer—or if an endorser has been paid or given something of value to tout the marketer's product—the ad is misleading unless the connection is made clear.

Under the guidelines:

- Endorsements must reflect honest opinions, findings, beliefs, or experience of the endorser.

- An endorsement message need not be phrased in the exact words of the endorser, but they may not be taken out of context, unless this is made clear.

- Where an advertiser uses an "expert or celebrity" for an endorsement, the advertiser may only continue to use such an endorsement so long as the endorser continues to hold the views expressed, imposing a requirement on the advertiser to secure the endorser's views at reasonable intervals.

- The advertiser may only continue to use an endorsement as long as it has "good reason to believe the endorser remains a bona fide user of the product."

- Advertisers are subject to liability for false or unsubstantiated statements made through their endorsements or for the failure to disclose material connections between themselves and their endorsers, and endorsers may be liable for their endorsement statements.

These advertising rules are not specific to the medium of social media—but they do apply to social media.

CAN A BLOG COMMENT OR A TWEET BE AN ENDORSEMENT?

Not only can a blog comment or tweet be an endorsement, but so too can a post to Facebook or Google+ or a video uploaded to YouTube.

An "endorsement" under the guidelines means "any advertising message." An "endorser" may be "an individual, group, or institution" providing an advertising message that consumers are likely to believe reflects the true opinions or experiences of the endorser, rather than statements supplied by the sponsoring advertiser.

It is the message that matters, not the medium used to convey the message. A tweet, Facebook update, or blog comment or chat room chat can trigger FTC scrutiny and enforcement as a regulated endorsement.

What ever happened to free speech?!

To quote the FTC:

If you are acting on behalf of an advertiser, what you are saying is commercial speech—and commercial speech can be regulated under the FTC Act if it's deceptive.

IF YOU'RE TRYING TO CREATE A "SOCIAL" EVENT, BE SOCIAL

On a side note, don't blow a big chance to tap into "social." You're hosting an event for over a thousand people in a major city? You've even gone through the trouble of creating an event hashtag and inviting bloggers at your guest? Don't drop the ball at the event!

Monitor hashtag mentions of your event. You're monitoring your reputation and creating advocates and a community when you do and you respond. When you don't, you just highlight the fact that you really aren't "social."

LEGAL LAND MINE

Don't think lawyers know about social media law just because they are lawyers.
— Ask.

WORKING WITH SOCIAL MEDIA INFLUENCERS TO ORGANIZE BLOGGING EVENTS

One of the easiest ways to create some buzz? Tap a social media influencer to help organize your social event.

LEGAL LAND MINES

Be alert to these potential problems.

- If you "sponsor" (i.e., give free stuff to) social media influencers and they fail to disclose their connection to you, it is you, not they, who risk being sanctioned by the FTC.

- If you entrust a social media influencer to organize an event on behalf of your brand, be sure that you have chosen carefully and have instructed your organizer well in the disclosure requirements, as any failure to disclose in a compliant manner could also entangle and alienate the other social media influencers in attendance.

> • If you are a "sponsored" blogger (i.e., you've gotten free stuff) and you fail to disclose your connection when tweeting, blogging, or vlogging (video blogging) about your cool stuff, travel, etc., although you are unlikely to be sanctioned by the FTC, you may, ultimately, find your reputation damaged and find yourself on a "Do Not Sponsor" list. (This is a list that should be made by brands that sponsor bloggers and discover that you don't disclose.)

The "Ann Tran Clan," as fans of social media blogger Ann Tran like to refer to themselves, is a big online community and getting bigger. With over 424,000 followers on Twitter, Ann Tran, who also blogs for the *Huffington Post*, has tapped into the power of social to share her passion for "inspiring the world through social media." Not surprisingly, luxury brands connect with Ann to ask that she organize tweet-ups where influential bloggers are wonderfully pampered and get to test-run some of the best vacation spots, sharing their experiences with their own sizable communities.

Ann Tran organized a Miami tweet-up at the luxurious Mandarin Oriental hotel. Ann was entrusted with putting together a VIP list of power bloggers to be treated to some of the finest pampering possible. Ann and her guests, all guests of the Mandarin Oriental, created quite a bit of online buzz as they blogged and tweeted about the event.

Ann Tran, as the influencer organizer, even created a video that was shared online by many of the attendees. An added benefit of tapping a social media influencer is that most are media and tech savvy, meaning that the chances are that not only will they tweet about your event; they'll likely also blog about it, and Facebook it, and Instagram it, and pin it—and maybe even create a video about it.

HOW DID @ANNTRAN_ DO ON HER DUTY TO DISCLOSE?

"Clear and Conspicuous" Disclosure

If you go to YouTube and search "Sizzling Miami TweetUp," you can watch the video Ann Tran made about the sponsored blogging event she organized. Note the following about the video:

- **On the video home page.** When you see the YouTube video, you notice that prominently below the "thumbs up" and share buttons, there is a disclosure— . and only a disclosure: "Please note that the Mandarin Oriental @MO_Miami invited us as their guests for the #SizzlingMiamiTweetUp extravaganza."

- **Readability.** The disclosure is easy to find and read.

- **Embedded disclosure.** In the narration of the video, Ann underscored the written disclosure, noting that they were "guests" and "treated" to their spa pampering.

- **Wrap-up disclosure.** The video concludes with a prominent, full-screen repetition of the disclosure that was found on the home page of the video: "Please note that the Mandarin Oriental @MO_Miami invited us as their guests for the #SizzlingMiamiTweetUp extravaganza." Large print. White lettering on black background. Easy to read and understand.

Speaking of disclosures. I should note that Ann and I are friends who met on Twitter. We have also met in real life at a social media conference. I have also shared with her some of my thoughts on social media compliance for bloggers, as she is keenly interested in the subject—something those who sponsor blogging events should be interested in finding in their influencers!

BEST PRACTICES FOR BRANDS WHEN WORKING WITH SOCIAL MEDIA INFLUENCERS

When you work with social media influencers, it is vital that you take these steps:

- **Vet your social media influencers carefully.** Look at their blogs and vlogs: do they contain conspicuous disclosures, or have they overlooked their obligation to disclose their material connections?

- **Be clear about your compliance expectations.** Since you, the brand, are on the hook with the FTC if disclosures are not conspicuously included in the content of sponsored bloggers, be sure that your influencer organizers are aware that you are entrusting them with their own compliance vetting process (you cannot abdicate your own responsibility, but it doesn't mean you can't strengthen the process by enrolling others in the task as well), as they will know their fellow bloggers better than you.

- **Don't rely on a single disclosure; provide several disclosures where you can.** Ann's video, for example, began with a static home-page disclosure, which the FTC has indicated is rarely enough to satisfy the duty of clear and conspicuous disclosure, as some viewers may overlook the static content and move right to the video. To guard against this, Ann then made mention in the video that she and her fellow bloggers were "guests" and "treated" to the pampering. She also ended the video with a very prominent restatement of the disclosure that she and the others were there as guests of the brand.

- **Don't ignore your duty to instruct sponsored bloggers of their duty to disclose simply because they are prominent.** Since so few seasoned marketers seem to know the social media disclosure rules, it is a bit much to expect that bloggers will have a better understanding of the rules. And in all instances, it is your responsibility to provide the instruction under the FTC rules, as there are no exceptions provided by the guidelines.

- **Set out the rules when you make your invitation.** Just as you would with a traditional blogging event, set out the disclosure rules in your invitation.

- **Consider requesting a signed acknowledgment of the disclosure requirements from your sponsored bloggers.** This may seem a bit over the top, but it really should not be. This can be included either in the invite acceptance or at the on-site registration.

- **If a blogger fails to make the required disclosure after being instructed to do so, add him or her to your own in-house "Do Not Sponsor" list.** You will be held responsible for inviting to sponsored events a blogger you know to be noncompliant. You are asking for trouble if you continue to invite to sponsored events a blogger you know is not making the appropriate disclosures. Don't do it.

COLLEGE STUDENT/EXPERT VIDEO GAMER/BLOGGER? YEAH, THE FTC'S TALKIN' TO YOU!

The college student who decides to spend his time at college playing video games and blogging about the games he plays does not escape the FTC's scrutiny. If he receives a free game from a manufacturer, the student, according to the FTC, should clearly and conspicuously disclose that he received the gaming system free of charge.

"That's silly."

That's an actual compliance example provided by the FTC. And it makes good sense.

The manufacturer, according to the FTC, must advise the student "at the time it provides the gaming system to the student that this fact must, in some way, be disclosed." The FTC even goes on to say that the manufacturer giving the gift should have procedures in place to monitor the blogger's postings for compliance.

The FTC noted that without such a disclosure from the student, readers of his blog would otherwise be unlikely to know of a factor that "likely would materially affect the credibility they attach to his endorsement." Simple enough!

IF A BLOGGER IS NONCOMPLIANT . . . THE FTC IS COMING AFTER . . . THE SPONSOR

"Say what?!"

You heard me right. Social media marketing compliance is all focused on the sponsor (i.e., advertisers), and not on the bloggers (i.e., endorsers). As the FTC would say, it's "just as it's always been."

When the FTC's social media guidelines were first announced in 2009, they created a firestorm from the blogosphere, as bloggers and social media commentators feared the worst, that bloggers would be subjected to hefty fines for not dotting every *i* and crossing every *t*, leaving the FTC to issue $11,000 fines at every blog post.

The FTC was swift in stomping out the firestorm, assuring bloggers that it would not be targeting them in its efforts to keep advertising in the social sphere honest and transparent. Instead the FTC explained that it would focus on those who were sponsoring bloggers for such compliance.

"So let me get this right: bloggers are told under the FTC's guidelines that they have a duty to disclose 'material connections' in a 'clear and conspicuous' manner—and if they don't . . . the FTC plans to do nothing about it?!"

Not exactly.

WHEN YOU HAVE A BIG QUESTION, GO TO THE SOURCE

I needed to get to the bottom of this question myself, as it was a question that had perplexed me for some time. Richard Cleland, assistant director at the Division of Advertising Practices, Bureau of Consumer Protection, was the FTC's chief spokesperson on the topic when the guidelines were first announced, in 2009, and when the firestorm started. He was the one who put the firestorm out by doing a blitz of interviews assuring everyone that no bloggers would be targeted under the new guidelines. So I decided to ask for an interview with the man himself.

"So is the FTC really still telling us that it's not going to go after bloggers who don't follow the rules [the FTC's social media marketing guidelines]," I demanded to know in the interview.

A seasoned interviewee, Cleland was quick to turn the table on his interviewer: "How many bloggers are there?" he calmly asked in response to my question.

"Well," I stammered, "seems to me pretty much everyone is a blogger these days."

"We have 40 lawyers in my group," said Cleland. "It is a question of prioritizing the use of resources and evaluating what is the likelihood that a single blogger is going to cause significant consumer injury." Like a smart general leveraging limited resources, Cleland explained that the FTC's goal is to get the sponsors to identify the bloggers who aren't complying with their disclosure obligations and to end their relationships with those who aren't.

Given the Commission's limited resources, Cleland explained, the FTC's enforcement strategy is one of "encouraging" the sponsors to "police their own marketing."

DON'T BE THE FIRST BLOGGER TO GET HIT WITH A CIVIL LAWSUIT

The fact that the FTC decides not to pursue an action against a blogger for deceptive conduct doesn't preclude someone who has suffered an injury from suing a blogger whose advice or recommendation was relied upon and contributed to the person's harm. Such a lawsuit will happen. It's just a question of when. The blogger's nondisclosure of a material connection with the brand might or might not make a difference to the litigation, but there is a good chance that it would, if the injury is substantial enough. It could well be considered for the purposes of awarding punitive damages to discourage others from similar misconduct.

Even when you state whom you work for in your Facebook or Twitter profile, the FTC still expects you to make a disclosure of whom you work for in the stream of the conversation if you are reviewing your company's products or services in the social space. The FTC has sensibly noted that most users of social media are focused on the social conversation, without necessarily stopping to look at the profiles of those doing the posting or tweeting.

Additionally, in an age of megacorporations, one might not expect that the company that makes contact lenses also makes contraceptives. It's about being "clear and conspicuous."

LEGAL LAND MINES

You are on dangerous ground if either of the two is true:

- You hire a marketing firm that doesn't understand the FTC's guidelines.

- You are a marketing firm, and you don't understand the FTC's guidelines.

"Amazing new game!"

"ONE of the BEST!"

"GREAT, family-friendly board game app"

With reviews like that, who wouldn't be interested in buying the game?

If you were then told that they were all written by a marketing firm being paid to promote the game, might it impact the weight you gave to the credibility of the reviews?

"Sure would."

"IT'S ABOUT THE CONNECTION"

The reviews you just read were actually posted by employees of a marketing firm, Reverb Communications, that had been hired to promote a mobile app game. The marketing firm stood accused of creating fake reviews for a client. The PR firm's owner, Tracie Snither, was quick to defend the actions of her employees, telling *CNET News* that the reviews weren't fake at all, but represented the true opinion of 7 out of her 16 employees who had actually purchased the game with their own money, played the game, and simply posted their true opinions about the game. Nothing fake here!

In her defense of her firm's actions, Ms. Snither conveyed a complete misunderstanding of the obligation of truthfulness under Section 5(a) of the Federal

Trade Commission Act: it imposes a duty to disclose material connections. It is not about the truthfulness of the reviews being offered, but rather about giving consumers a fair understanding of a relationship that would be reasonably expected to affect the weight given to an endorsement, however truthful that endorsement may have been.

The offense, as described by the FTC in its complaint, was all about the omission of relevant information, namely, the connection of the reviewers to the product being reviewed:

> Respondents failed to disclose that those reviews were written by employees of Reverb, a company hired to promote the gaming applications and often paid a percentage of the applications' sales. These facts would have been material to consumers in their purchasing decision regarding the gaming applications. The failure to disclose these facts, in light of the representation made, was, and is, a deceptive practice.

"Companies, including public relations firms involved in online marketing, need to abide by long-held principles of truth in advertising," said Mary Engle, director of the FTC's Division of Advertising Practices. "Advertisers should not pass themselves off as ordinary consumers touting a product, and endorsers should make it clear when they have financial connections to sellers." *In the Matter of Reverb Communications, Inc., et al. FTC File No. 092 3199.*

In its settlement with Reverb Communications, the FTC issued no fine, but it did require the firm to remove the posts where Reverb employees had failed to disclose their connection as a marketer of the online game. The settlement further prohibited Reverb employees from posting any further reviews without disclosing their connection to the manufacturer of the game.

BEST PRACTICES

The best practices to be learned here are these:

- Be certain to vet any agencies you may work with to be sure that they have a solid understanding of the FTC rules—and that their employees do as well.

- Be certain that your own employees are briefed on the FTC's guidelines.

Although FTC settlements tend to include a statement that a "complaint is not a finding or ruling that the respondent has actually violated the law" and that a settlement does not constitute an admission of any violation of the law, such points are generally lost on the public. Simply put, woe to those who fail to heed the FTC's guidelines—or who happen to be the first to clarify by example the specifics of the guidelines.

PERHAPS A DISCLOSURE-LEARNING SERIES REGARDING AFFILIATES WOULD BE HELPFUL . . .

Nashville-based Legacy Learning, producer of a popular guitar-learning DVD series, agreed to pay $250,000 to settle FTC charges that it "deceptively advertised its products through online affiliate marketers who falsely posed as ordinary consumers or independent reviewers."

Describing its complaint against Legacy Learning, the FTC alleged that the company used "an online affiliate program, through which it recruited 'Review Ad' affiliates to promote its courses through endorsements in articles, blog posts, and other online editorial material, with the endorsements appearing close to hyperlinks to Legacy's website." Affiliates received commissions for the referrals they generated.

MONITORING FOR COMPLIANCE: MONITORING TOP-PRODUCING AFFILIATES AND RANDOM SAMPLING OF OTHERS

In addition to the settlement sum, Legacy agreed both to monitor its top 50 revenue-generating affiliate marketers to make sure that they were complying with their duty of disclosure and to monitor a "random sampling" of another 50 of its affiliates. This provision in the settlement release may be instructive to those who might wonder about the scope of the duty to monitor sponsored bloggers. At the same time, those sponsoring bloggers would be well advised to weigh the FTC's refrain that all its reviews are case specific.

Commenting on the FTC's settlement, an FTC representative noted, "Advertisers using affiliate marketers to promote their products would be wise to put in place a reasonable monitoring program to verify that those affiliates follow the principles of truth in advertising."

TRUTHFULNESS AND TRANSPARENCY

Wading through all the guidelines, examples, and case studies, the FTC is demanding that bloggers and those that "sponsor" them adhere to principles of truthfulness and transparency. "Truthfulness and transparency" are guiding principles of new media, absent any FTC edit. The FTC, however, has made them marketing mandates, calculated to protect consumers in new media, where every consumer gets to have a powerful voice and every business gets to make powerful new connections with influencers.

HOW SHOULD A BLOGGER DISCLOSE AN AFFILIATE LINK?

Other than informing a blogger (vlogger, twitterer, pinner, Google+er, . . .) of his or her duty to disclose "material connections" (yes, affiliate links would unmistakably fit that bill!) in a "clear and conspicuous" manner, the FTC doesn't say how it should be done. The FTC does say you don't need to hire a lawyer to draft the language–and if you do (hire a lawyer to draft the language), that it shouldn't be in "legalese." Beyond that, it's up to you.

WHAT ABOUT THE FTC'S POSITION ON "LIKE-GATING"?

"What about 'like-gating'?" I asked Cleland; "like-gating" is the practice of getting others to "like" your Facebook page in return for something.

"The terminology is confusing," he said. "The whole issue is a gray area."

"It is 'endorsement-*like*,'" he went on to say, with a chuckle in his voice. "It is an evolving debate." Stay tuned.

STRAYED FROM THE FTC'S NEW SOCIAL MEDIA GUIDELINES?

The stationery for the Division of Advertising Practices of the FTC is very simple in design: logo, division name, and D.C. address. It is the most dreaded stationery for the marketing departments of most businesses to see, as it is the stationery that comes with the announcement of an "investigation."

According to the FTC:

> [T]he Commission may initiate an enforcement action if it has "reason to believe" that the law is being or has been violated. . . . The basic consumer protection statute enforced by the Commission is Section 5(a) of the FTC Act, which provides that "unfair or deceptive acts or practices in or affecting commerce . . . are . . . declared unlawful." *(15 U.S.C. Sec. 45(a)(1))*. See FTC.gov

THOU SHALT NOT "ASTROTURF": TELL US WHO'S PAYING YOUR BILLS

"Astroturfing" is the practice of deceptive marketing in which a marketer or company employee posts fake reviews by posing as an unbiased consumer endorsing a product or service; it is a practice prohibited by the FTC's revised guidelines.

So if you love to chat online and you also love your company's products, fine! Just don't mix the two without forgetting to tell us both facts—that you love the products *and* that you work for the manufacturer or marketer of the products you are posting about.

The FTC provided in its updated guidelines the example of an online message board dedicated to the discussion of new music download technology where a poster promoted his employer's products without disclosing his connection to the products he was promoting. Such conduct is deceptive under the guidelines.

As explained in the FTC example, where knowledge of a poster's employment "likely would affect the weight or credibility of her endorsement," that connection must be clearly and conspicuously made.

"FAKE" ITUNES REVIEWS PUT PR FIRM IN THE FTC'S HOT SEAT

The FTC has underscored its intolerance of astroturfing, or fake reviews, by initiating enforcement actions against those it believes violates this prohibition. Issuing a report on the settlement of one such action, the FTC succinctly explained the circumstances of its enforcement and issued an additional warning:

> A public relations agency hired by video game developers will settle Federal Trade Commission charges that it engaged in deceptive advertising by having employees pose as ordinary consumers posting game reviews at the

online iTunes store and not disclosing that the reviews came from paid employees working on behalf of the developers.

"Companies, including public relations firms involved in online marketing, need to abide by long-held principles of truth in advertising," said Mary Engle, director of the FTC's Division of Advertising Practices. "Advertisers should not pass themselves off as ordinary consumers touting a product, and endorsers should make it clear when they have financial connections to sellers." *In the Matter of Reverb Communications, Inc., et al. FTC File No. 092 3199.*

In its defense, Reverb Communications insisted that the online reviews of the game that were posted by its employees were posted by employees who had actually paid for and downloaded and played the games on their own initiative. The reviews, according the firm's owner, actually represented the true sentiments of the players who posted them, though they did not include any disclosure of their connection to the game developer. Such a defense, however, does not square with what is a rather unambiguous requirement of disclosure on this point.

In its settlement with Reverb Communications, the FTC issued no fine but did require the firm to remove the posts where Reverb employees had failed to disclose their connection as a marketer of the online game. The settlement further prohibited Reverb employees from posting any further reviews without disclosing their connection to the manufacturer of the game.

TAKEAWAYS

- Establish a social media policy and make sure that it covers the FTC's social media endorsement guidelines.

- Understand that if you are a business that provides a benefit to bloggers, you must inform the bloggers of their duty to disclose their "material connection" with you.

- A "material connection" is the existence of a relationship that would be likely to influence the weight or credibility the average consumer might give to an endorsement if the consumer knew of the otherwise undisclosed relationship between the business and the blogger.

- There is no dollar sum that triggers a "material connection." The FTC uses a case-by-case approach for such evaluations. Bloggers should consider the volume of "freebies" they may receive rather than the value of a single item they may receive.

- "Clear and conspicuous" disclosure of a "material connection" must be something more than a button or tab or link that takes you to a disclosure statement.

- A disclosure statement in a social network profile is unlikely to satisfy the requirement of "clear and conspicuous" disclosure.

- Notifying readers of a sponsored endorsement in Twitter "may" be accomplished by the inclusion of a hashtag alerting the reader, such as #ad or #paid. However, the FTC cautions that even the inclusion of a disclosure hashtag, such as "#ad," may not be enough, depending on the circumstances of a particular case, to meet the requirement of "clear and conspicuous" disclosure.

- There is no magic disclosure language: it is up to the blogger to decide what will work to inform the reasonable consumer of a relationship.

- The FTC review of social media marketing is on a case-by-case assessment; it will review each case on its own merits.

- A sign at an event informing bloggers of their duty to disclose a material connection with a sponsoring business will not satisfy a business's duty to inform bloggers of their duty to disclose their connection to the business when blogging about the business or its products or services.

- If you are a business that engages a network of affiliates to blog about your products or services, you must provide such bloggers with training on their disclosure and truthfulness obligations. (The manner of such training is not specified by the FTC.)

- "Bloggers" for the purposes of the FTC endorsement guidelines include Twitterers (i.e., microbloggers on Twitter), as well as vloggers (bloggers using video to convey their stories). Google+? Though the FTC social media endorsement guidelines were written before the advent of Google+, the network format of user content sharing would likely fall within the FTC's contemplated application of its guidelines if the content contains an "advertising message."

- Businesses that sponsor bloggers must monitor them for the truthfulness of their blogging about the business's products or services, as well as for disclosure of their material connection to the business. (The FTC does not say how or for how long this monitoring must take place.)

- Businesses must "follow up" if in their monitoring of sponsored bloggers they find "questionable practices." (The FTC does not specify what the form of the follow-up should be in such instances.)

- If a company has a "reasonable training and monitoring program," it is unlikely that the company would face an FTC law enforcement action due to the activity of a "rogue blogger."

- Marketers, affiliates, and employees of a company all have a duty to disclose their material connections when tweeting, blogging, Facebooking, vlogging, or Google+ing about products or services; they may not portray themselves as ordinary consumers.

- You are responsible for your blogging, chatting, posting affiliates!

- In monitoring sponsored bloggers for their disclosure of their material connections, a random sampling of such bloggers might satisfy the FTC monitoring requirement—though the FTC has offered no blanket statement of random monitoring and has said that each case would be examined individually.

- The FTC's principles concerning truth in advertising have not changed.

5

How to Make Required Disclosures in Digital Advertising

In March 2013, the Federal Trade Commission issued an update, its first since 2000, of its seminal digital advertising guidelines, known as the ".com Disclosures: How to Make Effective Disclosures in Digital Advertising." The update takes into "account the expanding use of smartphones with small screens and the rise of social media marketing," providing mock ads (some of which are "tweets") to illustrate the updated principles.

IF THE DISCLOSURE GUIDELINES ARE MERELY "GUIDELINES," DO WE REALLY HAVE TO FOLLOW THEM?

Let's attack the easy question first: "If these are simply 'guidelines' we're talking about, and not administrative regulations, do we really need to follow them?" This question is answered in a footnote to the document:

> Guides are "administrative interpretations of laws administered by the Commission." *16 C.F.R. § 1.5.* Although guides do not have the force and effect of law, if a person or company fails to comply with a guide, the Commission might bring an enforcement action alleging an unfair or deceptive practice in violation of the FTC Act. Pg. 2, Footnote 5, .com Disclosures

So follow these guidelines or risk an FTC enforcement action.

THE APPLICABILITY OF FTC LAW TO SOCIAL MEDIA

In updating its online advertising disclosure requirements, the FTC specifically noted that the FTC Act's prohibition on unfair or deceptive acts or practices "broadly covers advertising claims, marketing and promotional activities, and sales practices in general." *.com Disclosures, Sec. II.*

To the point, it noted that "[t]he Act is not limited to any particular medium." Social networking sites fall within the scope of the Act's regulatory power. *Id., 15 U.S.C. § 57a(a)(1)(B).*

WHAT MAKES DIGITAL DISCLOSURE SO DICEY?

What makes getting required digital disclosures right so difficult? A warning included in the updated .com guidelines sums up what makes digital compliance in the realm of advertising disclosure so dicey: "There is no litmus test for determining whether a disclosure is clear and conspicuous. . . ." *.com Disclosures, Sec. II.*

The core requirement for compliant digital disclosures is that they be "clear and conspicuous." In the absence of a "litmus test," everything becomes a case-by-case review, examining "specific facts at hand." *Id., Sec. I.* Even with an abundance of detail offered in the guidelines, a marketer is left to weigh what makes for a compliant disclosure. This means a need for marketers to look closely at each social media marketing campaign with a fresh eye toward compliant disclosure.

In a footnote to the guides, the FTC observes that "[c]opy tests or other evidence of how consumers actually interpret an ad can be valuable." *Id., Sec. III, A, pg. 5, Footnote 14.*

Articulating a best practice for marketers, the FTC does not elaborate on the point. Elsewhere in the document, however, the FTC does caution that the guide is not "intended to provide a safe harbor from potential liability." *Id., Sec. I.*

Whether a disclosure meets the FTC's detailed, yet amorphous, standard is measured by its "performance"—that is, how well a reasonable consumer would actually perceive and understand the disclosure within the context of the entire ad. What matters, according to the FTC, is the "overall net impression of the ad"— was the disclosure seen and comprehended; was the truth of the ad claims clear?

THE MEDIUM, PLATFORM, OR DEVICE DOES NOT MATTER TO THE OBLIGATION OF DISCLOSURE

Point 5 of the overview of the updated guidelines gives a warning that states pretty clearly the overarching obligation of the updated guidelines:

If a disclosure is necessary to prevent an advertisement from being deceptive, unfair, or otherwise violative of a Commission rule, and it is not possible to make the disclosure clearly and conspicuously, then that ad should not be disseminated. This means that if a particular platform does not provide an opportunity to make clear and conspicuous disclosures, then that platform should not be used to disseminate advertisements that require disclosures.

In other words, if your advertisement, i.e., "sponsored conversation" or tweet or blog post, requires a disclosure under any of the FTC guidelines, that disclosure must be "clear and conspicuous" whether it appears on a blog on someone's desktop or in a tweet as viewed on someone's smartphone.

"How can we do that?!"

Good question. The FTC leaves the answer up to you, though it does offer some parameters and benchmarks.

FOUR KEY POINTS FROM THE FTC'S LATEST DIGITAL ADVERTISING UPDATE

Lesley Fair, senior attorney with the FTC's Bureau of Consumer Protection, provided a summary of the FTC's updated digital advertising disclosure guidance. Fair's disclosure summary, *FTC Reboots .com Disclosures: Four Key Points and One Possible Way to Bypass the Issue Altogether,* distilled the 53-page PDF down to "four key points":

1. "The Most Important Thing About the New .com Disclosures Is What Hasn't Changed"

Simply put, traditional truth-in-advertising principles apply to digital marketing.

2. If the Disclosure of Information Is Necessary to Prevent a Claim in an Online Ad from Being Deceptive or Unfair, It Has to Be "Clear and Conspicuous"—Regardless of the Platform or Device

Here the mandate of "clear and conspicuous" disclosure is addressed with specific regard to mobile platforms and social media platforms, where the communication space may be limited due to the small size of a mobile device screen or the character limitations of a social platform, such as Twitter's 140-character limitation.

Under the updated .com Disclosures guidelines, advertisers are cautioned to be sure that their required disclosures are "clear and conspicuous on all devices and platforms that consumers may use to view their ads."

So what is a business to do if it can't reasonably provide a "clear and conspicuous" disclosure on a particular mobile device or social platform? The FTC has an easy solution: "then that ad shouldn't run on that device or platform." Period.

3. Disclosures Should Be "as Close as Possible" to the Relevant Claim. Hyperlinks Require Clarity, Conspicuousness, Detail—and Functionality Across Platforms and Devices

Let's examine these elements in greater detail:

- **Proximity.** Placement of disclosures in online advertising has become more demanding under the FTC's 2013 updated guidelines. Where the 2000 guidelines advised marketers to place their disclosures as "near, and when possible, on the same screen" as "the ad claims they explained or elaborated on," the new guidance is that "[d]isclosures should be 'as close as possible' to the relevant claim." A subtle, but important, distinction. Proximity matters.

- **Hyperlinks.** The FTC's 2000 guidelines addressed the issue of hyperlinks in disclosures and cautioned marketers to "avoid buried or generically labeled hyperlinks" and not use them to make disclosures of "key categories of information—for example, how much a product costs or certain health or safety information." These principles remain.

  The new guidelines go into great detail describing how hyperlinks should look and where they should be placed, calling for far greater clarity and conspicuousness in the use of hyperlinks. Hyperlinks, under the updated guidance, should be labeled as specifically as possible so that consumers easily understand the purpose and destination of the hyperlink.

- **Functionality of hyperlinks across platforms and devices.** Focusing on the pervasiveness of mobile devices and social platforms, the updated guidelines also call upon businesses to pay particular attention to how their disclosure hyperlinks will function across devices and social platforms. Knowing that a given disclosure on a website complies with the requirements of conspicuousness and clarity when viewed on a laptop, says little about its functionality on Facebook on a smartphone. It's the advertiser's responsibility to ensure that disclosures, particularly hyperlinks, retain their functionality across devices and social platforms.

4. Mobile Screens and Social Media Platforms Are Constraining Space for Disclosures—but the Responsibilities Remain the Same. Pop-Up Disclosures Are Out

Returning to the very first point of this summary, disclosure responsibilities remain essentially unchanged, despite the ascendancy of social and mobile platforms. Although the updated guidelines specifically recognize the challenges presented by the constrained spaces of social platforms and the smaller screens of mobile devices, the responsibility of clear and conspicuous disclosure remains unchanged.

In regard to pop-up disclosures, the online advertising summary succinctly addresses the issue of using pop-ups for disclosures with a simple question and answer in the negative:

What about conveying that information via pop-ups?

Not a good idea since there are so many technologies for blocking them.

WHAT ABOUT FAIR'S POINT ON "ONE POSSIBLE WAY TO BYPASS THE ISSUE ALTOGETHER"?

Correctly, Fair notes that "the need for a disclosure is really a warning sign that the underlying ad claim may contain some element of deception." Her solution, bypassing all the fonts and disclosures? "Rather than focusing on fonts, hyperlinks, proximity, platforms, and the whole disclosures rigmarole, how about stepping back and reformulating the ad claim to get rid of the need for a disclosure in the first place?"

Additional Best Practices from the FTC's Updated Guidelines on Digital Advertising

The updated guidelines offer other key points related to best practices.

You Have a Duty to Stay Abreast of New Studies Relating to Consumer Online Behaviors

One of the bullet points in the fourth point of the document's overview contains this seemingly simple statement: "Keep abreast of empirical research about where consumers do and do not look on a screen." *Id., Overview, Pt. 4.*

That simple bullet point is a very big and dangerous deal. It imposes a high standard on how advertisers must provide appropriate, mandatory disclosures. Let's suppose that a new, leading study demonstrates that on tablets or Facebook, consumers tend to look first at a particular part of the tablet, business blog, or Facebook screen. That discovery will beget the question of why you weren't aware of that study and weren't using it to meet your obligation of clear and conspicuous disclosure, should an issue of adequate disclosure arise.

"How big a study, how widely accepted, must it be to count or to require action from an advertiser?"

Unknown.

A general tenet of administrative interpretation is that such writings should be read in a manner to give the fullest effect to prevention of harm that they are intended to provide. In this instance, the FTC's update is not merely prescribing a habit of staying abreast of industry studies, but acting upon the information contained in those studies to further the protection of consumers.

Gone Are the Days of Buried Disclosures

The FTC states what we all know to be true. Consumers don't necessarily look at an entire screen. *Id., Sec. III, B, citing, Deception Policy Statement at 180-81.* Having to scroll down on a blog to find to a disclosure makes it more likely that the disclosure will be missed. *Id., Sec. III, B.*

Disclosures Near the Bottom of a Page Require "Cues"

When, for some reason, it becomes necessary to provide a required disclosure where a reader would be required to scroll down to it, the FTC instructs advertisers to "use text or visual cues to encourage consumers to scroll to view the disclosure." *Id., Overview, Pt. 4.* Those "cues" must be explicit and not vague. *Id., Sec. III, C(1)(a.).*

Optimizing Your Website for Mobile Becomes a Compliance Imperative

The mandate of clear and conspicuous disclosure follows a marketer's communication regardless of the device being used. As a consequence, the importance of optimizing a blog for mobile devices becomes important for meeting the mandated disclosures. *Id.* The guidelines even go so far as to consider how consumers may use their smartphones or tablets in either a vertical or horizontal position, changing further the screen view on a single mobile device. *Id.*

In short, "Simply making the disclosure available somewhere in the ad, where some consumers might find it, does not meet the clear and conspicuous standard." *Id., Overview, Pt. 4.* Bear in mind that the sort of "ad" we are discussing here is any marketing communication, including a corporate blog or business Facebook page. *Id., Overview.*

EXAMPLE: HOW TO GET AN FTC-MANDATED DISCLOSURE *WRONG* IN A TWEET

• **FTC's Mock Tweet, Example 14**: *Shooting movie beach scene. Had to lose 30lbs in 6 wks. Thanks Fat-away pills for making it easy. (Mock Link)*

The guidelines provide several examples illustrating the principles they enunciate. In this one (Example 14 in the .com Disclosures), the FTC shows how to get required disclosures wrong in a tweet, the 140-character space provided on Twitter for messages.

Here a person (a movie actress) on Twitter is being paid to endorse a dietary supplement and has tweeted that she has lost 30 pounds in six weeks, using the supplement; though she doesn't say so in her tweet, the average consumer could expect to lose much less using the same supplement under normal circumstances. The company sponsoring the tweet has provided a link in the tweet that leads to a disclosure that the person has been paid for her tweet and that typical results in using the supplement would be far less than those tweeted about by the celebrity.

Under the Guides Concerning the Use of Endorsements and Testimonials in Advertising, *16 CFR Part 255,* it is generally required that a person who has received a benefit from another must disclose that relationship in a clear and conspicuous manner. Additionally, as discussed throughout the .com Disclosures update, important qualifying information would also need to be provided to consumers in a clear and conspicuous manner.

Examining the scenario, the FTC warns that a link included in such a tweet—one that led directly to a disclosure informing consumers that the person sending the tweet was sponsored and that typical results from use of the dietary supplement might be far less than those reported by person in the tweet—would "not be adequate" compliance with its advertising disclosure requirements if consumers could purchase the touted supplement at a "brick and mortar store or from a third-party online retailer (a retailer that is not affiliated with the advertiser)." Why? The FTC explains that such a

(continued)

---

hyperlinked disclosure would be noncompliant because a consumer viewing the tweet "might not click through" to the disclosure and "thus would not see these disclosures."

EXAMPLE: HOW TO GET AN FTC-MANDATED DISCLOSURE *RIGHT* IN A TWEET

• **FTC's Mock Tweet, Example 15:** *Ad. Shooting beach scene. Had to lose 30lbs in 6wks. Thanks Fat-away pills for making it easy. Typical loss: 1lb/wk.*

Same person tweeting about the same scenario. Compliant. Why? All the important information is clear and up front. The first content in the tweet alerts the reader to the fact that it is a "sponsored tweet," an ad. Next, though the celebrity still notes her stellar results from using the supplement, the qualifying information is as close in proximity to the claim as it could possibly be, making it easy for consumers to see and understand the important qualifying information.

"What if the company had the person include the necessary disclosure information in a tweet that followed the first one about the effectiveness of the dietary supplement?"

That would be Example 16 from the update, and the answer is no. More particularly, the FTC explains,

Putting that information in a subsequent message is problematic, because unrelated messages may arrive in the interim. By the time Juli's disclosures arrive, consumers might no longer be reading these messages, or they simply might not realize that those disclosures pertain to the original message.

EVEN IN A TWEET, IT'S A CASE-BY-CASE REVIEW

The .com Disclosures are very detailed. Yet as noted above, the FTC expressly warns that its guidelines are not intended to create any "safe harbor" and that compliance with the letter of its guides may not result in compliance with the law, if the spirit of the disclosure obligation is not met, meaning that the average consumer would be unlikely to discern the truth of an "ad" or sponsored tweet.

In an additional example, Example 17, the FTC reviews how even the use of the disclosure "spon," as an abbreviation for "sponsored tweet," which might, under many circumstances, be an effective method of disclosure of the sponsored nature of a tweet, could be rendered ineffective due to its placement directly after another link or simply because "a significant proportion of reasonable viewers" would not understand the significance of the hashtag.

Just as the FTC will look at every ad for compliance on a case-by-case analysis, so should marketers, understanding that there is no magic formula, only a genuine effort to discern the reasonable impact of a sponsored communication on a consumer.

6

How to Run a Social Media "Contest" Without Losing the Prize

- You just announced your contest winner, and you've just been notified that you need to pay royalties for the song she's singing and for the picture she has in the background of the video.

- You just announced the winners for your incredibly successful Facebook charity contest, only to have three of the "losers" announce that they're suing you and your hot-shot digital marketing agency for "fraud," "breach of contract," and "intentional infliction of emotional distress." Seems you deprived the losing contestants of their rights, causing them substantial harm when you strayed from your own contest rules by allowing the prizes to go to "winners" who gamed your game.

Everybody's doing it: announce a contest; offer a prize; ask for likes, retweets or pins. Tons of new prospects start following your account; you announce a winner. Simple.

Not so fast. Many businesses are holding social media promotions without any sense of the law or the rules dictated by their favorite social network, putting at risk their reputations, social media accounts, and financial well-being. Even if it seems that many social media contests are running along just fine, they could well be headed for a train wreck. We'll explore how not to become that train wreck.

As you prepare to launch your social media promotion, you should study the rules of the social network you are going to use for your promotion and the laws relating to the geographic area you intend to include in your promotion. We will examine these points in more detail.

FOLLOWING THE LAWS OF SOCIAL MEDIA CONTESTS

Facebook guidelines on the subject of holding a contest or sweepstake on Facebook include an important warning to those sponsoring contests or sweepstakes: "Please note that compliance with these [Facebook] guidelines does not constitute the lawfulness of a promotion."

LinkedIn, as do many other social media sites, echoes Facebook's warning, cautioning that compliance with its guidelines on contests and promotion "is not a guarantee of lawfulness." The network warns: "Promotions are subject to many laws and regulations, some of which vary from jurisdiction to jurisdiction, and if you are unsure of the lawfulness of a proposed promotion, consult an expert."

As we'll see, advertising laws outside the United States have already taken down one Twitter-based giveaway for not following "the law of the land." And Facebook has already temporarily suspended the account of a major brand for getting Facebook contests wrong. Another brand has been cited by a regulatory authority for improper practices in sponsoring a Facebook contest.

PROMOTION RULES VARY FROM SOCIAL NETWORK TO SOCIAL NETWORK

Each social network, as we shall see, gets to set its own rules on how contests, sweepstakes, and giveaways are to be conducted on its network. Each may also impose whatever penalty it chooses to for violations—and most of the networks threaten the social media equivalent of a death sentence for violations: permanent suspension of *all* of a user's accounts, with no guaranteed right of appeal.

Be mindful, too, that though the social networks provide specific social media promotion (contest and sweepstake) guidelines, they all refer users to their general terms-of-service requirements, as well as to the respective privacy guidelines. The contest and sweepstake guidelines are obviously where we will turn for the general "dos and don'ts" of holding promotions, but a look at the more detailed terms of service and privacy policy is an equal necessity.

CHECK SOCIAL NETWORK PROMOTION RULES IMMEDIATELY BEFORE YOU BEGIN YOUR PROMOTION

Bear in mind that social networks are notorious for making major revisions to their terms of service with little notice and tend to make such changes frequently. This means that even if you have carefully examined the promotion rules of the social networks you will be using for your promotions, consult them one last time before you launch your promotion to be sure that they have not changed. This advice certainly applies to any "rules" cited within this chapter as well. Let's look at an example, using a made-up tweet from a candy company we'll call Company X.

> To celebrate Company X's grand opening, we are giving away 10 candy goodie bags. Follow and RT to win! #goodies

Now this just looks like the sort of giveaway you'd see about a hundred times in any given week on Twitter, but there are a few issues with it. The first problem is that the giveaway shows no sign of having followed Twitter's terms of service on the subject of promotions, which states that you cannot ask users to "RT [retweet] to win!" Beyond this, as we shall see, the "harmless, easy" giveaway also violated "the law of the land."

ONE COMPLAINT IS USUALLY MORE THAN ENOUGH TO TRIGGER A REGULATORY INVESTIGATION

If you were to review advertising enforcement actions by regulatory authorities, you would find that a single complaint often sets in motion an investigation that shuts down or beats up (or both) a major marketing initiative. You might even find that the regulatory agency itself, without any prompting whatsoever from a consumer complaint, starts the investigation on its own.

Often marketers will ask, "hypothetically speaking," of course, about the chances of their promotion running into trouble for noncompliance. The simple answer is that if a promotion doesn't follow the law of the land or the law of the given social network, there is a real risk of significant sanctions, well beyond reputational damage or a derailed competition.

Ultimately, though, such a question is not a legal one; it is a question about chance. So the answer might be to ask, in return, "Do you have the confidence that your promotion will not inspire even a single complaint to a regulatory authority?" With the steep price tag for getting a promotion wrong, the better question would be to ask, "How do we get it right?"

GETTING SOCIAL MEDIA "CONTESTS" RIGHT: TRANSPARENCY AND CLARITY

Though different states, different countries, and different social networks have different guidelines pertaining to promotions, there are two constants: transparency and clarity. Sponsors must be transparent and clear about the process of participation and prize winning. So as you examine your own promotion for compliance, ask if the process of participation and winning is transparent and clear: if it is not, go back to the drawing board.

From the tweet in the example above, it is clear that the sponsor intended the promotion to be a competition. It was also clear that those interested in winning a "goodie bag" were expected to follow the business's Twitter account and retweet the contest message. But how would the brand choose who would be lucky enough to receive those treats? The tweet did not say how the winners of the goodie bags would be chosen, and it provided no link to where the answer could be found in any competition rules. Under any standard, that's an unfair "competition," as it doesn't say how the prizes will be awarded. Participants are left to guess.

WHAT KIND OF PROMOTION ARE YOU HOLDING ANYWAY?

Regulators or a court might have viewed Company X's prize competition as something other than a competition, when the value of a follow and retweet is still evolving and could be deemed an act of value or legal consideration (concepts to be discussed shortly).

If the promotion is offering a "prize," asking people to do something with some measure of value ("consideration") for the chance to win a prize ("Follow and RT"), with the prizes being awarded on a completely random basis, with no alternative mode of entry, the promotion could well be deemed an unlawful "lottery," rather than a "giveaway" or "competition."

In a moment, we will look at the important distinctions that determine the type of game promotion that is being conducted under the law of the land. Note that though I have been using the term "contest" up until this point as if it applies to all sorts of competitions—it does not. Understanding the distinctions in the types of promotions will play a key role in compliant social media promotions.

"We really didn't have any rules for our 'competition.'"

An agency such as the British Advertising Standards Authority (which you will learn more about later in the book) would've noted the following deficiencies in Company X's competition:

- No terms and conditions were available.

- All applicable significant conditions for the promotion should have been communicated before or at the time of entry.

- "Applicable significant conditions" require information such as the closing date and the method of selecting winners.

- Participants should have also been able to retain conditions or easily access them throughout the promotion.

THE MORAL OF THE COMPANY X STORY?

A "simple" tweeted promotion that doesn't follow the law and prompts a single complaint can cause your business to be the subject of a regulatory investigation and, even if that investigation merely shuts down your promotion, can get your company noticed in negative way, causing reputational damage at the very least.

So let's focus on getting our promotion right!

STEP 1: Contest, Sweepstake, or Lottery—Know the Differences

Are you planning to hold a contest, a sweepstake, or a lottery? You need to know what makes each unique, or you could find yourself and your business in serious trouble, something far worse than merely having your social media promotion shut down.

I. A Lottery: Consideration + Chance + Prize = Unlawful Gambling (Unless Conducted by the State or with Limited, Special Permission)

Let's start with the promotion you *cannot* hold on any social network: a lottery.

A lottery is pretty well prohibited in every state of the United States, as well as in most other nations, unless it is being conducted by the government or, in very limited circumstances, by a charity.

WHAT MAKES A LOTTERY A "LOTTERY"?

The law defines a "lottery" as a game of chance that has three core elements:

- **Consideration** (legalese for something of value, whether an actual monetary payment or an action that has some "value"—and note that the law may leave undefined, except by sanction and court case, the type of actions that are contemplated under the broad umbrella of "consideration" that satisfy this one element of a lottery)

- **Chance** ("luck," i.e., random selection, not skill, decides the winner)

- **A prize** that is awarded

Knowing that a lottery is unlawful to hold and that it consists of three elements: (1) consideration, (2) chance, and (3) a prize, you must take great care to make sure that you eliminate one of these three elements from your promotion. This can be trickier than you might think.

Keep the Prize; Eliminate the Consideration or Chance

Since a promotion without a prize isn't going to generate much excitement, most businesses keep the element of a prize as part of their promotion. So you must either eliminate the element of consideration (i.e., the requirement of a payment or anything of value), which would leave you with a "sweepstake," or eliminate the element of chance, which would leave you with a "contest." And here's where it can all get a little tricky.

The three elements that make up a "lottery"—consideration, chance, and a prize—are generally very broadly defined under law, meaning, for example, that the element of consideration (i.e., that thing or act of value) really does not need to have much "value" attached to it.

While the expense of a postage stamp required to send in an alternative mode of entry form generally does not reach the level of value deemed to be "consideration," asking a consumer to send a text message or to fill out a survey might well be enough to complete the element of consideration.

Following, Liking, Retweeting, Pinning?

As of this writing, the jury is still out on whether these seemingly simple and nonsensical actions might actually be deemed to have sufficient value to trigger the element of consideration. An abundance of caution would attribute value to them and avoid using them in a sweepstake promotion, as we will discuss in more detail later. If you look at the "law of the social networks," you will find that these actions are already largely prohibited by the networks themselves.

II. A *Contest*: A Contest Is a Prize-Awarding Competition Based on Skill (Eliminating the Element of Chance) in Which a Qualified Judge (or Judges) Determines the Winner Based on Objective Criteria ("Consideration," i.e., Something of Value, May or May Not Be Required as a Condition of Entry)

Beware of community voting. Community voting seems a natural component for a social competition. The danger is that a community vote could be viewed as lacking in application of objective standards and qualified judging, leaving what was intended to be a contest, i.e., an assessment of skill, little more than a game of chance, with luck deciding the winners. In light of this, it could become rather easy for an unwary sponsor to wind up hosting an unlawful lottery even when the plan had been to hold a lawful contest. Remember that it is the elimination of chance that you are trying to remove to keep your gaming promotion from becoming a lottery. Community voting in this context could be viewed as community whim, with sometimes little connection to the contest's stated criteria or measurement of skill awarding the prize.

Compliant Contest Checklist

To be compliant:

- **Use measurable criteria.** Establish and announce objective, measurable criteria to assess the best display of skill(s).

- **Seek a legitimate skill.** Be sure that your contest is truly judging a legitimate skill, such as the ability to solve a puzzle, rather than to merely guess at an answer. The classic example of a guessing game masquerading as a test of skill is the challenge of asking how many jelly beans are in a jar. Although mathematical ability might bring someone close to the jelly bean answer, the element of chance or luck is usually deemed to be the deciding factor in answering such a question, as opposed to skill or mathematical ability.

- **Judge your judges.** Create a panel of judges made up of people who possess generally accepted skill, training, or experience to professionally judge the announced, objective criteria. (Do not simply resort to using company employees.) Establish an odd number of judges to avoid ties in winner selection. Designate backup judges in the event that any primary judges are unable to complete their task of judging due to an illness, late-discovered conflict, or the like.

- **Eliminate chance; stick with skill.** Review your rules to ensure that under no circumstances will the contest resort to chance to determine the winner(s).

- **Address fraud.** Address voter or participant disqualification in your rules in the event of fraud. Understand that you cannot determine your contest winners at random because you have detected fraud; your contest rules must provide for how the contest will objectively determine the winner(s) based on skill even in the face of fraud. Know that you can't simply modify the rules in the middle of the competition.

- **State the number of rounds needed to win.** In a clear and conspicuous way, inform contestants how many rounds of the contest they must participate in to win the grand prize, and specify the time frame for the contest.

- **Get permission to use the contest winner's work.** Your judges just selected the winning photos. Be sure you included a consent from your entrants that allows you to showcase the winning works without the need to pay any royalties.

- **Require confirmation of original work and noninfringement.** Have your contestants attest to the fact that any work that they have submitted is an original work and does not infringe in any way on the copyright or trademark of another. Watch for so-called ancillary infringements, where contestants may have included in their photos or videos brand logos or the like. Your rules should dictate disqualification as the penalty for a violation of either prohibition.

What Are Some Other Items That Should Be Included in Your Game Promotion Checklist, Whether You Are Holding a Contest or Sweepstake?

Add these to your checklist:

- **Include the sponsor's name and address.** This is a must.

- **Specify the general eligibility rules.** Include age and geographic scope.

- **List restrictions on participation.** These restrictions apply to employees, their family members, and sponsor vendors.

- **Note limitations on participation and voting**. State the number of entries or votes permitted.

- **Identify the timing of the competition**. Specify when entry acceptance begins and when it will end, choosing a time zone for clarity (and giving consideration to any alternative mode of entry you may have designated if you have designated one).

- **Describe the prizes.** Include the retail values.

- **Include the familiar "Void where prohibited by law."** This catch-all phrase should help you stay on the right side of the law in the event that you may have missed something in planning your competition, such as a change in the law in a given jurisdiction.

- **State how you will notify winners.** Specify how the winners will be notified and where and when participants can look to find a list of winners.

- **Obtain permission** to announce and use the winners' names and likenesses (i.e., their picture) without compensation. You can do this the same time you get their permission to use their work.

- **Register with the states** of Florida, New York, and Rhode Island. These three states have special registration requirements (see the sidebar).

FLORIDA

Florida's special registration requirements include the following.

Registration, Fee, and Bonding

Florida requires game promotions offering *prizes totaling more than $5,000* to be registered with its Department of Agriculture and Consumer Services, Division of Consumer Service (*Section 849.094, F.S.*), *seven days prior to the start of the promotion,* along with **a** *$100 nonrefundable filing fee.* An exception to the registration requirement exists where promotion operators have "conducted game promotions in Florida for at least 5 consecutive years and they have had no civil, criminal or administrative actions instituted against them for a violation of s. 849.049 F.S. during that 5-year period."

Florida also mandates that the "material terms of the rules must be published in all advertising copy" and that a list of winners must be provided to all who request it at no charge.

A *trust fund* or *surety bond* is required for the prizes that are to be awarded.

A seven-page Promotion Filing Packet for filing online is provided by Florida:

Florida Department Agriculture and Consumer Services

P.O. Box 6700

Tallahassee, Florida 32314-6700

You can call Florida's Division of Consumer Affairs at 850-410-3800.

Penalties for violations of Florida's promotion rules include "a civil penalty of up to $1,000 per violation, an injunction and, in some cases if appropriate, referral for criminal prosecution."

To review the latest version of Florida's gaming laws online, visit:

---

https://www.flrules.org/gateway/chapterhome.asp?chapter=5j-14 and

http://www.freshfromflorida.com/Divisions-Offices/Consumer
-Services/Consumer-Resources/Consumer-Protection/Game-Promotions
-Sweepstakes

NEW YORK

New York has its own special registration requirements, though they are not that different from Florida's.

Registration, Fee, and Bonding

Like Florida, New York requires registration of promotional games where the retail value of *prizes exceed $5,000*. Game sponsors are required to file their application, along with a *$100 filing fee, 30 days before the start of their promotion.*

New York provides a five-page application online at http://www.dos
.ny.gov/forms/corporations/0255-a.pdf.

A trust fund or surety bond is required for the prizes that are to be awarded.

RHODE ISLAND

The special requirements for Rhode Island sometimes make it not worth the while to meet, as you will see below.

Registration, Record Keeping, and a Fee

If the "total announced value" of the *prizes exceeds $500*, the state of Rhode Island *(Title 11, Chapter 50 of Rhode Island General Laws)* requires registration (using a form provided by the secretary of state), record keeping, and a *fee of $150*.

Rhode Island provides a PDF online with the state's laws and registration form at *http://sos.ri.gov/documents/business/misc/GamesofChance.pdf*. A copy of the required filing form, Form No. 659, may also be obtained by writing the Office of the Secretary of State, Corporations Division, 148 West River Street, Providence, RI 02904-2615.

(*continued*)

For additional questions, you may call the Office of the Secretary of State at (404) 222-3040.

Rhode Island's rules also include a requirement of posting certain information in retail stores related to the competition, which could create an additional logistical hurdle for sponsors. This should be reviewed with an attorney.

Psst . . . rather than go through the registration process, you might want to exclude the residents of the state of Rhode Island from your contest. You wouldn't be the first. Many contest sponsors simply choose to exclude the residents of Rhode Island (which has a population of slightly more than a million) from their game promotions. Why? Simply put, the state's promotion requirements are triggered by the modest sum of $500 in prizes, when some contest sponsors look to bypass Florida's and New York's registration requirements by keeping the total retail value of prizes under $5,000. Without having the sort of redeeming population size of a Florida or New York, Rhode Island often finds itself sidestepped by game promotion sponsors.

- **Keep a record of winners.** Maintain a record of your prizewinners for a period of four years, as some states that do not require game promotion registration do require promotion sponsors to maintain a record of prizewinners for up to four years.

- **Get an affidavit from winners.** Winners should be asked to complete an affidavit (i.e., a sworn statement witnessed by someone authorized to perform oaths, such as a notary) acknowledging their consent to and compliance with the contest terms, as well as providing their essential information, including—when prizes awarded are valued at $500 or more—their social security number, as you will be required to provide winners, in such instances, with tax filing information.

- **Send IRS Form 1099-Misc to anyone winning a prize valued at $600 or more.** (Yes, Uncle Sam always wins!) It doesn't have to be a cash prize of $600 to trigger the filing obligation, but any type of prize valued at $600 or more.

III. A *Sweepstake:* No Judges. No Test of Skill, and "No Purchase or Fee Necessary to Enter or Win!"
Always a good idea to include the "no-purchase-necessary" phrase up-front in your sweepstake rules! A prize or prizes awarded purely on the basis of chance.

Buying a product or service doesn't increase your chances of winning. (Be sure to note this point in your rules!) Selection by chance, but a process of random selection that withstands scrutiny for its integrity. Welcome to a "sweepstake"!

Sweepstakes are promotions that retain the element of chance, which means that extra care must be taken to ensure that a "sweepstake" does not become a "lottery" by requiring anything of entrants that might be deemed a thing or act of value, even if that "thing" or "act" might appear trivial to some. With social media and social media law still evolving, the understanding of what has "value" is also evolving. Getting this wrong could be costly.

Include an Alternative Method of Entry for Your Sweepstake

Creating a secondary, cost-free method of entering a sweepstake, by providing for a mailed-in or other online entry, is the traditional method of providing a protection to avoid any claim that "consideration" (i.e., a thing or act of value) was an element of the promotion. And before you ask, know that an alternative method of entry (AMOE) can become another legal land mine if not done right.

Getting the AMOE Right

If you are going to provide an AMOE for your sweepstake—and you should— you must not bury the AMOE in your sweepstake rules, and you must not make the alternative method complicated. It is a good idea to mention the AMOE early in your rules and to accentuate at least the section heading in all caps and bold. Be mindful that a regulatory agency or court is likely to shoot down the protective value of the AMOE if it is deemed to have been "hidden" in the contest rules or if it included any unnecessary hurdles to participation.

Participants must also understand that AMOE participants have an equal chance of winning any and all prizes.

Compliant "Sweepstake" Checklist

In addition to the other promotion checklist items reviewed in this chapter, here are some specific to sweepstakes:

- **Use all caps and boldface to broadcast the message "NO PURCHASE OR FEE REQUIRED TO ENTER OR WIN!"** This should be announced clearly and conspicuously at the top of your sweepstake rules.

- **Maintain parity for AMOE.** The chances of winning must be the same whether or not an entrant makes a purchase or completes a survey, etc.

- **Be "bold" with your AMOE.** *This information must not be buried in fine print!* Best to put it in caps and bold lettering.

- **Specify the odds of winning.** Define the participants' odds of winning.

- **Remember that a "random" winner selection requires professional procedures.** You may be tempted to think that selecting a winner "at random" would be an easy task. So how will you answer the attorney for the participant who did not win and sues, when asked to provide the details of your method of winner selection and how it ensured that everyone who entered was given an equal chance of winning prizes? Did you use true-and-tried, industry-approved software? A respected third party? Be ready to answer the question.

- **Do not require your sweepstake participants to do even "little" things.** Don't even ask them to complete surveys or provide referrals or to even like you on Facebook, if you wish to lessen the chances of your compliant sweepstake spiraling into an unlawful lottery. ("RT" and "like" in order to be eligible to win are actions prohibited, in any event, by the respective social networks as a contest function.)

- **Skip the handling fees for prizes.** Do not require shipping or handling fees, or fees of any kind, for any reason associated with your sweepstake, as to do so could be viewed as reintroducing the element of consideration into your promotion, making it an unlawful lottery.

ESTABLISH A PRIVACY POLICY FOR YOUR SOCIAL MEDIA PROMOTION

Since you will be collecting consumer data during the course of your promotion, create a social media policy that informs consumers how you will be using and protecting their data. Know that if you fail to live up to the standards set in your own privacy policy, your conduct may be deemed fraudulent and misleading under FTC advertising standards, exposing your business to sanctions, as well as legal action by consumers.

KEEP IN MIND THAT NOBODY "LIKES" A SOCIAL MEDIA CONTEST MORE THAN AN INTERNET PRANKSTER (EXCEPT, MAYBE, A GAMER OR TROLL)

Let's just say that your social media contest may take you places you never imagined . . . For example, when Walmart announced that its store with the most Facebook likes would be getting a special visit from Miami-based hip-hop artist Pitbull, a prankster, journalist David Thorpe, apparently decided that it would be funny to turn Walmart's contest upside down by sending the music star not to one of Walmart's largest or busiest stores, but to one of its smallest and most remote stores, a store located on "the frozen Alaskan island of Kodiak." The campaign to highjack the Walmart social media contest came complete with a Twitter hashtag, #ExilePitbull.

So how effective was the prankster in derailing Walmart's scrupulously orchestrated social media competition? A headline from the *New York Daily News* tells how the contest ended: "Pitbull heading to Walmart in Alaska after Internet prank." The city of Kodiak, Alaska, population 6,100, was surprised and proud to discover that its Walmart store was voted the most "liked" Walmart in all America, with over 70,000 likes.

One can be sure that the promotion's outcome wasn't exactly what Walmart or the pop star had in mind when the social media promotion was launched. Nonetheless, both the hip-hop artist and contest sponsor took the social media prank in stride, with Pitbull even inviting the prankster to join him in his visit to Alaska.

In an interview with the *New York Daily News*, the prankster, Thorpe, explained that his #ExilePitbull campaign was simply a plan "to disrupt a corporate social media campaign, since they really set themselves up for it." Hmmm. Underscoring the point that social media promotions can have unpredictable outcomes for everyone, even the prankster, Thorpe was found to lament in his interview that "everyone on the corporate side will probably spin this [his hijack of the Walmart promotion] as a Big Social Media Win, which is kind of gross."

In the end, because of Thorpe's prank hijacking of Walmart's social media contest, the promotion likely achieved much more publicity than if it had not been hijacked, offering an important lesson in responding to online social media contest disruptions. By not kicking up a fuss in the face of a powerful online hijack of its promotional campaign, Walmart actually did succeed in achieving a "Big Social Media Win," however "gross" such an outcome might have been for the prankster Thorpe.

Trolls Do Troll for Competitions

In another instance of a hijacked social media contest, Internet trolls took to "liking" the Horace Mann School for the Deaf after Papa John's and Chegg sponsored a contest that promised to send pop singer Taylor Swift to perform a concert at the school with the most Facebook likes. In a swell of online activity, thousands of votes poured in for Horace Mann for the concert location.

After noting massive fraud in the voting, the competition sponsors chose to eliminate the Horace Mann School from the competition, though they also graciously decided to provide the school with some meaningful donations. The moral of the story is to recognize that social media contests come with inherent, often overlooked and unexpected risks. Now you know better.

Dealing with Pranksters, Spammers, and Trolls in Your Competition

Your IT team should be able to help you spot fraud or spamming early on in an online contest. You need to have a plan in place to deal with both. Addressing the topic in your promotional rules is a good place to start, giving yourself the authority to disqualify contestants and votes where there is evidence of fraud or conduct "contrary to the spirit" of the promotion.

The sponsors of both the Walmart competition and Taylor Swift competition demonstrated how agility and gracefulness can deflect what might otherwise have been disastrous outcomes to hijacked promotions.

Speaking of disasters . . .

FACEBOOK CONTEST GETS CLIPPED BY REGULATORY AGENCY

One of the most popular recipes for a Facebook contest: Submit a photo. Get the most likes. Win an iPad.

A popular recipe, but a bad one, as Facebook's contest rules prohibit the use of wall postings and likes as contest-voting mechanisms.

Nonetheless, in 2012, Spain-based Piingwin decided to hold its first-ever Facebook competition by inviting fans to upload a great picture of a penguin. The picture that received the most votes would win a new iPad.

The promotion seemed simple enough, apart from its flagrant violation of Facebook's contest rules. However, as we have already seen, a noncompliant promotion may skirt the watchful eyes of the very social network platform from which the promotion is being conducted, yet get clipped by the law of the land, with the punishment meted out by a regulatory authority, in this instance, the British Advertising Standards Authority (ASA).

What went wrong? Not surprisingly, the ASA was unconcerned about the company's noncompliance with "the law of the social network." Instead, the ASA concerned itself with the law of the land. In particular, Piingwin's contest ran aground and afoul of the United Kingdom's promotion rules when the promotion sponsor announced that it could not, as it had promised it would, select the iPad winner based on "the most votes." The sponsor, it seems, found itself with "a large amount of complaints regarding the veracity of the votes of some of our candidates," a crisis that the company was able to confirm by its own investigation.

To remedy fraudulent voting in its contest, Piingwin decided to use judging instead to pick the winner. Sounds reasonable . . . only it's not what the contest rules provided for, and it's not what the law allowed.

PIINGWIN PARTICIPANT CRIES "FOUL"

Learning of Piingwin's midcontest judging revision, a participant lodged a complaint, petitioning the ASA to review whether amending the rules in the middle of the promotion was fair, even though it was done to address fraudulent voting.

Answering the complaint, Piinwing explained to the ASA that the social media contest was the company's first attempt at a Facebook promotion. Piingwin noted that its rules had specifically called for only one vote per Facebook profile. Despite this precaution, the company received complaints of cheating, discovering that "some people were actively exchanging or buying votes, with many votes originating from the same IP addresses."

To remedy the fraud, the Piingwin decided that instead of the winning photo being chosen by the most votes received, the winner would be selected by a panel of five employees, basing their selection on the funniest and most entertaining entry and the effort put in to the picture. The company said that the winner of the promotion was selected from "the ten finalists [who] were the entries that received the most votes after the disputed votes were removed from the participants' count." The company disqualified multiple votes received from identical IPs. (And the company also informed the U.K. regulator that based on its unfortunate experience, its first Facebook competition was likely to be its last.)

Wings Clipped: U.K. Regulator Finds Company Violated Fairness Standards

Sympathetic to the contest sponsor's plight, the U.K. regulatory authority began its ruling on the Facebook contest by saying that it "understood" why the sponsor changed its competition rules during the competition. Yet the ASA quickly went on to say that "altering the judging criteria had put many participants at a significant disadvantage."

The ASA also observed that the sponsor's remedy for the fraudulent voting was to create a panel of judges using five employees, a violation of the United Kingdom's code, which requires either "an independent judge or a panel to include one independent member when the selection of a competition winning entry is open to subjective interpretation," as in the determination of "the funniest and most entertaining entry," as well as "the effort" put into the picture.

THE SAME COMPETITION WOULD HAVE RAISED LAW-OF-THE-LAND ISSUES IN THE UNITED STATES, EVEN WITHOUT THE RULE CHANGES IN THE MIDDLE OF THE COMPETITION

If the Piingwin contest had been scrutinized under U.S. law, a similar outcome could have been anticipated by a U.S. regulatory review of the competition's mid-promotion rule changes. But legal issues would have been raised even if the competition had gone along as planned.

To the point, allowing a competition to be decided by "the most votes" would be unlikely to satisfy any legal notion of objective criteria, making the promotion a sweepstake, or game of chance, rather than a competition, or objective assessment of skill. Add to this the question of the value of "likes," and a court could well decide, though none has to date, that the competition combines chance, a thing of value, and a prize, making it an unlawful lottery. Not becoming the first case study is always a good goal with compliant social media.

CONTEST AND PROMOTION RULES FOR THE NETWORKS— "THE LAW OF THE NETWORKS"

As you prepare your promotion, bookmark the rules for the social networks you will be working with to more easily determine if they change along the way—and keep checking!

FACEBOOK CONTEST RULES: BUSINESSES "LIKED" THE 2013 REVISION

Here are the 2013 contest rules revision in a nutshell:

- Businesses can hold a contest directly from their business page, where before they were required to create or pay for an application to do so.

- Businesses can use likes and timeline comments as a method of contest participant entry, something previously prohibited. (One year later, in August of 2014, Facebook announced in a post on its Developer's Blog a prohibition on "offering rewards" to "incentivize" people to "like a Page." Though the blog post did not discuss the subject of Facebook contests, the prohibition on incentivized "likes" was broad and would seem to encompass their use in contests. This policy change, buried in the post of a developer's blog, underscores the hazards of keeping pace with the "Law of the Networks"—in particular, the rules of Facebook. Though there remains a question mark as to whether Facebook might at some point soon announce another change to make an exception for the use of "likes" in contests, the blog post prohibition, with a stated effective date of November 5, 2014, seems to be the latest law of the social network.)

Elaborating on the policy change prohibiting incentivized "likes," the developer's blog post stated, in part:

> You must not incentivize people ... like a Page. This includes offering rewards, or gating apps or app content based on whether or not a person has liked a Page. It remains acceptable to incentivize people to login to your app, check in at a place or enter a promotion on your app's Page. To ensure quality connections and help businesses reach the people who matter to them, we want people to like Pages because they want to connect and hear from the business, not because of artificial incentives. We believe this update will benefit people and advertisers alike. See: Graph API v2.1 and updated iOS and Android SDKs *(https://developers .facebook.com/blog/post/2014/08/07/Graph-API-v2.1/)*

The August 2013 Facebook contest rule changes dramatically simplified the process of holding a contest via a Facebook business page. No longer would businesses have to decide between using an often-costly, third-party application to run their contest or undertaking to develop such an application themselves. While still allowing businesses to use an application to run their Facebook contests, the new rules allow brands to simply run a contest directly from their own business page, in a seemingly uncomplicated manner.

Under the revised rules, enterprises are required to make it clear that:

1. It is the business's contest.

2. Facebook has nothing to do with the contest.

Businesses must also get participants to acknowledge their understanding of points 1 and 2, as well as obtain a release of liability of Facebook from all participants.

Sounds pretty straightforward, and it essentially is, provided one keeps in mind all the other rules that govern contests generally, as in the law of the land. The law of the land always trumps the law of the social network.

Facebook's Contest Rules Are Outlined in Four Points

You can refer to the complete set of Facebook contest rules at https://www.facebook.com/page_guidelines.php. Let's discuss the four points here:

1. "You Are Responsible for the Lawful Operation of That Promotion . . ."
Facebook leads with the most important point first: it is up to you to figure out the law of the land and to make sure that your contest complies with it.

Please refer to this chapter's discussion of contests and the law of the land, and be reminded that it is there to provide some highlights of legal issues that are subject to change—it is *not* legal advice. Facebook cites examples of compliance issues such as determining "registration and obtaining necessary regulatory approvals," as well as including the rules of the contest. Consultation with an attorney from your jurisdiction before holding a contest is always well advised.

2. You Must Get a Release of Facebook *and* an Acknowledgment from Each Participant that Facebook Has Nothing to Do with Your Contest
While telling businesses that they must get a release and acknowledgment from participants, the revised rules do not say how this must be done. A review of

scores of contests appearing on Facebook suggests large-scale noncompliance with these two requirements. This should not be considered in any way an invitation for you to do the same, as Facebook maintains the right of selective enforcement, meaning giving others a pass while sanctioning your page, which would most likely mean the suspension of your business page.

In the absence of guidelines on how to obtain the necessary release and acknowledgment, some businesses are simply including a statement in the contest announcement that repeats language set forth in the rules, to the effect:

> By participating in this contest, you acknowledge that it is in no way sponsored, endorsed or administered by, or associated with, Facebook AND you completely release Facebook from any and all claims that may arise from this contest.

Again, in the absence of Facebook expressly saying how the release and acknowledgment should be obtained, there remains a question mark about whether or not such language, by itself, actually complies with Facebook's rules.

3. Promotions May Be Administered on Pages or Within Apps on Facebook

Contests must be run from a business page or an application—it may not be administered from an individual's personal page. Additionally, though Facebook permits the use of likes and comments as ways of joining a Facebook contest, it expressly prohibits businesses from asking would-be participants to share something on their own timeline to enter the contest or to share something on a friend's timeline to get additional entries. This, too, is a provision that you will see routinely violated in many Facebook contests; yet the violation of any of the rules invites a sanction.

You Can Still Use an App for Your Facebook Contest

Why go through the trouble or expense of using an application to administer your Facebook contest? For some, the ability to provide a more customized user experience and the ease of collecting participant e-mails are seen as the chief advantages of using an application rather than a business page's timeline. An application may also provide greater compliance opportunities with the ability to more easily and prominently provide required rule information.

4. "We Will Not Assist You in the Administration of Your Promotion . . . You Do So at Your Own Risk"

Again, pretty straightforward: you're welcome to run a contest on Facebook, but if anything goes wrong, you have assumed the risk of the consequences, and Facebook will not assist you in resolving problems. Planning, preparation, and execution in holding a Facebook contest fall squarely with the sponsor.

Always keep in mind the potential amplification that social media can bring to any subject. Always ask, "What if this contest for some reason goes viral, becomes really big; will we be able to meet our obligations?"

GOOGLE+ CONTESTS AND SWEEPSTAKES

Circle this: No contests or sweepstakes on Google+.

> You may display a link on your Google+ Page to a separate site where your Promotion is hosted so long as you (and not Google) are solely responsible for your Promotion and for compliance with all applicable federal, state and local laws, rules and regulations in the jurisdiction(s) where your Promotion is offered or promoted.

The Google+ Dos

- *Do* host your promotion on a separate site.

- *Do* accept responsibility if anything goes wrong with your promotion and guarantee that you will cover any costs Google+ might incur in connection with any claims associated with your promotion, even if you terminate your Google+ account or Google terminates it for you!

Google+ Buttons Policies

> Publishers may not promote prizes, monies, or monetary equivalents in exchange for Google+ button clicks.

Penalties for Getting Your Google+ Promotion Wrong

At a minimum, if Google thinks that your promotion isn't following Google's rules, it reserves the right to "to remove your Promotion content from Google+

Page for any reason." Beyond that? Google "does no evil," but a denial of account services is not beyond the range of penalties that could be imposed.

Google+ References

- Contests, Applications, and Ads, http://www.google.com/intl/en/+/policy/pagesterm.html

- Google+ Pages Contest and Promotion Policies, http://www.google.com/intl/en/+/policy/pagescontestpolicy.html

- Google+ Buttons Policies, https://developers.google.com/+/plugins/buttons-policy

PINTEREST IS A POPULAR PLACE TO HOLD A CONTEST!

The social media landscape changes quickly. Pinterest, a site where users get to "pin" visual posts to "boards" they get to create, has become the social media site de jure, driving enormous traffic and motivating consumer purchases. It is also new territory for contests and promotions.

Ad Age profiled one of the earliest, large-brand Pinterest-based contests. In the article "With Pinterest-Fueled Photo Contest, Panasonic Wades into New Social Waters," *Ad Age* reported how Panasonic launched a Photo of the Year contest, announced through e-mail, with a camera as a prize to be awarded to the winning photographer, as well as one to be awarded to one of the people who repinned (shared on their Pinterest account page) the winning photograph. Within two weeks, the contest garnered over 10,000 submissions, pointing to a high level of consumer interest in pinning and repinning as a winning online contest formula. *Ad Age* noted that social contests had previously been all about Facebook likes but now had become "all about the repin."

Pinterest's Promotion Guidelines

Pinterest's guidelines on holding a promotion are a model of simplicity:

> If you use Pinterest as part of a contest or sweepstakes, you are responsible for making sure it complies with all legal requirements. This includes writing the official rules, offer[ing] terms and eligibility requirements (ex: age and residency restrictions), and complying with marketing regulations

(ex: registration requirements and regulatory approvals). These rules can vary from place to place, so please work with a lawyer or other expert to make sure you're in compliance. You should also always comply with our Terms of Service. Please note that Pinterest isn't responsible or liable in any way to you if you use us as part of your promotion.

Pinterest also provides it's own set of dos and don'ts for holding a promotion:

The Pinterest Dos

- Encourage authenticity: Reward the quality of pinning, not just the quantity of it.

- Promote your contest: Link to your Pinterest account or contest board from your website, social media and marketing channels.

- Prevent spam: Read up on our anti-spam measures to help keep your contest fun and useful.

- Make getting involved easy: Create clear instructions and a simple process.

The Pinterest Don'ts

- Encourage spam: Steer clear of contests that encourage spammy behavior, such as asking participants to comment repeatedly.

- Run a sweepstakes where each pin, repin, or like represents an entry.

- Ask pinners to vote with a repin or like.

- Overdo it: Contests and promotions can be effective, but you don't want to run a contest too often.

- Suggest that Pinterest sponsors or endorses you: Make sure you don't say or imply this anywhere in your marketing materials or branding.

Pinterest guidelines for hold a promotion may be found at http://business .pinterest.com/logos-and-marketing-guidelines/#ads.

TUMBLR

The Tumblr Dos

- *Do* get Tumblr's permission for contests, sweepstakes, or giveaways with prizes valued over $1,000 (U.S. dollars); they aren't allowed without Tumblr's permission.

- *Do* "[f]ully disclose all of the contest, sweepstakes, or giveaway's rules including, for example, eligibility restrictions, all entry methods, information about your prizes (including retail value), and odds of winning."

- *Do* include in your rules a full release of Tumblr by each person participating.

- *Do* include in your rules an acknowledgment that "the contest, sweepstakes, or giveaway isn't associated with Tumblr (including, without limitation, that it isn't administered, sponsored, or endorsed by Tumblr)."

- *Do* include in your rules a statement that each person participating is giving information to you and not to Tumblr.

The Tumblr Don'ts

- *Don't* allow entry by individuals younger than 18.

- *Don't* direct and open your contest, sweepstakes, or giveaway to people who don't live in your country.

- *Don't* use Tumblr's "social features (like following, reblogging, and liking) as entry methods."

Communicating on Tumblr About Off-Site Contests, Sweepstakes, and Giveaways

On the subject of off-site contests, sweepstakes, and giveaways, Tumblr says, "Communicating on Tumblr about a contest, sweepstakes, or giveaway that happens off-site is generally OK," provided you "provide all the information" contained in the Tumblr contest guidelines, as noted above.

Tumblr's promotion guidelines may be found at http://www.tumblr.com/policy/en/contest_guidelines.

TWITTER PROMOTIONS AND CONTESTS

Before starting your Twitter promotion, bookmark and review Twitter's rules—they're subject to change; you'll find the rules at https://support.twitter.com/articles/18311-the-twitter-rules and the contest guidelines at https://support.twitter.com/articles/68877-guidelines-for-contests-on-twitter.

Twitter Sanctions for Promotion Violations

It is common for businesses, especially members of the Fortune 500, to have numerous Twitter accounts, some for recruiting, others for customer relations management, etc. *Be warned*: If you violate Twitter's rules on compliant promotions, you risk having *all* your business Twitter accounts suspended.

"That sounds rather harsh."

It is. So let's try and avoid it by understanding and following the rules.

The Twitter Dos

- *Do* include in your contest or promotion rules a rule stating that "anyone found to use multiple accounts to enter will be ineligible." (A promotion *participant* who ignores this may get all his or her accounts suspended.)

- *Do* include a rule stating that "multiple entries in a single day will not be accepted."

- *Do* include a rule stating that all contest-related tweets must include the hashtag #contest. (This rule aims to address the FTC's requirement of disclosing sponsored communications and tweets.)

- *Do* tell contestants to include your @username in their entry tweet so that you will see their tweet when it comes to picking a winner, as "a public search may not show every single update, and some contestants may be filtered from search for quality."

The Twitter Don'ts

- *Don't* offer prizes for tweeting a particular update.

- *Don't* offer prizes for following a particular user.

- *Don't* offer prizes for posting updates with a specific hashtag.

- *Don't* set rules to encourage lots of duplicate updates (e.g., "whoever retweets this the most wins").

- *Don't* encourage contestants to add your hashtag to totally unrelated updates.

YOUTUBE CONTESTS

There are two essential steps you need to follow to run a contest on YouTube.

STEP 1: Become a YouTube Partner

To hold a contest on YouTube, you must first become a YouTube "partner." According to YouTube, it's "easy and free." You can find out how to become a partner at https://support.google.com/youtube/topic/14965?hl=en&ref_topic=2676320.

STEP 2: Follow YouTube's Contest Guidelines

Contests only, please. Yes, I did say "contest" guidelines. YouTube does not permit you to hold a sweepstake on its platform. You may only provide "a game of skill where the winner is determined by a set of clear judging criteria."

The YouTube contest guidelines may be found at http://support.google.com/youtube/bin/answer.py?hl=en&answer=1620498.

YouTube begins its promotion guidelines with a reminder that any contests or promotions must also follow the platform's privacy policy, terms of service, and community guidelines. As noted before, the contest and promotion guidelines are a layer of rules in addition to those that already police your conduct on the social network. To help focus your attention on this point, it should be noted that all the networks take a stern view on spamming and prohibit spamming as a general "no-no." For some reason, when businesses begin to hold a contest on a social platform, they spring into action by spamming. *Do no spam.* It's against the law of the social networks, and it violates the law of the land.

Contest Interrupted

You are no doubt familiar with the Twitter "fail whale," the iconic whale diagram that would appear whenever Twitter experienced a disruption of services.

Such disruptions on social networks, thankfully, have become far less frequent. Be aware that they do happen, though. YouTube wants you to understand that if you happen to be holding a contest on its platform when such an interruption of services occur, "YouTube is not responsible for any issues with your contest. . . ." You absolve YouTube from any bugs, errors, or omissions. Got it?

The YouTube Dos

- *Do* have a set of official rules that include links to the YouTube terms of service and community guidelines and make it clear that entries that don't comply will be disqualified.

- *Do* accept entries only from "users aged 18 and up, or, the age of majority in the jurisdiction(s) where your contest is offered or promoted if it is over 18."

- *Do* make your contest *free* to enter.

- *Do* make sure that your contest really is a game of skill where the winner is "determined by a set of clear judging criteria."

- *Do* "clearly state that YouTube is not a sponsor of your contest and ask users to release YouTube from all liability related to your contest."

- *Do* include a "legally compliant privacy notice in your Official Rules which explains how you will use any personal data you collect for the contest and adhere to that use."

- *Do* "immediately remove any entry and disqualify any entrant suspected of violating the Official Rules or if their entry violates the YouTube Terms of Use."

- *Do* remember who runs YouTube (*hint:* not you) and know that "[o]nce the contest has ended, YouTube may close your account and you may no longer be able to directly retrieve entries." (I don't make the rules; I just report them!)

- *Do* know that videos entered in your contest "will be available on YouTube, both during and following the completion of your contest."

- *Do* get any contest submission "gadgets [YouTube's term] . . . approved by YouTube's technical and policy teams before it can go live."

The YouTube Don'ts

- *Don't* ask participants "to give all rights for, or transfer the ownership of, their entry to you."

- *Don't* use "channel functions, such as video likes or view counts, to conduct your contest."

- *Don't* use any data collected from entrants for anything other than contest administration purposes; you "cannot re-use the data for marketing purposes (even if the user has expressly opted-in to that use)." *This is an important point.* Most businesses sponsor contests for the data gold the contests provide to them for later marketing. YouTube wants to keep the data to itself, even if your participants expressly consent to connecting with you for marketing as part of your contest. YouTube, for its part, doesn't care what sort of consent you get from your participants for later marketing; it strictly forbids the use of the data you have collected for a YouTube contest for anything other than the administration of the contest. Anyone listening?

- *Don't* use the YouTube embedded player or YouTube API to run a contest offsite.

YouTube Penalties

"Where'd my contest go?!"

YouTube has the right to remove your contest for any reason.

"Where'd my YouTube account go?!"

"YouTube may terminate any user account, at any time and YouTube is not liable to you for termination of any account, the removal or reposting of any video or our failure to terminate an account or remove or report a video."

If either of these two penalties is imposed . . . too bad. You agreed that YouTube has the unfettered right to exercise either penalty, with all consequences falling on "You."

And if anyone decides to sue you and YouTube for your YouTube contest . . . You agree to defend and indemnify (pay for a lawyer—and cover any and all costs if you lose the lawsuit) YouTube, its parent company (Google—yes, even Google needs a good lawyer every now and then!), etc. Nothing different in this "defend and indemnify" clause that isn't found pretty much in every social network's promotion rules.

KNOW WHAT YOU'RE GETTING YOURSELF INTO

The bottom line: Know what you're getting yourself into. Tapping a "preferred" vendor and an attorney who can guide you through the latest rules and regulations is a smart investment when it comes to holding a social media contest. It is complicated and requires a lot of contingency planning. A sweepstake or contest gone wrong can be a lot more expensive than the costs associated with getting a game promotion right.

7

Thou Shalt Not Spam (on Social Networks)

One advertiser's marketing may easily be deemed social media spam if carefully spelled-out rules are not followed. The price for spamming on a social network is much more than simply the risk of losing the privilege of having an account on a social network. While spamming is an offense that can quickly get a business's social media account suspended, that sanction pales in comparison with the other sanctions that can be meted out against a business that simply doesn't know the rules governing electronic and wireless communications with consumers.

Know that social networks are getting much better at identifying and combating spammers—and much more aggressive about bringing them to court.

Twitter's rules make it clear that it intends to remain agile and vigilant in its fight against spammers, recognizing that "[w]hat constitutes 'spamming' will evolve as we respond to new tricks and tactics by spammers." So just because your clever marketing technique doesn't exactly break the rules when it comes to the laws against spamming, realize that the social networks themselves are fully entitled to take action against those companies that they believe to be spamming.

Additionally, despite the massive use of social media for marketing, know that you may even be deemed a spammer if your account simply isn't "social" and just spends its time churning out business deals. Twitter addresses this point in its rules against spamming by including in the definition of what constitutes spam (and what can get an account permanently suspended) the following: "If your updates consist mainly of links, and not personal updates."

Moving on to more blatant instances of spamming . . .

FACEBOOK SPAMMER HIT WITH RECORD $873 MILLION JUDGMENT. MYSPACE SCORES $234 MILLION JUDGMENT AGAINST SPAMMER

In two separate cases, within the span of six months, two courts made it eminently clear that the U.S. antispam law, known as the CAN-SPAM Act, would apply to social networking messages. The first case, from 2008, involved spamming on MySpace. The second case involved Facebook. Hundreds of thousands of users were getting messages that attempted to "harvest" e-mails by sending false messages to network users. Lawsuits were initiated by the respective social networks. Judgments were entered. MySpace was awarded a paltry $234 million. Facebook was awarded a whopping $873 million, a record award under CAN-SPAM.

Interestingly, both cases had as their chief culprit the same defendant, Sandford "Spamford" Wallace, the "spam king," a marketer with a notorious history of spamming. While Wallace took the judgments in stride, promptly filing for bankruptcy, both cases made it eminently clear that spammers on social networks are subject to the sanctions of the U.S. antispamming law, that they may face legal action by the social networks they spam on, and that social media spamming can come with a hefty price tag. And not surprisingly, if deemed a spammer, you may also see yourself and your business permanently banned from using the offended social network—or any social network—by order of the court.

COURT REAFFIRMS THE APPLICATION OF THE CAN-SPAM ACT TO SOCIAL NETWORK MESSAGING

In September 2011, Facebook was forced to revisit the issue of whether the CAN-SPAM Act applied to social networking sites, in the case of *Facebook v. MaxBounty*, when the alleged spammer, MaxBounty, filed a motion to dismiss the case, contending that the law did not apply. The court in that case rejected the alleged spammer's motion to dismiss, reinforcing the right of consumers and social networks to seek sanctions for social media spamming under the CAN-SPAM Act.

The sanctions provided under the CAN-SCAM Act include not only monetary fines and injunctive relief (i.e., the court can prohibit a spammer from doing certain acts), but also imprisonment.

UNREQUESTED COMMERCIAL MESSAGES ON SOCIAL NETWORKS ARE ILLEGAL UNLESS . . .

Getting right to the point, if you are a business and you think that it might be cool to tap into the power of social media marketing by sending a message blast to your new "friends" on Facebook, think again: it's against the law unless you comply with the CAN-SPAM Act. (And you'll also want to comply with the European Union's directive on the subject, as well as Canada's new antispam legislation that specifically includes social media marketing. More on both at the end of this chapter.)

Consent of the recipient of a commercial message is at the crux of the CAN-SPAM Act. The Act specifically requires the "affirmative consent" of a recipient to receive the message, "either in response to a clear and conspicuous request for such consent or at the recipient's own initiative."

"PRIMARY PURPOSE" RULE DETERMINES WHAT MESSAGES ARE COVERED BY THE CAN-SPAM ACT

In assessing whether an electronic message must comply with the CAN-SPAM Act, the FTC applies the "primary purpose" rule, which asks whether the primary purpose of the message is a "commercial advertisement or promotion of a commercial product or service."

The CAN-SPAM Act does not apply to messages that are deemed to have as their primary purpose "transactional or relationship" communications. The FTC offers that a message is covered by this exception if the message:

consists only of content that:

1. facilitates or confirms a commercial transaction that the recipient already has agreed to;

2. gives warranty, recall, safety, or security information about a product or service;

3. gives information about a change in terms or features or account balance information regarding a membership, subscription, account, loan or other ongoing commercial relationship;

4. provides information about an employment relationship or employee benefits; or

131

5. delivers goods or services as part of a transaction that the recipient already has agreed to.

"What If a Message Combines Commercial Content and Transactional or Relationship Content?"

The FTC also provides some guidance for situations where a message combines both commercial and transactional or relationship content, explaining:

> If a recipient reasonably interpreting the subject line would likely conclude that the message contains an advertisement or promotion for a commercial product or service or if the message's transactional or relationship content does not appear mainly at the beginning of the message, the primary purpose of the message is commercial. So, when a message contains both kinds of content—commercial and transactional or relationship—if the subject line would lead the recipient to think it's a commercial message, it's a commercial message for CAN-SPAM purposes. Similarly, if the bulk of the transactional or relationship part of the message doesn't appear at the beginning, it's a commercial message under the CAN-SPAM Act.

A $16,000 FINE IS AUTHORIZED FOR *EACH* MESSAGE SENT IN VIOLATION OF THE CAN-SPAM ACT . . . AND THE ACT ALSO PROVIDES FOR UP TO FIVE YEARS IMPRISONMENT

When in doubt about whether your message has as its "primary purpose" a commercial or a transactional or relationship message, bear in mind the hefty penalties for getting your assessment wrong. The full measure of penalties allowed under the CAN-SPAM Act should give any business pause: each separate message sent in violation of the CAN-SPAM Act is subject to a fine of $16,000, and the law also provides for the imposition of imprisonment for up to five years.

"It wasn't us; it was our marketing firm" might sound like the perfect defense in the event of a CAN-SPAM Act enforcement action, but it isn't. The Act allows for more than one party to be held responsible for each violation. As the FTC explains, "For example, both the company whose product is promoted in the message and the company that originated the message may be legally responsible."

FTC CAN-SPAM Act Compliance Checklist

The FTC has provided businesses with a CAN-SPAM Act compliance checklist:

1. **Don't use false or misleading header information.** Your "From," "To," "Reply-To," and routing information—including the originating domain name and email address—must be accurate and identify the person or business who initiated the message.

2. **Don't use deceptive subject lines.** The subject line must accurately reflect the content of the message.

3. **Identify the message as an ad.** The law gives you a lot of leeway in how to do this, but you must disclose clearly and conspicuously that your message is an advertisement.

4. **Tell recipients where you're located.** Your message must include your valid physical postal address. This can be your current street address, a post office box you've registered with the U.S. Postal Service, or a private mailbox you've registered with a commercial mail receiving agency established under Postal Service regulations.

5. **Tell recipients how to opt out of receiving future email from you.** Your message must include a clear and conspicuous explanation of how the recipient can opt out of getting email from you in the future. Craft the notice in a way that's easy for an ordinary person to recognize, read, and understand. Creative use of type size, color, and location can improve clarity. Give a return email address or another easy Internet-based way to allow people to communicate their choice to you. You may create a menu to allow a recipient to opt out of certain types of messages, but you must include the option to stop all commercial messages from you. Make sure your spam filter doesn't block these opt-out requests.

6. **Honor opt-out requests promptly.** Any opt-out mechanism you offer must be able to process opt-out requests for at least 30 days after you send your message. You must honor a recipient's opt-out request within 10 business days. You can't charge a fee, require the recipient to give you any personally identifying information beyond an email address, or make the recipient take any step other than sending a reply email or visiting a single page on an Internet website as a condition for honoring an opt-out request. Once people have told you they don't

want to receive more messages from you, you can't sell or transfer their email addresses, even in the form of a mailing list. The only exception is that you may transfer the addresses to a company you've hired to help you comply with the CAN-SPAM Act.

7. **Monitor what others are doing on your behalf.** The law makes clear that even if you hire another company to handle your email marketing, you can't contract away your legal responsibility to comply with the law. Both the company whose product is promoted in the message and the company that actually sends the message may be held legally responsible.

EUROPEAN UNION REQUIRES "OPT-IN SYSTEM" FOR COMMERCIAL COMMUNICATIONS

Under Article 13(1) of the European Union's "Privacy and Electronic Communications Directive," member states are required to "prohibit the sending of unsolicited commercial communications by fax or e-mail or *other electronic messaging systems* such as SMS and MMS unless the prior consent of the addressee has been obtained." (Emphasis added)

The EU's rule does provide an exception for sending messages within the context of an "existing customer relationship," where there had been a previous sale to the recipient and the sender is sending marketing information on a product or service previously sold to the recipient. Any such subsequent communication, however, should still include "an easy way for the customer to stop further messages (opt-out)." Member state rules should be reviewed for specific guidance.

Canada Ups the Ante on Social Media Spam: Follows EU Model

Putting to rest the question of the applicability of its antispam legislation to social networking communications, Canada has amended its antispam rules to specifically include social media. Canada's Electronic Commerce Protection Act, more commonly referred to as Canada's Anti-Spam Law (CASL), like the model outlined in the EU's antispam directive, creates an "opt-in" rather than an "opt-out" commercial communications legislative scheme. With the majority of the changes in law coming into effect as of July 1, 2014, Canada's Anti-Spam Law provides for a fine of up to $1 million per incident for an individual and $10 million per incident for a business.

CASL Requires Consent for Commercial Messages

Under the Canadian antispam law:

> It is prohibited to send or cause or permit to be sent to an electronic address a commercial electronic message unless the person to whom the message is sent has consented to receiving it, whether the consent is express or implied.

CASL Requires Transparency in Commercial Communications

Commercial messages, under CASL, must:

> (a) set out prescribed information that identifies the person who sent the message and the person—if different—on whose behalf it is sent;
>
> (b) set out information enabling the person to whom the message is sent to readily contact one of the persons referred to in paragraph (a); and
>
> (c) set out an unsubscribe mechanism.

To Obtain Lawful Consent Under CASL

CASL stipulates that requests for consent must "clearly and simply" provide the following information:

> (a) the purpose or purposes for which the consent is being sought;
>
> (b) prescribed information that identifies the person seeking consent and, if the person is seeking consent on behalf of another person, prescribed information that identifies that other person.

CASL's Standard for "Implied Consent"

Consent is implied under CASL only if:

> (a) the person who sends the message, the person who causes it to be sent or the person who permits it to be sent has an existing business relationship or an existing non-business relationship with the person to whom it is sent;
>
> (b) the person to whom the message is sent has conspicuously published, or has caused to be conspicuously published, the electronic address

to which the message is sent, the publication is not accompanied by a statement that the person does not wish to receive unsolicited commercial electronic messages at the electronic address and the message is relevant to the person's business, role, functions or duties in a business or official capacity;

(c) the person to whom the message is sent has disclosed, to the person who sends the message, the person who causes it to be sent or the person who permits it to be sent, the electronic address to which the message is sent without indicating a wish not to receive unsolicited commercial electronic messages at the electronic address, and the message is relevant to the person's business, role, functions or duties in a business or official capacity.

Broadly, CASL defines an "existing business relationship" as one "arising from the *purchase or lease* of a product, goods, a service, land or an interest or right in land, within the two-year period immediately before the day on which the message was sent." (Emphasis added)

Canada has provide a user-friendly, online reference site for the updated law that includes a section on "Frequently Asked Questions": http://www.crtc.gc.ca/eng/casl-lcap.htm

A GLOBAL TREND TO STOP SOCIAL MEDIA MARKETING SPAM SHOULD TRIGGER STRICTER COMPLIANCE POLICIES AND PRACTICES

Courts in the United States have already made it clear that while the U.S. antispam law, the CAN-SPAM, contains no specific reference to social media marketing spam, its intent and language, broadly construed, give courts the authority needed to impose the full weight of the law against those who would spam using social media. The EU's broad antispam scheme, likewise, seems to reasonably encompass social media spam. New legislation, such as Canada's Anti-Spam Act, can also be expected to more specifically address social media marketing spam, closing loopholes that may be found to exist and upping the penalties for those who violate the rules. Businesses would be well advised to tread carefully when it comes to business development techniques in social media marketing, investing more time, effort, and resources in content marketing and compliance than relying on marketing techniques that stray too close to the limits of the law.

By the Way, the United Kingdom's Information Commissioner's Office Is on the Hunt for Texting Spam—and Ready to Issue Its First Monetary Fines

As marketers continue to look for the newest and most effective means of reaching consumers, text messaging has become fertile grounds for marketing—and spamming. In the United Kingdom, the Information Commissioner's Office (ICO), an independent body set up by the government to promote data privacy for individuals, is encouraging consumers to contact it with information about unwanted text messages, even if the only information a consumer has to provide is the phone number from which the text message was received. The ICO is eager to put together the pieces needed to identify marketers spamming via text messaging so that unwanted text messages may be rewarded with substantial fines.

Recently, the ICO announced on its blog that it was preparing to issue its first fines for text spamming, in the sum of "six figures" against two text spammers it had tracked down using consumer complaints.

THE UNITED KINGDOM'S RULES FOR TEXT MARKETING

According to the ICO, under the United Kingdom's laws, namely, the Privacy and Electronic Communications Regulations of 2003, organizations may only send direct marketing by electronic means, including by text message, when:

- The sender has obtained the consumer's details through a sale or negotiations for a sale.

- The messages sent are about similar products or services offered by the sender.

- The sender gave the recipient an opportunity to refuse the texts when the consumer's details were first collected, and if the consumer did not refuse then, the consumer is also given a simple way to opt out in all the text messages sent.

UNDER U.S. FCC RULES, CONSENT OF CONSUMERS TO RECEIVE COMMERCIAL TEXT MESSAGES MUST BE "IN WRITING"

As with the U.K. text-messaging rules, the U.S. rules likewise require the consent of the consumer before a commercial text message may be sent to that person.

According the U.S. regulatory authority that governs text messaging, the Federal Communications Commission (FCC), the consent of a consumer to receive a commercial text "must be in writing (for example, in an email or letter)"; and "for non-commercial, informational texts (such as those by or on behalf of tax-exempt non-profit organizations, those for political purposes, and other noncommercial purposes, such as school closings)," the consent of the recipient may be oral.

According to the ICO's investigations, much of the spam text messaging is being done by "lead generation companies—companies that are trying to find people who will respond so they can sell those people's details to claims or debt management firms. The companies behind these messages are looking to earn money by selling these leads." From a lawyer's perspective, even the use of such ill-gotten data by a company, even if the company had no role in the collection of such data, would create legal liability issues.

KEEP AN EYE ON HOW EACH SOCIAL NETWORK DEFINES "SPAMMING"

Nations, as we have learned, are outlining rules with many common touchstones when it comes to the definition and prohibition of spamming. Understand, however, that each social network has its own definition of what constitutes spamming, and each is free to set its own boundaries on how you market and expand your presence within its network.

Twitter's rules on what constitutes spamming help convey the importance of reviewing each network's specific definition of spam. According to Twitter's rules, you are spamming:

- If you have followed a large amount of users in a short amount of time;

- If you have followed and unfollowed people in a short time period, particularly by automated means (aggressive follower churn);

- If you repeatedly follow and unfollow people, whether to build followers or to garner more attention for your profile;

- If you have a small number of followers compared to the amount of people you are following;

- If your updates consist mainly of links, and not personal updates;

- If you post misleading links;

- If a large number of people are blocking you;

- [If there are a] number of spam complaints that have been filed against you;

- If you post duplicate content over multiple accounts or multiple duplicate updates on one account;

- If you post multiple unrelated updates to a topic using #;

- If you post multiple unrelated updates to a trending or popular topic;

- If you send large numbers of duplicate @replies or mentions;

- If you send large numbers of unsolicited @replies or mentions in an attempt to spam a service or link;

- If you add a large number of unrelated users to lists in an attempt to spam a service or link;

- If you repeatedly post other users' Tweets as your own;

- If you have attempted to "sell" followers, particularly through tactics considered aggressive following or follower churn;

- [If you are] [c]reating or purchasing accounts in order to gain followers;

- [If you are] [u]sing or promoting third-party sites that claim to get you more followers (such as follower trains, sites promising "more followers fast," or any other site that offers to automatically add followers to your account);

- If you create false or misleading Points of Interest;

- If you create Points of Interest to namesquat or spam.

Instagram, by comparison, defines spam as "repetitive comments, as well as service manipulation in order to self-promote, and extends to commercial spam comments, such as discount codes or URLs to websites."

8

A Word About (Mobile) Apps

TAKE A BITE OUT OF THIS: APPLE USERS HAVE DOWNLOADED MORE THAN 15 BILLION APPS

In the summer of 2011, Apple announced that more than 15 billion mobile applications had been downloaded from its App Store, at that time offering users "425,000 of the coolest apps" to choose from. If your business doesn't already have an app, it will. Why? Because your CEO will want one.

One Nation Under Apps

In 2012, Pew Internet Research Center released a landmark study on "Privacy and Data Management on Mobile Devices." Interestingly, the study found a "consistency" across age and gender groups when it came to concerns about mobile applications and personal privacy: "app users of all ages are equally likely to remove (or to avoid downloading) an app based on privacy concerns."

Among those had downloaded apps, according to the study:

- 54% of app users have decided to not install a cell phone app when they discovered how much personal information they would need to share in order to use it.

- 30% of app users have uninstalled an app that was already on their cell phone because they learned it was collecting personal information that they didn't wish to share.

- Taken together, 57% of all app users have either uninstalled an app over concerns about having to share their personal information, or declined to install an app in the first place for similar reasons.

Pew's findings reveal that U.S. mobile app users are deeply concerned about the protection of their personal data and the risk of exposure of such data by the use of mobile apps. The nation's primary consumer protection authority, the Federal Trade Commission, shares in that concern and has already outlined best practices for app developers and those who market apps or use them to promote their business.

It is important for social media marketers who integrate apps into their marketing toolbox to recognize that not only is it the law to protect consumer privacy, but protecting consumer privacy will also go a long way in improving user experience—and use—of a mobile app. So here, once again, we see the convergence of consumer data protection best practices, user experience, marketing success, and the law.

FTC PUBLISHES GUIDE TO HELP MOBILE APP DEVELOPERS OBSERVE TRUTH-IN-ADVERTISING, PRIVACY PRINCIPLES

The FTC has outlined best practices for those developing or promoting apps:

- **Tell the truth about what your app can do.** "Whether it's what you say on a website, in an app store, or within the app itself, you have to tell the truth," the publication advises;

- **Disclose key information clearly and conspicuously.** "If you need to disclose information to make what you say accurate, your disclosures have to be clear and conspicuous."

- **Build privacy considerations in from the start.** Incorporate privacy protections into your practices, limit the information you collect, securely store what you hold on to, and safely dispose of what you no longer need. "For any collection or sharing of information that's not apparent, get users' express agreement. That way your customers aren't unwittingly disclosing information they didn't mean to share."

- **Offer choices that are easy to find and easy to use.** "Make it easy for people to find the tools you offer, design them so they're simple to use, and follow through by honoring the choices users have made."

- **Honor your privacy promises.** "Chances are you make assurances to users about the security standards you apply or what you do with their personal information. App developers—like all other marketers—have to live up to those promises."

- **Protect kids' privacy.** "If your app is designed for children or if you know that you are collecting personal information from kids, you may have additional requirements under the Children's Online Privacy Protection Act."

- **Collect sensitive information only with consent.** Even when you're not dealing with kids' information, it's important to get users' affirmative OK before you collect any sensitive data from them, like medical, financial, or precise geolocation information.

- **Keep user data secure.** Statutes like the Graham-Leach-Bliley Act, the Fair Credit Reporting Act, and the Federal Trade Commission Act may require you to provide reasonable security for sensitive information. The FTC has free resources to help you develop a security plan appropriate for your business.

FTC COMMISSIONER REINFORCES BEST PRACTICES IN THE DEVELOPMENT AND PROMOTION OF MOBILE APPS

During a talk on privacy, FTC commissioner Julie Brill issued a warning to app developers, marketers, and the businesses using apps:

> As our enforcement actions concerning privacy practices gain more attention, app developers, app service providers and others in this space realize that they need to think more about privacy issues.

Brill went on to explain that, in addition to going after major social networks for privacy violations, the FTC has taken enforcement actions against app marketers and developers due to privacy-related offenses, namely, the failure "to sufficiently protect the private information of consumers."

FTC's Guiding Principle for Mobile App Developers: "Bake in Privacy"

Commissioner Brill articulated a general principle of guidance for mobile app developers:

> Our guidance encourages app developers to bake privacy into their app from the start.

This notion of "baking privacy" into an application "from the start" is consistent with the FTC's larger principle of "privacy by design," a regulatory mandate that consumer privacy should be taken into consideration by businesses from the start of and throughout the process of any marketing campaign or product development.

Commissioner Brill, in her talk about online privacy, gave some specific guidance to help those in the app space better understand her principle of "baking in" privacy. To "bake in privacy," according to Brill, developers should do the following:

1. Limit information collected by the app to the information needed for the proper functioning of their app.

2. Ensure the security of the information they do collect.

3. Collect sensitive information—financial, medical, precise geolocation—only with a user's affirmative consent.

4. Comply with the provisions of the Children's Online Privacy Protection Act in connection with children's information.

5. Be transparent about privacy practices.

6. Provide users with choices that are "easy to use and understand, and the choices should, of course, be honored."

Commissioner Brill's elaboration on the meaning of "baking in privacy," not surprisingly, closely follows the guidance offered in the FTC's mobile app guide.

You Have a Duty to "Disclose Key Information Clearly and Conspicuously"

Signaling an important trend in regulatory policy, the FTC's mobile application guide warns:

> Generally, the law doesn't dictate a specific font or type size, but the FTC has taken action against companies that have buried important terms and

conditions in long licensing agreements, in dense blocks of legal mumbo jumbo, or behind vague hyperlinks.

Whether your business already has an app or is contemplating developing one, the FTC's report on the topic is a must-read: *Marketing Your Mobile App: Get It Right from the Start.*

9

Legal Issues for Blogs and Bloggers

IF YOU STAND STILL, YOU JUST MAY GET SUED

If you stand still, you just might get sued. Why? Because someone may take offense at where you are standing, and although there are protections against frivolous lawsuits, there is still an abundance of silly lawsuits. So in an age when search is social and sharing is community and content driven, if you don't blog, you and your business may never get found. Blogging is a powerful medium to project your expertise and to build your online community. So the question really becomes, not *whether* to blog, but *how* to blog and minimize your risks of being sued or sanctioned while blogging or hosting a blog.

To be fair, there are more than a few legal mine fields for bloggers to be aware of beyond those previously discussed under the FTC's social media guidelines for sponsored bloggers.

SOME LEGAL LAND MINES FOR BLOGGERS

What you need to keep in mind about blogging:

- Blogs are megaphones for anything you do or say wrong.

- Your blog is a permanent record that cannot be deleted.

(continued)

- People may actually read your blog, and if they do and if your information is inaccurate, you risk getting sued if someone suffers a loss as a result of your bad advice or bad information.

- If you fail to disclose your material connections in your blogging, you could be sanctioned by your state or sued by another.

- If you invite guest bloggers, their inaccuracies or failure to disclose material connections can create problems for your business's reputation, as well as entangle you in legal problems.

- While you may be an excellent investigative journalist in your reporting, you may not be given the protections that give reporters a greater freedom from defamation lawsuits than an average person or blogger would receive, unless that blogger were to be recognized as a journalist.

- You may not be able to keep your "confidential" sources confidential.

- If you defame someone, you may get sued.

- Depending on the topic you choose to blog about, you may find yourself being sanctioned by a state regulatory agency if you are not licensed in the field you have chosen to blog about, such as nutrition.

- If you are a sponsored blogger or if you are sponsoring bloggers, the details of such sponsorships may become the fodder of courtroom litigation and be publicized.

- If you edit blog posts on your blog site improperly, so as to change their meaning, you may have destroyed immunity against damages under federal law for content users who post to your site.

- If a visitor to your site posts copyrighted content to your blog, you could be sued if you have not created a "safe harbor."

- You risk being sued if you use someone else's likeness without the person's permission.

- You risk being sued if you intrude upon someone's privacy, disclose embarrassing private facts about the person, or create a false impression about him or her based on faulty information.

IF YOU DO GET YOUR BLOG CONTENT WRONG, YOU MAY GET SUED OR SANCTIONED

I'm not going to review the FTC's social media marketing guidelines again, but I strongly recommend that you really study the chapter about them and be mindful of them when you do blog. Even if the FTC sticks to its plan of not coming after wayward bloggers in its enforcement actions, a failure to disclose a material connection in your blogging not only can damage your reputation but could well serve as a basis for someone to ask your state attorney general to go after you for consumer fraud. And there are other legal risks as well for careless blogging.

Do know that if you overstate the benefits of a product or service, or otherwise get use limitations wrong, and someone gets hurt, you expose yourself to a lawsuit as a consequence. If you simply give bad advice and someone gets hurt or loses money or wastes money, based on the promises or descriptions or projections you have provided, a court could well ask whether you exercised reasonable care in providing the information you shared from your blog. And if you hold yourself out to be an expert in a field, a court will look at all that you blog with a higher degree of scrutiny.

LESSEN LEGAL RISKS BY ADDING COMPLIANCE TO YOUR BLOG CALENDAR

If your business creates a blog content calendar, with regular meetings, someone from your compliance department should be copied on the topics to be blogged about and even given a chance to read the posts before they go out.

Think about it. It makes sense. Legal and compliance need to pick up the pace, meaning that they've got to understand that a speedy turnaround is vital in the world of social media. If they are on board with this, they shouldn't be slowing you down. We're talking about blog posts. This means quick reads by someone from compliance. (Or photo reviews or video reviews.)

Businesses need to understand that members of their legal and compliance teams will only be able to work well with social media if they understand it. Most don't. They should be required to attend some to the social media training opportunities that come up so that they can begin to understand the importance, techniques and strategies of social media.

Adding compliance to you blog calendar will only benefit the process if compliance understands social!

GUEST BLOGGERS SHOULDN'T GET A PASS ON COMPLIANCE

Inviting guest bloggers to blog on your site is a great way to broaden your blog community. Keep in mind, though, that you can't give your guest bloggers a pass when it comes to social media compliance. The FTC disclosure rules can't be ignored because it's your guest who is ignoring them. It's also your reputation and your blog.

In a moment, we're going to review a law that extends blog and community hosts a strong measure of immunity from the content shared by others on their site. Don't be confused by that discussion to think that it applies to those you invite to blog as a guest on your site. By extending the invitation, even if you don't exercise editorial control over the content, you would likely expose yourself or your business to liability, through the doctrine of "entanglement," though you could conceivably fashion an argument about why that doctrine of liability should not apply.

BLOG THIS: YOUR PRESS PASS DOESN'T NECESSARILY MAKE YOU A JOURNALIST

You get press passes. That's all nice. Just don't make the mistake of thinking that getting the perks of a journalist necessarily gives you, as a blogger, the protections of a journalist. At the moment, the decision about whether a blogger should be afforded any of the special protections that apply to journalists varies from state to state and country to country. The issue of whether a blogger is a journalist has profound implications at least in the United States when it comes to being sued for defamation, i.e., causing damage to the reputation of another due to the spreading of false or erroneous information.

In *New York Times Co. v. Sullivan, 376 U.S. 254, 279–280 (1964)*, the U.S. Supreme Court extended to members of the press a powerful defense against defamation lawsuits brought by public figures as it established a standard that required "actual malice," a showing that "the statement was made with knowledge of its falsity or with reckless disregard of whether it was true or false," before an award of damages for defamation could be rendered. This heightened threshold for defamation suits has been deemed a necessary breathing space for the conduct of a free press. Whether a court deems a blogger a journalist, and therefore able to have the protection of the higher threshold, could mean the difference of, let's say, $2.5 million, as we'll see in a moment.

According to the Reporters Committee for Freedom of the Press, 40 of the U.S. states have also adopted press shield laws that protect members of the press from having to reveal their confidential sources. What is not uniform among those 40 states is whether bloggers would qualify for the shield.

"INVESTIGATIVE BLOGGER" ORDERED TO PAY $2.5 MILLION FOR A SINGLE POST

The headline from *Courthouse News Service* was a thunderbolt: "Investigative Blogger Must Pay $2.5 Million." The opening paragraph from the story that followed seemed even worse for bloggers who thought that they might receive the same protection of a journalist against defamation lawsuits when they engaged in "investigative blogging":

> A self-described investigative blogger must pay a financial company $2.5 million for a single blog posting in which she accused it of tax fraud, after a federal judge refused to grant her request for a new jury trial.

It is a story that gripped the blogging community with fear that all their efforts to bring earnest reporting to the blogosphere would be for naught if they found themselves subject to the prospect of staggering fines as a penalty for their investigative work. The judge in this case, however, was quick to dispel the notion that bloggers could not be considered reporters or afforded the special protections of a reporter against defamation lawsuits (i.e., a showing of "actual malice") brought by public figures. He made it clear that his decision applied narrowly to the facts of the case he was presented with, in which the self-proclaimed "investigative blogger" actually offered to provide the victim of an online smear campaign—one the "investigative blogger" had single-handedly conducted herself—with "reputation management" services for the very reputation she had smeared.

In addition to rejecting the blogger's contention that she should have been deemed a journalist, the judge also rejected the blogger's arguments that she had raised a matter of "public concern" and that the victims of her misdeeds were "public figures," elements considered when weighing an argument for the *NY Times vs. Sullivan* "actual malice" standard.

DON'T LET SHOCK TV AND RADIO HOSTS BE YOUR GUIDE FOR YOUR BLOG—UNLESS YOU WANT TO GET SUED

There are talk show hosts and celebrities who make a career out of being shocking and controversial. Please don't think that a blog provides you with any immunities; it doesn't. A blog does, however, magnify everything you say, increasing the importance of getting things right when you do blog.

IF YOU ARE GOING TO BLOG ABOUT NUTRITION . . . YOU JUST MIGHT NEED A LICENSE

Steve Cooksey writes a blog at http://www.Diabetes-Warrior.net, sharing his story of beating obesity and diabetes by following a "low-carb primal" diet. In January 2012, the North Carolina Board of Dietetics/Nutrition opened an investigation into Cooksey's blog, stating that Cooksey was not allowed to advise people through postings—whether publicly or privately, for compensation or for free—as he did not have a State license as a nutritionist. The Board threatened to take him to court if he did not comply with its warnings.

To address the Board's warnings, Cooksey said that he stopped his advice column, took down information on diabetes support, and made his disclaimer more prominent.

As a consequence of Cooksey's actions, the Board concluded that Cooksey was in "substantial compliance" and closed its investigation. However, according to Cooksey, the Board's closure letter still threatens to monitor him.

The Board, for its part, has provided on its website a full-page press statement called "Setting the Record Straight," noting that "a number of inaccuracies have been presented to the public regarding a complaint that was submitted to the North Carolina Board of Dietetics/Nutrition (the NCBDN) concerning Steve Cooksey, an unlicensed person."

The Board stated that it had received a written complaint "alleging that Steve Cooksey was providing nutrition care services in North Carolina without a license," which triggered a mandatory investigation under North Carolina law.

While insisting that it was not suggesting that a blogger would need to be a licensed nutritionist to blog about nutrition, it did offer the following observation in its lengthy defense:

It has been reported that the NCBDN maintains that Mr. Cooksey needs a license to advocate certain dietary approaches.

In and of itself, advocating a certain type of diet or dietary approach is not a violation of the law. The specific diet Mr. Cooksey promotes is not, and never has been, under investigation. However, unless a person is otherwise exempt, a license is required to provide nutrition care services, which is defined as:

- Assessing the nutritional needs of individuals and groups, and determining resources and constraints in the practice setting.

- Establishing priorities, goals, and objectives that meet nutritional needs and are consistent with available resources and constraints.

- Providing nutrition counseling in health and disease.

- Developing, implementing, and managing nutrition care systems.

Further explaining its version of events, the Board stressed that it had "never made any formal decision that Mr. Cooksey's blog violated state law or commenced any type of legal action against him." Plainly, this statement from the Board leaves open the possibility that the Board could have concluded that Cooksey's blog violated state law if it had not decided to close its investigation in response to the measures Cooksey had taken.

The Board's "Setting the Record Straight" seems to be, unintentionally or not, an additional warning shot to other unlicensed "nutrition" bloggers. It is likely to have a chilling effect on other bloggers in the state who might have an interest in blogging about diet and nutrition but do not hold a license in the state. Will this incident benefit consumers in the state of North Carolina—or hurt consumers by having a chilling effect on a broader debate on the subject of nutrition and diet? The answer may depend on one's perspective.

It should be noted that the state does have a legitimate interest in protecting the public from unsafe health-related information. It should equally be noted that imposing a requirement that those who blog about nutrition must be licensed to offer nutritional advice, an oversimplification of the issue, could pose serious impediments to healthy public debate and access to alternative dietary and nutritional information.

BLOGGING FOR DOLLARS? A COURT MAY ORDER IT DISCLOSED

Big companies are investing big dollars in sponsoring bloggers. As we know from our examination of the FTC social media guidelines, such connections between bloggers and their sponsors are supposed to be disclosed when a blogger is blogging about the sponsor.

An unusual court order issued in August 2012, in a major patent and copyright case between Oracle and Google, raised questions about a darker underbelly of the world of sponsored blogging. The order, from the trial judge, informed the parties:

> The Court is concerned that the parties and/or counsel herein may have retained or paid print or internet authors, journalists, commentators or bloggers who have and/or may publish comments on the issues in this case. Although proceedings in this matter are almost over, they are not fully over yet and, in any event, the disclosure required by this order would be of use on appeal or on any remand to make clear whether any treatise, article, commentary or analysis on the issues posed by this case [is] possibly influenced by financial relationships to the parties or counsel. Therefore, each side and its counsel shall file a statement herein clear[ly] identifying all authors, journalists, commentators or bloggers who have reported or commented on any issues in this case and who have received money (other than normal subscription fees) from the party or its counsel during the pendency of this action.

Importantly, it should be noted that the court's order applies not only to the tech giants but to their lawyers as well.

One prominent "independent" blogger, who had blogged extensively about the Oracle-Google litigation, disclosed "that Oracle has very recently become a consulting client of mine."

SECTION 230: "THE LEGAL MAGIC BULLET THAT PROTECTS TWITTER AND YELP"—AND YOUR PERSONAL OR BUSINESS BLOG

"Section 230," as it is commonly referred to, is a federal, legislative immunity provided to those who host online "interactive" services, a phrase broadly defined to include blogs, from lawsuits because of content posted by users of their interactive services. *47 USC § 230(c)(1)*. It has been called "the legal magic bullet that protects Twitter and Yelp" and similar user review and content-sharing sites because of the expansive immunity from lawsuits it provides.

It is a protection that was part of a larger legislative act, the controversial Communications Decency Act (CDA or Act), which had as its purported goal the protection of minors from explicit material online. Ironically, although nearly all the "anti-indecency" sections of the CDA were eventually invalidated by the Supreme Court as unconstitutional, what has remained in full force and effect of the Act is Section 230, which has at its core the protection of service providers from the content that users of their interactive sites post.

In particular, Section 230 largely protects any interactive service, such as a forum, chat room, blog, or social networking site that allows users to post their own content, from being sued because of defamation (libelous, i.e., published falsehood that injures the reputation of another) or inflammatory or harassing comments or content posted by users. *47 USC § 230(c)(1)*.

SECTION 230(C)(1): "THE SILVER BULLET"—WHAT IT SAYS

Section 230(c)(1) of the Communications Decency Act states:

> No provider or user of an interactive computer service shall be treated as the publisher or speaker of any information provided by another information content provider.

In other words, you, as someone hosting a blog or online community, cannot be held liable (i.e., be successfully sued in court) because of what someone else has posted to your blog or forum or other interactive site—generally speaking. You've always got to watch for the exceptions in a law, and so we explore them here!

Four Exceptions to the Immunity Provided by Section 230

Section 230 does go on to provide exceptions for four categories of content:

1. **Violations of federal criminal statutes**, *47 USC § 230(e)(1)*. Though this subsection specifically mentions crimes "relating to obscenity" or the "sexual exploitation of children," it includes "any other Federal criminal statute."

2. **Intellectual property infringements**, *47 USC § 230(e)(2)*. Copyright and trademark infringements posted to a blog or forum are not covered by the "magic bullet" of Section 230 and may expose a business blog or other interactive service provider to legal liability if other steps are not taken to create a "safe harbor," a protection that will be discussed following the exploration of Section 230.

3. **State law that is consistent with this section**, *47 USC § 230(e)(3)*. This is not really an exception to the immunity provided by Section 230, as any state law "consistent" with Section 230 would provide a similar immunity to interactive service providers. What is really significant about this

subsection is that it makes clear that state or local law may not trump or pierce the immunity of Section 230. Verbatim, this subsection provides:

Nothing in this section shall be construed to prevent any State from enforcing any State law that is consistent with this section. **No cause of action may be brought and no liability may be imposed under any State or local law that is inconsistent with this section.** *(Emphasis added)*

4. **Communication privacy laws**, *47 USC § 230(e)(4).* This subsection generally refers to protections found in the Electronic Communications Privacy Act of 1986 (ECPA), *18 U.S.C. §§ 2510–2522*, or similar state laws. The ECPA essentially prohibits the interception or tapping of electronic communications while they are in transit or stored on computers.

SECTION 230 DOES *NOT* PROTECT THE PERSON POSTING WRONGFUL COMMENTS

Let's be clear on this point: if you host a blog or a forum, Section 230 provides you with a strong immunity from legal claims because of the comments posted by others.

For example, if you host a restaurant review site and a person posts a comment saying horrible things about a particular restaurant and all the terrible claims made in the comment are false, you still should get a pass from any court, as you merely created an interactive service, forum, or blog and had nothing to do with the content of the comment that was posted.

What about the son of the owner of the neighboring restaurant who posted the pack of lies about the competing restaurant? Well, if the restaurant that was defamed (i.e., had its reputation damaged because of the communication of lies to third parties) decides to go after the person who posted the false and malicious post, it can. Its attorney would likely subpoena the service provider for details of the identity of the heretofore "anonymous" commentator and begin a lawsuit that might still include the service provider.

"Wait! What about the Section 230 immunity for service providers?!"

The immunity should prevail to get the provider dismissed from the lawsuit early on, but lawyers must generally err on the side of including anyone in a lawsuit who might plausibly have some responsibility for the harm. The service provider, in turn, would likely, quickly, submit a motion for summary judgment with a certification making it clear that he or she had no connection at all with the party who posted the defamatory comment. It is a motion that would likely not be objected to and would likely be granted.

SECTION 230(C)(2) ALLOWS BLOG OR ONLINE COMMUNITY HOSTS TO REMOVE "OBJECTIONABLE" CONTENT OR COMMENTS WITHOUT FEAR OF LEGAL LIABILITY

This subsection of Section 230 gives forum and blog hosts the freedom to remove or edit content where the material posted is deemed by the host to be "objectionable":

> 2) Civil liability
>
> No provider or user of an interactive computer service shall be held liable on account of:
>
> (A) any action voluntarily taken in good faith to restrict access to or availability of material that the provider or user considers to be obscene, lewd, lascivious, filthy, excessively violent, harassing, or otherwise objectionable, whether or not such material is constitutionally protected; or
>
> (B) any action taken to enable or make available to information content providers or others the technical means to restrict access to material described in paragraph (1)

Here Section 230 gives forum and blog hosts the ability to police their own forums and blogs for content they deem to be objectionable and to delete the material or edit it as desired.

CREATIVE EDITING OF BLOG COMMENTS CAN WAIVE SECTION 230 IMMUNITY

Although Section 230(c)(2) gives those hosting a blog or community the right to edit comments that are posted to an interactive site, editing that changes the meaning of a comment can cause the immunity of the subsection to be waived, potentially exposing the editor to liability. For example, editing a comment to delete the word "not" in the following sentence would be sure to expose the editor to lawsuits from both the commentator and the subject of the comment: "Tom is not a liar." Obviously, this example blatantly turns upside down a comment, but other, more subtle, editing that makes a significant change in the meaning of a comment, depending on the circumstances, could be equally problematic in terms of legal liability.

BE MINDFUL OF THE RIGHT OF PRIVACY WHEN YOU BLOG

In the law, rights often bump up against each other, requiring courts to consider the circumstances of a given case to weigh which right should yield. There is a fundamental right to privacy that each of us enjoys, and yet it is a right that must yield to other, more compelling rights at different times. Knowing when and where they apply may, in part, be a function of where you live, as some of these rights have even been codified into state or national law.

As a blogger, you should be aware of the four basic types of privacy—which offer four causes of action for a claim of invasion of privacy—that are generally recognized by the courts, thanks to the scholarly work of the eminent law school dean William Lloyd Prosser, whose writings on the subject remain a primary reference.

Four Types of Privacy

1. **Intrusion upon the plaintiff's seclusion or solitude, or into his or her private affairs.** In this sort of claim, the "intrusion" into the privacy of another is pretty blatant, such as a bank employee who releases information about a customer's finances.

2. **Public disclosure of embarrassing private facts about a person.** Here the information shared must truly be private, not a matter of public knowledge or a matter of true newsworthiness, and highly offensive to a reasonable person.

3. **Publicity that places a person in a false light in the public eye.** A "false light" invasion of privacy typically requires a finding that the person charged with the offense had knowledge of or acted in reckless disregard as to the falsity of the publicized information and that the portrayal of the offended person would create a false impression and be highly offensive to a reasonable person.

4. **Appropriation of a person's name or likeness for the person's disadvantage, commonly referred to as the "right of publicity."** California, the land of Hollywood, places a premium on the right of publicity, having enacted a state statute to protect its citizenry against such dastardly thievery. The code, *CAL. CIV. CODE § 3344 : California Code—Section 3344*, reads in part:

> Any person who knowingly uses another's name, voice, signature, photograph, or likeness, in any manner, on or in products, merchandise, or goods, or for purposes of advertising or selling, or soliciting purchases of, products, merchandise, goods or services, without such person's prior consent, or, in the case of a minor, the prior consent of his parent or legal guardian, shall be liable for any damages sustained by the person or persons injured as a result thereof.

California's "right of publicity" was recently tested and stood firm against Facebook, leading to a $10 million settlement payment by the social networking giant for the misappropriation of members' images, without the permission of users, in so-called Sponsored Stories, with users finding their likenesses being used in Facebook ads.

HOW TO CREATE A "SAFE HARBOR" AGAINST COPYRIGHT COMPLAINTS FOR COPYRIGHTED CONTENT POSTED TO YOUR BLOG BY USERS, *17 U.S.C. SEC. 512*

As we discussed before, Section 230 provides a strong immunity for those who host a blog against legal claims from the content posted there by users or third parties. We also learned that under 47 USC § 230(e)(2), copyright and trademark infringements posted to a blog or forum are not covered by the magic bullet of Section 230 and could expose a business blog or other interactive service provider to legal liability if other steps are not taken to create a safe harbor.

SECTION 512 OF THE DIGITAL MILLENNIUM COPYRIGHT ACT CRITERIA FOR THE CREATION OF A SAFE HARBOR AGAINST COPYRIGHT CLAIMS

To receive the safe harbor protection against copyright claims due to the content posted by users or visitors to a blog, blog hosts must not be aware of the infringing content or have had a role in it and should have designated an agent with the U.S. Copyright Office to receive infringement complaints. The designated agent's contact information should be easily accessible to blog visitors, and the blog host must be "expeditious" in removing infringing content when it is flagged.

The following points must be met to achieve a safe harbor:

1. The blog host has no actual knowledge that the material on the network is infringing.

2. The blog host is unaware of facts or circumstances from which the infringing activity is apparent.

3. Upon learning of the copyright infringement, the blog host acts expeditiously to remove the infringing material or disable access to it.

4. The host or service provider does not receive a financial benefit directly attributable to the infringing activity, in a case in which the service provider has the right and ability to control such activity,

5. The blog host must also have designated an agent with the U.S. Copyright Office to receive copyright infringement complaints and have made that agent's contact information accessible to the public with the following information:

    (A) the name, address, phone number, and electronic mail address of the agent

    (B) other contact information which the Register of Copyrights may deem appropriate

It is important to note that this safe harbor against copyright infringement claims only applies to content posted by third parties. It does not provide a protection against claims for content posted by the blog host.

THE STREISAND EFFECT

A term coined in 2005 by Mike Masnick of *Techdirt*, the "Streisand effect" refers to an online phenomenon of frenzied interest that occurs when someone attempts to censor something. In the unfortunate case of singer, superstar Barbra Streisand, the viral interest was unleashed when she sued a photographer for invasion of privacy after his photographs of her spectacular Malibu home were published. The lawsuit inspired intense interest in the photos—far more interest than ever would have existed without the attempt to quash them.

The photos of the star's sprawling mansion were actually taken as part of a program to document changes in the California coastline. Though the lawsuit to take down the photos failed, it did generate enough publicity in the month after the lawsuit to attract more than 400,000 visits to the site where they were posted.

A GREAT EXAMPLE OF A COMMUNITY GUIDE: THE *WALL STREET JOURNAL*'S "JOURNAL COMMUNITY RULES"

When it comes to traditional media "getting" social and "being" social, the *Wall Street Journal* is a marvel of agility. It has made the transition remarkably well by embracing social media. Care to comment online to a *WSJ* post? The newspaper has community rules, much as one would for any blog site or social community.

Examining the *Wall Street Journal*'s community rules provides a nice list of must-haves for blog or community moderation:

Welcome. Statement of Rules

- Requirement of using real names. There is no "right or wrong" on this point. It is a preference you as a "community" or corporate blog must decide upon.

- Necessity of staying on topic. For the benefit of everyone, this is a must. It lessens the likelihood of spam and trolls and improves the search engine optimization of your blog by keeping your content focused on your niche. It also makes it easier to spot and eliminate content that may be troublesome from a legal perspective.

- Respect for others.

- Staying civil. No personal attacks, wishing harm, stalking, or harassing of others.

- No obscenity, profanity, vulgarity, bigotry, or invasion of privacy.

- No self-promotional links.

- No comments in all caps or objectionable profile photos. (Kudos to the *WSJ* on creating a provision that is usually a way to spot spammers.)

Getting them off your blog early is good for your community, as the content they share is likely to be offensive, to be spam, and to include content that infringes on the rights of others.

- No spam. Ditto—though you still want to confront it head on.

- No uploading malware. This one may seem kind of silly, but including it provides a clear basis for banning individuals from your community or blog if they do.

- Compliance with all applicable laws. This is a must, especially in a medium where the law is evolving.

- No sharing of content that infringes upon trademark, trade secret, copyright, or other proprietary rights of any person.

- Catch-all statement reserving the right to remove any content at any time.

- Reporting of abuse. One of the best ways to police your blog for abusive content that is prone to create legal issues is by crowdsourcing the task with your own community. Be sure to provide a clear, easy-to-reach contact for this purpose.

- Statement reserving the right to ban anyone who violates the rules.

- Provision for further assistance—for example, "For help, contact Moderator@_____.com." To achieve the safe harbor protection against user content that infringes upon copyright, this contact may also be designated the clearinghouse for copyright infringement claims.

SOME BEST PRACTICES FOR BLOGS AND BLOGGERS

There's no better way to end this chapter than with this list of best practices:

- Blog as if your blog post is going to appear on the front page of the *Wall Street Journal*: be as accurate as you possibly can be!

- Remember that when you blog, you are creating a permanent record.

- Don't exaggerate in your blogging.

- Disclose your material connections in a clear and conspicuous manner and insist that your guest bloggers do the same.

- Carefully vet your guest bloggers.

- Know the rule in your jurisdiction about whether or not you may receive any protections extended to journalists.

- Remember that blogging is *not* a defense against defamation!

- Look into whether or not the subject matter you have chosen to blog about is within a field that ordinarily requires a license within your jurisdiction. If the subject matter you blog about covers a licensed profession, know the limits of what you are allowed to say or do on your blog.

- If you are a sponsored blogger or you are sponsoring bloggers, recognize that the details of such sponsorships may become the fodder of courtroom litigation and may be publicized.

- If you edit blog posts on your blog site, do not change their meaning, as you might destroy your Section 230 immunity against damages under federal law for content posted by visitors to the blog.

- Create a "safe harbor" against copyrighted material posted to your blog or forum by designating and registering an agent to receive copyright infringement claims. Be sure that the contact information for the designated copyright claims agent is easily viewable from your site and that you "expeditiously" remove copyrighted content when you receive a notification of infringement.

- Do not use someone else's likeness without his or her permission.

- Be respectful of the privacy of others.

10

"Business to Government": Social Media Best Practices for Large Organizations and Social Compliance in Government

B AE Systems is a global company that, among other things, builds really big weapons systems—as in the company is a multibillion-dollar, multinational defense contractor. It has about 88,700 employees, with a presence in Australia, India, the Kingdom of Saudi Arabia, the United Kingdom, and the United States.

Surely there's no point to a defense contractor being "social." This is the defense industry! All downside, no upside. Plus, what about the firewalls?!

Think again.

BAE SYSTEMS, INC. (DEFENSE CONTRACTOR): "WE'RE 'B TO G,' BUSINESS TO GOVERNMENT"

Steve Field, director of digital communication at BAE Systems, Inc., who once served as a public affairs specialist with the U.S. Army at the Pentagon, explained just why a defense contracting firm would want to be "social":

> We are a "B-to-G" company, a business to government company. Governments are our customers and governments are made up of people. Social makes sense.

Field explained that the company is able to leverage social media's powerful ability to connect to relevant key opinion leaders who are interested in the multimedia content BAE shares through social media about its products and services. The content shared by BAE, according to Field, is regularly viewed by high-ranking members of defense departments worldwide and helps them to understand the quality and importance of the systems BAE develops. Field also mentioned that social media plays an important role in the company's talent recruitment.

If one of the largest multinational defense firms finds a substantial return on being social in "business to government," i.e., "business to people," there might well be business applications for others . . .

But What About the Firewalls and All the Risks Generally Associated with Going Social?

Field was quick to share that his boss, Price Floyd, was the one who was able to get the mammoth defense company to think and be social. Floyd, however, isn't your average communications guy. Oh, he's done communications for a while, but he didn't start out as a cub reporter for a small-town newspaper.

EXPERIENCE AND CREDENTIALS MATTER IN GETTING C-LEVEL BUY-IN

Floyd earned his communications stripes with the U.S. Department of State, from 1989 until 2007, traveling to more than 50 countries, including service as the first Bosnia desk officer from 1993 to 1994. He earned the State Department's Superior Honor Award for his work during the Bosnian war.

He eventually went to work at the Pentagon, serving as the principal deputy assistant secretary of defense for public affairs. Recognizing the importance of social media and believing that it would benefit the objectives of the Department of Defense (DoD), Floyd took the bold initiative of bringing the U.S. Armed Forces into the world of social media. National Public Radio would describe him as "the Department's 'social media guru.'"

How did he do it? How did he overcome all the objections and naysayers?

It was Floyd's simple and direct approach. As to how he was able to cut through all the red tape to get the Pentagon "social," Floyd explains that, at that time, the Department of Defense had no social media policy. "If there's no policy," Floyd tells an audience in a deadpan delivery, "you get to do whatever you want," only half joking.

BALANCING THE BENEFITS AND RISKS OF SOCIAL

In 2009, it was Floyd who announced that the DoD was about to establish a social media policy, explaining to the public:

> I think there are two issues that need to be balanced. No. 1, you need to recognize the benefits taking part in social networking sites and social networking media give you, as well as the risks involved. And I don't want in any way to shortchange the risks.

To lessen the risks, the DoD embarked on a vigorous program of creating open-platform guides for members of the armed forces to hone their social media communications skills—and to understand the risks and rules of social networking.

Speaking to the risks associated with social media, Floyd, in the DoD announcement, warned:

> The problem now with social networking is that when you Twitter that information that might be sensitive . . . or put it on your Facebook page, thousands of people see it immediately, and then thousands more could see it as it's forwarded on to others. The ramifications of making a mistake, of putting things that shouldn't be on there on those sites, are even greater than they used to be.

THE PROCESS OF MAKING THE PENTAGON . . . AND A MULTINATIONAL DEFENSE FIRM—SOCIAL: AN INTERVIEW WITH PRICE FLOYD

Floyd, the once principal deputy assistant secretary of defense for public affairs and now serving as a communications strategist for Blue Engine Media, comments on social media in his former and current job.

Q. What was the first step you took to make the DoD "social"?

A. *The first step was to get buy-in from the senior leadership. This was the simplest part because during my job interview, Secretary of Defense [Robert M.] Gates said that reaching his audience—both internal and external—was one of his priorities, and, therefore, mine. All of the new hires—or recruits in the military—have never known a world without social media. The trick was to get the middle management on board.*

(continued)

Q. What was the initial reaction to the first step?

A. *The initial reaction was for Strategic Command to announce that soon all access to "internet-based capabilities" was going to be blocked from all .mil accounts. This was a warning from the risk-averse crowd that they would not go quietly into the night. They had several concerns: increased security challenges—phishing (fraudulent attempts to collect user data), profiling, etc. . . . leaking of classified information . . . wasted time.*

Q. How did the DoD's social media launch progress from there?

A. *When I launched the new Defense Department website eight weeks after I arrived, I had them add links to social media platforms and started my own Twitter account and had it added to the home page of the website as well. This allowed all who accessed the site to see that we were embracing, even if tentatively, social media.*

Q. How quickly did you begin to see positive returns from bringing the DoD into new media?

A. *It was more a realization that the senior leadership and the eventual policy document once approved was catching up to the members of the Armed Services. They were already there. They could now access their social media sites from their .mil accounts. This allowed a more open and transparent process for all.*

Q. How has social media helped the armed forces?

A. *There have been a whole host of benefits: the ability of service members to stay in contact with their family and friends; lower cost and quicker training; better recruitment (the Army is the best here); ability to take part in ongoing discussions with senior leaders on the needs of the force (the last two Chairmen of the Joint Chiefs of Staff have had Twitter accounts); rapid dissemination of information; etc. . . .*

Q. How long before someone said to you, "Great job on getting us social"?

A. *Within hours/days of the new website with the added social media links going live.*

Q. Recommendations for service members using social media today (I'm thinking of the Marine sergeant discharged for his Facebook postings and service members generally) so that they don't get themselves in a jam?

A. *If you couldn't say it in a letter or in an interview with a reporter, you can't say it on social media. Think before you post.*

Q. How was the DoD's initial social media policy written, and how has it changed?

A. *Long, boring, bureaucratic story. No different than any other policy change. Not fun, but necessary.*

Q. You arrive at a defense firm [after] your service at the Pentagon; who brings up the topic of BAE becoming social?

A. *Linda Hudson, the President of our company, wanted to tap the knowledge and energy of the workforce and believes social media is one of the ways to help make that happen. This goes back to my previous statement on this being leadership driven.*

Q. What did it take to get company buy-in for entering the conversation?

A. *Proof that it works. It is simple the way communications works now. We use this tool to communicate with employees, the media, customers, do thought leadership, etc. . . .*

Q. What were you hoping to achieve with joining the conversation, and how have the realities matched your hopes?

A. *If you want to have an impact on what is being discussed about you, your products, the strategy, etc. . . . you have to be there as well. We just wanted to make sure we were being heard.*

Q. Recommendations for large organizations still debating on whether to start using social media?

A. *Wrong question. Your "organization" is already using social media. The only question to ask is do you know what "they" are saying and do you want to join as well.*

"UNCLE SAM WANTS YOU . . . TO BE SOCIAL!" THE DEPARTMENT OF DEFENSE SOCIAL MEDIA HUB

The U.S. Department of Defense has created a "social media hub" at http://www.defense.gov/socialmedia. The U.S. site explains that it is there "to help the DoD community use social media . . . responsibly and effectively; both in official and unofficial capacities."

Though the DoD social media hub was created for members of the military, its "Education and Training" section—featuring a combination of slides, videos, and PDFs and covering topics ranging from "Securing Your Account Settings," to "Customizing Your YouTube Channel," to "Twitter in Plain Language"—is a great, free resource for anyone interested in learning how to use social media responsibly and securely.

For DoD members, the hub covers topics such as "Dos and Don'ts for Feds on Social Media," operational security, and threats posed by geotagging. For members of the DoD, as well as others in the federal government, the hub is a must-visit site with solid information that should be carefully studied. As anywhere, social media missteps by members of the Department of Defense or others can come at a price.

COMPLIANT SOCIAL MEDIA STARTS WITH FOLLOWING THE RULES YOU ALREADY KNOW

Conduct Unbecoming an Officer and a Gentleman

Any commissioned officer, cadet, or midshipman who is convicted of conduct unbecoming an officer and a gentleman shall be punished as a court-martial may direct. *10 U.S.C. § 933 : US Code - Section 933: Art. 133*

For members of the U.S. Armed Forces, the Uniform Code of Military Justice forms the foundation of compliant conduct. As explained elsewhere in this book, when individuals or enterprises wish to embrace social media in a compliant manner, they should look to those rules and regulations that guide their conduct as members of a given profession or organization. For members of the U.S. military, it begins with the Uniform Code of Military Justice.

NEVER LOSE SIGHT OF YOUR ORGANIZATION'S KEY COMPLIANCE CODE

Article 134 is the catch-all article for military discipline. Do something wrong, and you may find yourself up on charges for violating Article 134. New recruits learn about this sledgehammer of military justice. Members of the U.S. Armed Forces who decide to tweet and blog and use Facebook should consider well the large net cast by Article 134 and guide themselves accordingly. Social media compliance begins with the basics.

> Though not specifically mentioned in this chapter, all disorders and neglects to the prejudice of good order and discipline in the armed forces, all conduct of a nature to bring discredit upon the armed forces, and crimes and offenses not capital, of which persons subject to this chapter may be guilty, shall be taken cognizance of by a general, special, or summary court-martial, according to the nature and degree of the offense, and shall be punished at the discretion of that court. *10 U.S.C. § 933 : US Code - Section 933: Art. 134*

WHAT YOU WOULDN'T SAY IN FRONT OF YOUR BATTALION COMMANDER, YOU SHOULDN'T SAY ON FACEBOOK

A few Facebook posts and a one-day hearing were all that was needed to officially end the 9-year career of a 26-year-old U.S. Marine who had served a tour of duty in Iraq. "Clarifying" an earlier Facebook post where he had said he would not follow orders from his commander in chief, the U.S. president, with a follow-up Facebook post adding that he would not follow an "unlawful" order, did nothing to prevent the service member from receiving an "Other Than Honorable Discharge," ending any hopes of a continued career in the military.

Superimposing the president's image on a "Jackass" poster on a social media site somehow escaped Sergeant Gary Stein's judgment as conduct that might be out of line with the Uniform Code of Military Justice. Additionally, a confused sense of the breadth of "free speech" provided by the U.S. Constitution to members of the military somehow led him to think that a Facebook post, "Screw Obama. I will not follow all orders from him," would not be out of bounds for a service member. For certain people, the best social media compliance training and resources will be wasted, with the consequences predictable.

Sergeant Stein did attempt to halt the discharge proceeding with an appeal to the U.S. district court. That application was denied.

BEST PRACTICES

There are a number of best practices to bear in mind when dealing with large organizations and government:

- Understand that "Your 'organization' is already using social media. The only question to ask is do you know what 'they' are saying and do you want to join as well." *Price Floyd, the guy who got the U.S. Department of Defense "social"*

- Recognize the benefits of taking part in social networking, but don't in any way . . . shortchange the risks." *Id.*

- A successful social media launch requires buy-in from the senior leadership. *Id.*

- "All of the new hires—or recruits in the military—have never known a world without social media." Once you get senior-level buy-in, work on getting middle management on board. *Id.*

- Understand that creating a social media policy may be a "bureaucratic" process and "no fun," but it's a necessary process. *Id.*

- Even if you are a large organization, don't be afraid to start small. (The U.S. Department of Defense started by simply adding an employee Twitter account to a website!)

- If governments are your customers, recognize that "governments are made up of people. Social makes sense." *Steve Field, director of digital communication at BAE Systems, Inc.*

- Bring seasoned communicators to the task of launching compliant social media.

- Identify and never lose sight of your organization's key compliance code—it is the key to social media compliance.

- Begin your social media launch and compliance training with a review of all the core enterprise conduct guidelines and make it clear that they all apply to social.

- Create an organizational social media hub with the organization's social media accounts listed, policies, dos and don'ts, FAQs, and contact information for unanswered questions.

- Provide social media hub resources that cover how to communicate effectively in social media, as well as compliantly.

- If you have no social media policy for your organization, your employees may perceive that they get to do whatever they want, putting them and your organization at risk.

- Repeat after me: "Put it on your Facebook page; thousands of people see it immediately."

- Provide detailed guidance on the most challenging and complicated compliance issues, as the U.S. Office of Special Counsel has done with the Hatch Act for public employees.

SOCIAL MEDIA AND THE HATCH ACT: A BIG LAND MINE FOR CERTAIN PUBLIC EMPLOYEES

The Hatch Act limits certain political activities of employees of the executive branch of the federal government, employees of the District of Columbia government, and some state and local employees who work with federally funded programs. The restrictions apply whether the covered employees are on or off duty. The rules are a bit complicated, and violations of them can result in a loss of public employment. *5 U.S.C. § 1501 et seq.* Social media only heightens the risks.

U.S. OFFICE OF SPECIAL COUNSEL OFFERS GUIDANCE ON HATCH ACT SOCIAL MEDIA COMPLIANCE

Recognizing the special risks and unique questions posed by social media with regard to Hatch Act compliance, the U.S. Office of Special Counsel, an independent federal investigative and prosecutorial agency, in 2012 provided detailed guidance on the topic of covered public employees, "political activity," and compliant social media. For a list of frequently asked questions regarding social media and the Hatch Act, please visit https://www.osc.gov/haFederalfaq.htm.

11

Digital Legacy (Who Gets Your Twitter and Other Digital Accounts When You Quit Your Job or When You Die)

ARE YOU SURE YOU OWN YOUR TWITTER ACCOUNT? SETTLE THE QUESTION BEFORE A LAWSUIT

"I'm quitting, and, of course, I'm taking my Twitter account *and* its 17,000 followers with me."

"*Your* Twitter account? . . . Since when is it *your* Twitter account. That account belongs to the company, and it's staying with the company."

"So sue me!"

Ah, there were once simpler times. Now the question of who owns a Twitter account or LinkedIn account is no longer merely the debate of social media aficionados; it has become the subject of real courtroom disputes.

So what's changed? Perhaps a simple recognition that there is a business value to a social media community.

THE INFAMOUS CASE OF @PHONEDOG_NOAH

This particular issue, over who really owns a social media account, was brought to the fore by the infamous case of @Phonedog_Noah, a legal battle over the ownership and value of a Twitter account with a following of 17,000. It was an account started by Noah Kravitz, when he was a happy employee of Phonedog .com. When he decided to leave his post, he decided to take his Twitter account with him. Therein lies the rub. His company believed that the Twitter account and its followers belonged to the company. That was way back in 2010, and two years later the dispute was still in litigation, with the business placing a value on the following of 17,000 in excess of $300,000. (The case was finally settled out of court at the end of 2012.)

The moral of the story? Make sure you spell out in a binding document who owns your business's social media accounts!

THE CULT OF THE SOCIAL MEDIA PERSONALITY: "YAH, I'M BIG ON TWITTER"

It's not just Justin Bieber (55 million–plus Twitter followers) or Lady Gaga (67 million–plus Facebook likes) who seem to amass strong followings on social networks; it's also people quite different from both. There are tech writers, YouTube vloggers, and food critics who have garnered immense followings on various social networks.

Back in 2009, Peter Cashmore, CEO of the popular social media Mashable, asked the question, "As he tweets out his latest story to his 1.1 million Twitter followers, does David Pogue need *The New York Times*, or does *The New York Times* need David Pogue?" Now PBS Nova host, Pogue's Twitter flock has grown to over 1.5 million.

STEPS TO TAKE TO AVOID A LAWSUIT OVER WHO OWNS YOUR LINKEDIN OR TWITTER (OR PINTEREST OR FACEBOOK . . .) ACCOUNTS

There are steps you can take to ward off a lawsuit:

- Establish in writing who owns a given social media account. A written agreement spelling out the ownership of an account will lessen if not eliminate the "He said, she said" that becomes the fodder of courtroom battles.

- Include the issue of social media account ownership in your business's social media guidelines.

- Create a separate agreement, beyond your social media policy, defining ownership of social media accounts, especially when they are branded accounts. Make sure that the agreement includes the core elements that make a contract binding: offer, acceptance, consideration (a statement of the mutual benefits received from the branded account). Be sure to include in your "Agreement of Social Media Account Ownership" a statement that oral agreements shall not modify this written agreement. (The absence of such a statement will allow an unscrupulous party to create fanciful tales about the modification of the original agreement.)

- Get your employees or partners to sign a written agreement defining ownership, control, and conduct governing any social media account that is being used for a business purpose. You should also include an acknowledgment of their having read and understood the company's social media policy.

- Define the circumstances under which the account must transfer to another or to the business.

- Define what the employee or partner must do when, under the terms of the ownership agreement, a request is made to completely relinquish control of the account to another.

- Include in the agreement that the agreement shall remain binding on the heirs of the employee, with the employee's understanding and intention being that the account does not belong at any time to the employee, but that ownership at all times remains with the business despite the status of management of the account.

"BUT WHAT HAPPENS TO MY SOCIAL MEDIA ACCOUNTS WHEN I DIE?"

Looking at this topic first from the business's perspective, you may recall that during our discussion of how to create a social media policy, I had suggested that in addition to addressing the issue of social media account ownership in the company's social media policy, it would be best to spell it out in a separate agreement on the issue of social media account ownership. Such a document could be particularly helpful in resolving quickly any questions from a deceased worker's or partner's estate concerning account ownership.

You might think that ownership of a social media account becomes moot once a business associate or employee passes on to that great social network in the sky. Think again. Even if you have the account password and it is a branded account, someone handling the decedent's estate just might have a different view of this issue and consider it to be an asset of the estate—and one worth fighting for to keep.

In the PhoneDog case, $340,000 was the business value placed on the business-branded Twitter account in dispute. Accepting that figure as even coming close to a true valuation of a business-branded social media account, for our discussion, would make such an account an asset that an estate's attorney would unquestionably need to consider claiming as part of the decedent's estate for purposes of accounting, preservation, and distribution. It could well be a breach of an attorney's fiduciary duty if this were not to be done. (*Estate attorneys:* Add digital assets when doing your estate planning and ask about digital assets when doing your inventory of a decedent's estate!)

BUSINESSES: SPELL OUT OWNERSHIP OF SOCIAL NETWORK ACCOUNTS IN THE EVENT OF DEATH

So for businesses, to give yourselves the best protection possible from digital legacy disputes, spell out the ownership issue in the event of death in a signed document and make it clear that business-branded accounts, even ones managed and co-branded by an employee, belong to the business even upon the individual manager's passing and must not in any way be considered a shared asset by anyone.

After You Decide Who Inherits Your Corvette, Consider Who Gets Your Music Collection on iTunes, Your Library on Your Kindle—and Your $340,000 Twitter Account

Yes, your family and friends have already told you that they want your sports car when you pass on, but they may not have thought about your massive iTunes collection or your Twitter account valued at $340,000. (Twitter terms of service disallow the sale of Twitter accounts; rumor has it that this limitation has been sidestepped with licensing agreements.) Don't penalize your heirs for their lack of appreciation for the value of your digital assets. Surprise the music lover in your family with your iPad and iTunes account password, and leave to the budding marketer in your firm the username and password for your Twitter account.

So don't let your digital assets go to waste. They can have a real and substantial value. Include them in your inventory of "who gets what" when you pass on. As you would with any other asset, identify such assets with clarity (e.g., I bequeath my TWITTER ACCOUNT: Twitter.com/SocialMediaLaw1 PASSWORD: ___) to my niece . . .

The person who inherits your Twitter account, by the way, gets to change the password, profile, biography, and background *and*, most importantly, gets to keep your valuable following.

DIGITAL INHERITANCE RULES ARE EVOLVING

Please note that digital services and social networks themselves are still trying to sort out the subject of digital inheritance. Some terms of service (the agreement that users never read but agree to as a condition of getting to use a digital service or social network) suggest or say that a social network or digital account cannot be passed on to another user. As we know, however, such policies are subject to regular revisions. *Bottom line:* Don't neglect your digital assets in your estate planning!

A Grief-Stricken Mother Demands Access to Her Deceased Son's Facebook Page

In 2005, when 22-year-old Loren Williams was killed in a motorcycle crash, in Tempe, Arizona, his mother sought access to his Facebook account. It is reported that she hoped that access to her son's account would give her new insights into her son's life and would help her with her grieving. Initially Facebook denied the request, citing "the federal 1986 Electronic Communications Privacy Act, which prevents disclosing stored communications unless there's a court order." In what is believed to be the first case of its kind, Loren's parents sought a court order compelling Facebook to give them control of their son's account. Only when a court order was signed, did Facebook consent to providing Loren's parents with the access they sought.

Courts and legislatures, and even social networks, have still not settled how best to balance the interest of protecting a decedent's privacy expectations and wishes, from when an account was first opened, against the wishes of a grieving family. Some states have begun to codify standards to resolve the issue, trumping network terms-of-service agreements.

FACEBOOK "MEMORIAL" ACCOUNTS

Facebook does provide a procedure to change an active Facebook account into a "memorial" account upon the death of the account holder.

Facebook explains:

> We may memorialize the account of a deceased person. When we memorialize an account we keep the profile on Facebook, but only let friends and family look at pictures or write on the user's Wall in remembrance.

How Does a Facebook Memorial Account Work?

According to Facebook:

> Memorializing an account sets the account privacy so that only confirmed friends can see the profile (timeline) or locate it in search. Friends and family can leave posts in remembrance. Memorializing an account also prevents anyone from logging into the account.

How Do You Create a Facebook Memorial Account?

Even if you are not a deceased person's next of kin, you may request that an active account be changed to a memorial account by:

- Visiting http://*www.facebook.com/help/contact.php?show_form=deceased*

- Identifying how you are connected to the decedent

- Providing proof of death, in the form of either an obituary or news article about the death

- Including the e-mail address that is associated with the subject Facebook account

Only Next of Kin May Request That a Facebook Account Be Closed

To close a Facebook account upon a member's passing, as opposed to creating a memorial account, a formal request must be submitted by the decedent's next of kin.

WHO SAYS YOU CAN'T KEEP ON TWEETING AND FACEBOOKING AFTER YOU DIE?!

Don't want to trouble your survivors with issues about who gets or who closes your social network accounts after you pass on? Maybe you'd even like to keep tweeting from the other side of the pearly gates? Well, there's an app for that! It actually allows you to continue Facebooking after you've gone to that great, big Facebook following in the sky.

DeadSoci.al promises to allow users to place their Twitter and Facebook accounts into the care of a service that allows messages from beyond the grave—literally. Explaining how the app works, the creators use the case of a fictional Facebook account owner, "Gabriel." With the service under way, the company explains that "His widow is even the recipient of an inappropriate joke from time to time."

Creepy?

Just a little, though it is certainly one way to address the issue of control of a Twitter or Facebook account, postmortem. (*A caveat:* Compliance with a social network's terms of service and any app is something that should be examined before signing up to use an app. This book makes no representations concerning this app or any other app.)

12

Going Global: International Social Media Law

SOCIAL MEDIA MARKETING AND INTERNATIONAL LAW

Social media used to be called the "Wild West" of the Internet, a reference to a time and place of lawlessness in the western United States as migration pushed into new frontiers. Before social media became "social business," many social media users seemed to ignore many conventions of common sense and adherence to principles of fair conduct on the web. With the realization that social media is now social business, regulatory authorities across the globe are seeking to impose a much higher degree of accountability and responsibility on the social web.

In the world of advertising, self-regulatory organizations (SROs), bodies created nationally by the advertising industry, govern fair and honest marketing on the web by marketers from within their national boundaries. These authorities, generally independent of governmental regulatory agencies, though often working "in tandem" and alongside them, have taken their roles seriously, recognizing that the health of their industry depends on the trust of consumers. Like governmental regulatory authorities, SROs have been playing catch-up with the platforms, techniques, and technologies of social media. As this chapter will discuss, SROs, on a global scale, are catching up with social business. Marketers, brands, and media beware!

SELF-REGULATION OF THE ADVERTISING INDUSTRY GLOBALLY: THE ICC MODEL

In the advertising world, industry self-regulation is the standard internationally. The leading organization in this space is the International Chamber of Commerce (ICC). Since 1937, the ICC's self-regulatory advertising guidelines have served as a point of reference and a model for self-regulatory advertising and marketing frameworks around the world. Last updated in 2011 to include digital interactive marketing and new technologies, the Consolidated Code of Advertising and Marketing Communication Practice (ICC Code or ICC Consolidated Code) continues to serve as a touchstone for ethical advertising around the globe.

ICC'S ADVERTISING CODE EMERGES AS THE MODEL CODE GLOBALLY

The ICC's Commission on Advertising and Marketing focuses its efforts on "promoting effective self-regulation that is harmonized to best practice around the world." According to the ICC:

> Self-regulatory systems with rules based on the ICC Code are operating in over 35 countries, across 6 continents, spanning Canada, Mexico, most of Europe, Brazil, India and South Africa. Also, the ICC Code is being used to develop rules and new self-regulatory systems in a half dozen other countries including China, Serbia, Croatia and the Ukraine.

Demonstrating the continued importance, vibrancy, and broad acceptance of the ICC's Code as "the" international standard for self-regulatory advertising codes, China, in 2011, established its own regulatory advertising code, called the Responsible Marketing Code, using the ICC's Code as the reference for its own. China's Marketing Code expressly acknowledges the ICC's Code as a reference document.

CHINA'S RESPONSIBLE MARKETING CODE

So how does China's Responsible Marketing Code match up to its ICC model code? Though only 2 pages long, as opposed to the ICC's beefy 57-page PDF, China's Marketing Code actually captures the core points presented in the ICC Consolidated Code.

Speaking in terms of its own advertising industry's "self-discipline," rather than the term "self-regulation," the Chinese Code, like the ICC Code, emphasizes truthfulness and honesty as a basis for protecting both consumers and the reputation of marketers. It likewise addresses a concern for honesty, copyright protection, heightened protection for children, privacy protection, and clarity in data collection, all points found within the ICC Code.

Though the Chinese Code does not mention "social media" or "interactive digital marketing" by name, it does state that it covers Internet advertising and "other forms of communication by marketers," thereby encompassing advertising in social media.

MARKETING COMMUNICATION SHOULD BE DISTINGUISHABLE AS SUCH

For some reason, some brands still have a problem understanding one of the most basic propositions in advertising compliance: "marketing communication should be distinguishable as such."

The Chinese Code gets it: "Marketing communication should be distinguishable as such, legal, honest, truthful and decent." If you want to get social media marketing right, memorize that statement. Follow it. If you do, you will avoid one of the most common pitfalls in social media marketing. Transparency is a basic principle of effective, compliant, and sustainable social media marketing. It is a mandate of social media marketing in the European Union, the United States, and all nations following the ICC model. It is a core standard of ethical social media marketing.

What is the effect of this principle? If a blog post is sponsored or a tweet, post, or pin is incentivized, it must be disclosed as such.

The ICC notes that effective industry self-regulation, in addition to its obvious role in the protection of consumers through the establishment of ethical advertising standards, is also important for "the protection of individual companies' goodwill and reputation."

> Over the years, the ICC Code has served as the foundation and building block for self-regulatory structures around the world. These self-regulatory systems have built trust with consumers by assuring them of advertising that is honest, legal, decent and truthful and quick and easy redress when transgressions occur.
>
> —ICC Advertising Code

AN OVERVIEW OF THE ICC'S CONSOLIDATED CODE OF ADVERTISING AND MARKETING COMMUNICATION PRACTICES

In 1937 the International Chamber of Commerce established the International Code of Advertising Practice. Since that time, the ICC Code has been the model and reference point for advertising self-regulatory frameworks worldwide. Under its 2011 revision, its eighth version—and now called the Consolidated Code of Advertising and Marketing Communication Practice—the ICC Code has expanded to a 57-page PDF that contains 26 articles governing advertising and marketing communication practice. It also includes five detailed chapters, one of which is "Advertising and Marketing Communications Using Digital Interactive Media."

The general articles of the Consolidated Code cover topics ranging from data protection to transparency in commercial advertising and marketing. Overall, the latest revision emphasizes the applicability of the rules to "digital interactive marketing communications," i.e., social media, and recognizes the impact of "the rapid evolution of technology and technologically enhanced marketing communications and techniques."

The ICC's Code has, at its core, basic principles that have gone unchanged since the creation of its very first code in 1937: advertising should be "honest, legal, decent and truthful," with a "quick and easy redress when transgressions occur."

NEW CODE RECOGNIZES IMPACT OF TECHNOLOGY AND INTERACTIVE DIGITAL MARKETING

An underlying theme of the Consolidated Code is that rapid advancements in communications technologies and the interactive nature of digital advertising increase the need for greater responsibility in marketing.

In defining the purpose of the 2011 version of the ICC Code, the ICC states, as it did in earlier versions, that the document is "intended primarily as an instrument of self-regulation for commercial communications" but that "it may be used by the Courts as a reference document within the framework of applicable legislation."

Attempting to achieve broad applicability and usefulness for the Code, the ICC states, in the section on the scope of the Code, that it is "to be applied against the background of whatever legislation may be applicable." With this flexibility, the Code recognizes "variations in culture and societal rules and norms" while still enhancing "harmonization and coherence" in the regulation of marketing and advertising. As the ICC has explained to regulators, the Code always works alongside and "in tandem with local and national regulation."

At a minimum, the ICC Code should be used as a "global foundation of best practices in marketing and advertising communications." *ICC Regulator FAQ.*

THE ICC'S LATEST EDITION OF THE ADVERTISING CODE APPLIES TO SOCIAL MEDIA

The newest version of the Code specifically states that it applies to all "digital interactive media techniques, platforms or devices." The Code defines "digital interactive media" as:

> any media platform, service or application providing electronic communications, using the Internet, online services, and/or electronic and communication networks, including mobile phone, personal digital assistant and interactive game consoles which allows the receiving party to interact with the platform, service or application.

Interestingly, in addition to addressing mobile marketing, the Code also includes within its scope even "interactive game consoles," a multibillion-dollar industry of its own that some have considered to be outside the purview of advertising self-regulation. This provision puts to rest any question on the subject.

Summarizing its guidance for online behavioral advertising (OBA), the ICC calls for "clear and readily understandable information about how to use and collect data; the need for and use of choice mechanisms; and controls over sensitive data." *ICC Regulator FAQ.*

ONLINE BEHAVIORAL ADVERTISING DEFINED

Addressed at length in Chapter D, Article D7, the section of the Code devoted to digital interactive media, the Code defines OBA as:

> the practice of collecting information over time on users' online actions on a particular device across different unaffiliated websites in order to create interest segments or to allocate such viewing behaviour against interest segments for the purposes of delivering advertisements to and by that web user's interests and preferences.

The ICC Code sets strict standards for OBA:

- **D7.1 Notice.** "Clear and conspicuous" disclosure of data collection and use practices must be provided with an "easy to use mechanism for exercising choice" with regard to OBA.

- **D7.2 User Control.** OBA data collectors should obtain a user's "explicit consent" for behavior data tracking with an "easy to use mechanism". . . . "to withdraw their explicit consent and use of the data."

- **D7.3 Data Security.** Data protection safeguards should be maintained at all times, and the data collected "should only be retained as long as necessary for the business purpose stated in the explicit consent."

- **D7.4 Children.** Very simply, children 12 and younger should not be targeted for OBA data collection.

- **D7.5 Sensitive Data Segmentation.** Marketers and others who wish to use sensitive data, generally defined as the sort of information that could be used in an improper, discriminatory manner, such as a person's ethnicity, health, sexual orientation, or political affiliations, must obtain a web user's "explicit consent."

TECHNOLOGY AND SOCIAL MEDIA INCREASE THE NEED FOR SELF-REGULATION

Touching on the topic of digital interactive media, the Code notes:

> The rapid evolution of technology and technologically-enhanced marketing communications and techniques means that the importance of producing responsible marketing communications has never been more important for companies in preserving their "license to operate."

Self-regulatory schemes are always mindful that the ultimate consequence of the failure to produce and comply with ethical standards that keep pace with changing technologies and techniques is a loss of the right to practice within the industry that the regulatory schemes propose to regulate, in this case, marketing and advertising.

The Code states that it is "to be interpreted in the spirit as well as to the letter." This statement is highly important to courts and regulatory authorities, as it gives authorities broad latitude in the interpretation of the Code to advance the goals of the Code. In practice, this means that if an advertiser were to attempt to sidestep the Code by citing a technicality or loophole to avoid application of the Code, the enforcement authority could look to the "spirit" of the Code to resolve any ambiguities or challenges.

This principle of interpretative construction is reflected in the United Kingdom's Advertising Standards Authority's own self-regulatory code.

ADVERTISEMENTS SHOULD BE JUDGED BY THE "REASONABLE CONSUMER" STANDARD

According to the Code, "Communications should therefore be judged by their likely impact on the reasonable consumer, having regard to the characteristics of the targeted group and the medium used." This is a shifting standard of care that looks to the level of sophistication or vulnerabilities of the target audience.

Factors that should specifically be considered by a reviewing authority include the "knowledge, experience and discriminatory ability of the typical consumer." While children would naturally be given a higher measure of protection and consideration due to their "natural credulity and inexperience," members of a profession would be presumed to have a higher measure of knowledge in their given field and, generally, held to a higher standard of care when involved in advertising disputes related to their field.

JURISDICTION IN CROSS-BORDER ADVERTISING: "IT'S COMPLICATED"

The ICC Code notes that one of two sets of rules generally applies in cross-border advertising: "either the rules of the country from where the message or activity originates apply, or those of the country (or countries) receiving it."

From the ICC's perspective:

> [T]he rational and effective order would be for the principle of origin to take precedence, and ICC recommends it be implemented in the context of self-regulation. However, the question of legal jurisdiction, i.e. what national laws would be applicable in a given case, is de facto a complicated matter. Marketers are therefore urged to assess the legal situation with regard to where they target their marketing communications, and to familiarize themselves with the rules and regulations of the various relevant jurisdictions.

THE MEDIUM MATTERS—A HIGHER STANDARD OF CARE FOR SOCIAL MEDIA?

Importantly, while regulatory authorities in the United States tend to state that "the medium doesn't matter" in the application of the law or regulatory standards, the ICC Consolidated Code expressly states that the medium does matter and should be considered in the application of the Code. In practice, this could well mean a higher standard of care would be imposed in social media marketing, as advertisements are not as readily apparent as they would be in print or broadcast media. Additionally, social medium on personal connection, however attenuated, would also tend to argue for a higher standard of care in commercial communications.

GENERAL ICC CODE PROVISIONS ON ADVERTISING AND MARKETING

The following articles all apply to social media marketing. The guidelines they provide should be considered the minimum standards globally.

Article 1—Basic Principles

"All marketing communications should be legal, decent, honest and truthful." This is the first line of the first article of the ICC Consolidated Code, and it essentially encompasses the balance of the code, which fleshes out and applies this basic statement of principles. The concern expressed in this article is that advertising communication should do nothing to "impair public confidence in marketing."

Article 2—Decency

This article is an admonition for marketers to be sensitive to the "standards of decency currently prevailing in the country and culture concerned."

Article 3—Honesty

Beyond the obvious, this article also expresses a concern that marketers not exploit a consumer's "lack of experience or knowledge." This conforms to a basic principle and expectation of self-regulatory codes that marketers must consider variations in their target audience, making adjustments depending on the degree of knowledge or experience possessed by the target of the communications.

Article 4—Social Responsibility

Here the ICC's concern is respect for "human dignity" by not inciting or condoning any form of discrimination or exploitation of fear, misfortune, suffering, or superstition.

This article also prohibits the use of marketing communications that would "appear to condone or incite violent, unlawful or anti-social behaviour."

Article 5—Truthfulness

"Marketing communications should be truthful and not misleading" is the opening line and essence of this article, which speaks to exaggerations as well as omissions or ambiguities that would be likely to mislead consumers.

Article 6—Use of Technical/Scientific Data and Terminology

This article is actually about the misuse of such data and terminology to mislead.

Though this article, like the others, uses the phrase "should not," as opposed to "shall not," the former being permissive, the latter being compulsory, marketers would be well advised to recall that the general principle of interpretive construction for the articles and Code is one that captures the "spirit" as well as the "letter" of the Code. In other words, don't think that because the articles use "should not" versus "shall not," there is some wiggle room for marketers—there isn't, if the communication in question violates the spirit of the Code.

Article 7—Use of "Free" and "Guarantee"

"Free" should include no obligations, nor should it require postage charges that exceed the marketer's actual shipping costs. Terms like "guarantee" and "warranty" should not suggest something additional to those provided by the law when it does not, and the terms of the guarantee or warranty should be easily available.

Article 8—Substantiation

Advertising claims should be capable of substantiation, and substantiating evidence should be readily available.

Article 9—Identification

"Marketing communications should be clearly distinguishable as such, whatever their form and whatever the medium used." It is a standard by which all social media marketing campaigns should be examined. It is the standard that has tripped up big, smart brands in both the United States and the United Kingdom. Don't let it trip you up.

Article 10—Identity

With the exception of "teaser advertisements," the identity of the marketer should be apparent with contact information. Suffice it to say that the teaser-advertisement exception it discusses should be narrowly construed and generally avoided, as in most instances it would tend to violate the spirit of the Code and, very likely, national self-regulatory advertising codes.

Be mindful that the ICC Code is to be considered in tandem with local law and does not override local law. Whichever standard is stricter is the standard that should be followed.

Article 11—Comparisons

They should be fair and factual.

Article 12—Denigration

Like Article 4, which addresses social responsibility and human dignity, this article calls upon marketers to not "denigrate" others, i.e., look to bring "public contempt or ridicule" on "any person or group of persons."

Article 13—Testimonials

Testimonials should be "genuine, verifiable and relevant" and not "obsolete or misleading through the passage of time."

Article 14—Portrayal or Imitation of Persons and References to Personal Property

Don't do it unless you have the permission of the subject.

Article 15—Exploitation of Goodwill

Don't use another's goodwill unless you have prior consent.

Article 16—Imitation

Imitation is not flattery in the world of marketing. Don't mislead or confuse consumers by adopting the "distinctive marketing" of another, whether in text, layout, slogan, or sound.

Article 17—Safety and Health

Situations that "show a disregard for safety or health" should not be used. Safety warnings must be used when there is an exception to this prohibition. This article and Article 18 address the heightened care that must be used in marketing aimed at or using children.

Article 18—Children and Young People

The Code is emphatic that marketing should not exploit the "inexperience and credulity" of children and that it should consider parental consent. Chapter D, which addresses digital interactive media, addresses this concern further and in greater detail.

Article 19—Data Protection and Privacy

The ICC Code reflects data protection concerns that have been championed and legislated by the European Union. These protections currently those found within the United States, but should still be considered "best practices" in data protection. In the event that there is a breach of security and a loss of sensitive data, courts, even in the United States, would no doubt consider the practices commended on this topic by the ICC Code.

Article 19 addresses seven distinct topics concerning data protection and privacy:

1. **Collection of data and notice.** Consumers should be aware of the existence and purpose of data collection, as well as the same relating to any third parties.

2. **Use of data.** Data should only be collected for a legitimate purpose, and the amount of data obtained and retained should be relevant to the purpose of the collection and not excessive, and not retained longer than necessary for the stated purpose.

3. **Security of processing.** Security measures to prevent unauthorized access to data collected are the objective, and it should be established that any third parties with access to the data will follow similar security measures.

4. **Children's personal information.** Data protection guidance should be provided to parents, and parental permission should be obtained to collect data on any child 12 or younger. The data collected should only be as much as is necessary "to enable the child to engage in the featured activity."

Identifiable personal information about children should not be shared with third parties without parental consent.

5. **Privacy policy.** Those who collect data online should have a privacy policy that should be readily available to consumers with a clear statement that data collection is taking place.

6. **Rights of the consumer.** Marketers must provide consumers with a clear ability to opt out of marketing, to control whether their data is shared with third parties, and to correct incorrect data that may be stored concerning them.

7. **Cross-border transactions.** Data protection rights should follow consumers when data are transferred to another country.

Article 20—Transparency on the Cost of Communication

When there is a communication cost to consumers, it must be clear, and the billed communication must be efficient.

Article 21—Unsolicited Products and Undisclosed Costs

Unsolicited products or marketing that appears like an invoice should not be sent to consumers.

Article 22—Environmental Behavior

Marketing should not condone actions that contradict generally accepted standards of environmentally responsible behavior.

Article 23—Responsibility

These articles apply to all forms of marketing communications, and responsibility for those communications rests with (1) the marketer whose products are the subject of the communication, (2) the communications practitioner or agency, *and* (3) the publisher or media owner.

Importantly, Article 23 also imposes responsibility on the individual who is employed by any one of the three groups listed above. In other words, no one gets to duck responsibility for noncompliant marketing communications—and no one gets to pass the buck for noncompliant advertising.

Article 24—Effect of Subsequent Redress for Contravention

Subsequent correction of noncompliant marketing is "desirable" but does not cure the violation. In other words, although a marketer, agency, or media owner takes steps to make noncompliant marketing communications compliant, the correction does not remove the fact that a violation has occurred and that sanctions might follow.

Article 25—Implementation

This article is a general call for adoption of the Code by SROs, as well as by companies and individuals involved in the marketing process.

Article 26—Respect for Self-Regulatory Decisions

This article calls upon all to be respectful of the decisions of an SRO and to not be a party to any communications found to be noncompliant by an SRO.

CHAPTER D: ADVERTISING AND MARKETING COMMUNICATIONS USING DIGITAL INTERACTIVE MEDIA

The ICC has rewritten Chapter D to ensure that it covers "all digital interactive media techniques, platforms or devices." To be clear, that means social platforms and social media marketing. The ICC predicted that this revision would have a "significant" impact on the scope of duties and "rules of regional and national code compliance schemes across the globe." This is a change that empowers and, indeed, calls upon regional and national SROs to include social media marketing in their advertising compliance vigilance and enforcement.

General Provisions on Advertising and Marketing Communication Practice, as Well as Direct Marketing, Apply to Digital Interactive Marketing

Chapter D begins by noting that it should be read in conjunction with the General Provisions on Advertising and Marketing Communication Practice. Interestingly, it also begins by noting that it should be read, as well, in conjunction with the Code's section on direct marketing, perhaps an expression of the ICC's understanding of the nature of social media marketing.

Duty of Disclosure in Digital Interactive Marketing

The first article of Chapter D contains a crucial admonition that has been mentioned before and remains one of the most critical compliance points in social media marketing:

> The commercial nature of product endorsements or reviews created by marketers should be clearly indicated and not be listed as being from an individual consumer or independent body. *ICC Consolidated Code, Article D1*

In the United States, under the FTC social media endorsement guidelines, this is known as the duty to disclose "material connections." The failure to make this disclosure tends to render a sponsored blog, tweet, vlog, etc., misleading, fraudulent, and sanctionable.

MARKETERS MUST RESPECT THE RULES AND STANDARDS GOVERNING SOCIAL SITES

Marketers are urged to be respectful of the rules and standards of social media sites, whether blogs, forums, wikis, etc. Specifically, marketers are warned not to post advertising communications to such sites unless "the forum or site has implicitly or explicitly indicated its willingness to receive such communications."

The balance of Chapter D calls upon marketers to demonstrate particular care with regard to children and covers at length obligations relating to online behavior advertising and data protection.

Digital marketers are also told to be respectful of the "sensitivities of a global audience."

THE EUROPEAN UNION WORKS TO ESTABLISH A LARGER GLOBAL PRESENCE IN THE ADVERTISING INDUSTRY'S SELF-REGULATORY SPACE

Although the ICC continues to dominate the advertising self-regulatory space, the European Union, representing 27 member nations, has its own self-regulatory organization, the European Advertising Standards Alliance (EASA). EASA describes itself as "the single authoritative voice on advertising self-regulation issues" in the European Union. Aiming to promote more standardized advertising guidelines among member nations, it also coordinates cross-border complaints for efficient resolution. At the same time, EASA notes that it is not itself an SRO, but rather it maintains an educational, informational, coordinating, and advisory role.

Serving in an advisory capacity to the EU Commission and Parliament on the subject of advertising industry self-regulation, EASA facilitates coordination among 28 national advertising SROs, including those of all the member states of the European Union, and 13 industry federations, covering advertisers, agencies, and media.

Recognizing the foundational role of the ICC within advertising industry self-regulation, EASA notes that "[a]ll national codes, in an extensive system of advertising self-regulation across the globe, are based on the ICC Code."

EASA reports that its member states' SROs receive and resolve about 50,000 complaints annually.

The SRO Process

Generally, consumer complaints concerning an advertising communication are reviewed by the national SRO. If a communication is found to be noncompliant, the advertiser will be asked to remove or change the communication. There is generally an appeals process in place if the advertiser wishes to challenge the decision of the SRO. If, in a rare case, a marketer remains noncompliant, the SRO may refer the dispute to the statutory authorities, who have the power to prosecute the advertiser if there is a violation of law related to the marketer's conduct. Most advertisers, however, abide by SRO decisions, which are typically published for transparency of process.

THE EUROPEAN UNION'S INTERNATIONAL COUNCIL ON ADVERTISING SELF-REGULATION

Despite EASA's deference to the ICC, EASA has set up its own International Council on Advertising Self-Regulation (ICAS), which first met in May 2008. According to ICAS, its goal is to "facilitate information exchange, best practice discussions and communication among advertising SROs around the world." EASA members are automatically members of the International Council.

EASA does, however, continue to recognize the strong tradition and success of the ICC Code and holds it up as the standard in the absence of a national, industry self-regulatory code:

> A general pan-European code is not in effect. Each country has a set of national rules or principles which are suitable for advertising practice according to the local culture, economy and society. These rules are based heavily on the ICC's code of practice. ICC principles are applied in areas where codes do not exist.

CROSS-BORDER COMPLAINTS

Since 1992, EASA has had a cross-border complaint system to address marketing communications that originate in a given member nation, but problems arise when the communications are carried in media in a different member nation.

Two basic principles guide EASA's cross-border complaint system:

1. **Country of origin.** "An advertisement must comply with the rules of the country where the media is based."

2. **Mutual recognition.** "EASA Members agree to accept advertisements which comply with the self-regulatory rules in the country of origin of the media, even if those rules are not identical to their own."

Concerned About Compliance and Your Pan-European Campaign? Get a Confidential Compliance Review

Concerned about meeting the self-regulatory, marketing compliance requirements for a pan-European campaign? Not to worry; there's a pretty simple solution for that as explained by EASA:

> Since November 2009, an online one-stop shop exists enabling advertising professionals to get advice on whether an ad is compliant with the local advertising code in one or several of the 15 European countries that take part in the facility. This European Copy Advice/Pre-Clearance Facility can be accessed on www.ad-advice.org.
>
> Once registered for the online facility, advertisers and agencies can submit requests for copy advice to one or more advertising self-regulatory organisations of the 15 European countries taking part in the project for one or more media. All requests are treated in complete confidentiality and are on a non-binding basis. The facility can also be used to submit pre-clearance requests; either the site directly submits your request to the organisation responsible for pre-clearance, or it will direct you to the relevant on-line resource. Any special requirements or fees that apply are flagged, as some countries require payment for this service.
>
> The following countries have national advertising self-regulatory bodies that currently participate in the online facility: Austria, Belgium, Czech Republic, France, Greece, Hungary, Ireland, Italy, Netherlands, Poland, Portugal, Slovakia, Slovenia, Spain, United Kingdom.

EASA'S BLUE BOOK

Semiannually, EASA also publishes a book of compliant marketing best practices internationally. Known as the *Blue Book*, it is sold directly by EASA.

TAKEAWAYS

- The International Chamber of Commerce, which established the world's first advertising industry's self-regulatory Code, back in 1937, updated its Code in 2011 to specifically include "digital interactive marketing," i.e., social media.

- The ICC Code revision is a call for all SROs to include social media within their monitoring and enforcement charge.

- "Marketing communication should be distinguishable as such, legal, honest, truthful and decent."

- The revised ICC Code is to be used as a reference document for court and, in the absence of a national SRO, serve as the point of reference for issues relating to advertising communications, including those in social media.

- All the general provisions of the ICC Consolidated Code apply to social media.

- Responsibility for compliance with the updated ICC Code rests not only with the marketer, the brand being marketed, and the medium or medium of communication, but also with the individual employed by each who may have a role in the creation or implementation of a marketing communication. (The ICC seems to have made a decision to include a code of personal responsibility within the overall Code.)

- In 2011, China created its own national advertising SRO Code and expressly acknowledged the ICC's Code as a foundational document. EASA, the European Union's parent organization for its member state SROs, likewise has acknowledged the foundational and continuing importance of the ICC Code, which has been credited in all the continents as a foundational reference document for national SROs—meaning that a worldwide, generally accepted standard of social media marketing conduct is well under way.

- The ICC calls upon individual marketers to familiarize themselves with the ICC Code—and they should.

- Marketers directing social media marketing campaigns in Europe should look to EASA for compliance guidance, both from its seminal *Blue Book* and from its online compliance review opportunity.

- Those wishing to stay on the right side of social media marketing "law" should closely adhere to the letter, as well as the spirit, of the ICC's Code.

- The ICC, like EASA and the U.S. FTC, imposes a higher standard of care on any marketing that uses or is directed to children 12 and younger than on marketing that targets those who are older.

- Data collection relating to children is prohibited in the absence of parental consent.

- Online behavioral advertising in the European Union comes with a whole host of responsibilities not found in the United States.

- OBA generally requires "explicit consent" and a high standard of care for data protection; data deemed to be "sensitive," relating to matters such as health, ethnicity, sexual orientation, or political affiliation, requires an even higher standard of care.

- Presence of OBA data collection must be "clear and conspicuous," with an "easy to use mechanism for exercising choice" with regard to OBA.

- If a blog post is sponsored or a tweet, post, or pin is incentivized, it must be disclosed as such—wherever you are in the world, under a unifying principle of disclosure.

- If you are looking to start a social media campaign targeted anywhere in the European Union, you should consider requesting a Confidential Compliance Review through EASA—and get a copy of EASA's latest *Blue Book*.

- Social media law, especially related to social media marketing, is evolving and harmonizing, with readily accessible standards and a predictable pattern and process of enforcement.

- In nations that have not established social media marketing guidelines, the ICC Code should be deemed as setting a minimum standard of conduct.

13

Nike: A Lesson in International Social Media Nondisclosure

Wayne Rooney is an English "footballer" (i.e., soccer player, for those of us in the United States) for Manchester United, and he is considered to be England's best player. He's popular, very popular. He has over 10 million followers on Twitter and about 25 million friends on Facebook.

A second English footballer, Jack Wilshere, is a midfielder for Arsenal, an English Premier League football club. He's a star player, too, with over 1.6 million followers on Twitter (he had deactivated his Twitter account following the incident to be described) and over 3 million friends on Facebook.

In January 2012, both posted tweets with the hashtag #makeitcount and included a link to a Nike website selling Nike "Fuelbands," a wrist band that measures the wearer's activity and calories burned.

The problem in those tweets was that they were not sponsored by Nike. The advertising rules in the United Kingdom are like those that govern social media conduct in the United States: if it's a sponsored tweet, it must be disclosed in the tweet. Simple stuff. Nike knows it. Rooney probably did not.

THE ROONEY TWITTER ACCOUNT HAD NO BRANDING TO SUGGEST A NIKE SPONSORSHIP

Looking at Rooney's Twitter account in 2012, it was not branded in any way that would link it to Nike. There was no mention of an affiliation with Nike in the account profile, nor was there any reference to it in the Twitter background, which could be customized to contain information that the user wished to add. (Be aware that in the United States the FTC has made it clear that profile disclosures are not enough for its standard of "clear and conspicuous" disclosure of "material connections." It is also doubtful that under the ASA's standards, such account branding would have inoculated the sponsored tweet from being deemed an infraction of the ASA disclosure rules.)

The U.K. advertising industry is self-governed by codes of practice that are "designed to protect consumers and create a level playing field for advertisers."

These codes of practice are the responsibility of two industry committees: the Committee of Advertising Practice (CAP) and the Broadcast Committee of Advertising Practice (BCAP) and are independently administered by the Advertising Standards Authority (ASA).

WHAT IS THE ASA?

The ASA describes itself as "the UK's independent regulator for advertising across all media, our work includes acting on complaints and proactively checking the media to take action against misleading, harmful or offensive advertisements." Over 50 years old, the institution addressed 31,458 complaints in 2011, with 4,591 ads changed or withdrawn in 2011 as a result of ASA action.

ASA REGULATORS CONSIDER BOTH THE SPIRIT AND THE LETTER OF THE CODE

The ASA administers the rules in its Code, following the traditions established in the International Chamber of Commerce's model advertising self-regulatory rules; note that the rules of the ASA Code are to be interpreted with reference to both the "spirit" and the "letter" of the Code, making it almost impossible for advertisers to find loopholes or to get off on a technicality. This common-sense approach takes into account the nature of the product being advertised, the media being used, and the audience being targeted.

The ASA's own marketing materials tout the fact that a single complaint is enough for the self-regulatory agency to begin an investigation and, where appropriate, direct that an advertising campaign be stopped. In the case of Nike, the ASA's adjudication report of June 20, 2012, states that it received a single complaint about the Twitter campaign. It was enough.

Here is the ASA's statement of the issue presented:

Issue: The complainant challenged whether both tweets were obviously identifiable as marketing communications.

U.K. CODE RULES REFERENCED BY THE ASA IN MAKING ITS DECISION

The ASA cited the following rules from the twelfth edition of the UK Code of Non-broadcast Advertising, Sales Promotion and Direct Marketing (CAP Code) in rendering its decision concerning the Nike campaign:

2.1. Marketing communications must be obviously identifiable as such.

2.3. Marketing communications must not falsely claim or imply that the marketer is acting as a consumer or for purposes outside its trade, business, craft or profession; marketing communications must make clear their commercial intent, if that is not obvious from the context.

2.4. Marketers and publishers must make clear that advertorials are marketing communications; for example, by heading them "advertisement feature."

NIKE'S RESPONSE TO THE ASA COMPLAINT AND INVESTIGATION

Nike, according to the ASA, "believed the tweets should be viewed in the context in which they appeared." Noting that Twitter is a "more direct channel of communications between two parties than traditional media, Nike, according to the ASA, offered the defense that Rooney and Wilshere:

> were communicating to Twitter members who had chosen to "follow" them and that both footballers were well known for being sponsored by Nike, as were the teams for which they played; Manchester United and Arsenal respectively. They believed, therefore, that Wayne Rooney and Jack Wilshere's Twitter followers would not be misled about the relationship between the footballers and Nike.

Apart from the notion that fans of Rooney and Wilshere would already know that both players were sponsored by Nike, the retailer, according to the ASA, also contended that the tweets could be "objectively viewed" as marketing communications because of the presence of the Nike URL within the body of the tweet. Nike further contended that the presence of the Twitter hashtag #makeitcount, the advertising campaign tagline, made it sufficiently clear that those tweets were advertising.

THE ASA ASSESSMENT OF THE COMPLAINT AND NIKE'S RESPONSE

To begin with, the ASA noted that the tweets in question were in fact part of a sponsorship deal with Nike. As to the content of the tweets, it was reported that the footballers were both asked to submit their own ideas about what to write as part of their tweet. The ASA "understood that the tweet's final content was agreed with the help of a member of the Nike marketing team."

Keep in mind that advertising campaigns are nearly always reviewed by regulatory agencies from the perspective of the "average viewer," here a person who would be expected to follow "a number" (unspecified) of other Twitter accounts, and that the average Twitter user would receive a number of tweets throughout the day that would be scrolled through quickly. In this analysis, the ASA took into consideration the "average user" and, as well, looked at the manner in which the sponsored content would be presented and viewed: found within a stream of other messages that would all be scrolled through quickly, i.e., the nature of Twitter use.

UNDER THE CAP CODE, ADS MUST BE "OBVIOUSLY IDENTIFIABLE" AS SUCH

The issue presented by the unnamed complainant was "whether both tweets were obviously identifiable as marketing communications." In providing its assessment of the complaint, the ASA noted that "the Code did not just require ads to be identifiable as marketing communications but that they must be obviously identifiable as such." *CAP Code, Section 2.1*.

The ASA standard of review on this issue matches the "clear and conspicuous" standard imposed by the FTC's social media endorsement guidelines for the disclosure of sponsored endorsements. See *12 CFR Part 255.5, FTC Guides Concerning the Use of Endorsements and Testimonials in Advertising.*

The factors considered by the ASA in determining if the sponsored tweets were "obviously identifiable" as ads include:

- The Nike URL contained in the tweets which directed users to the Nike website

- The #makeitcount hashtag

- Nike's sponsorship of the footballers and their teams

And this is how the ASA reviewed the factors presented:

- The Nike reference was "not prominent and could be missed."

- Due to the timing of the launch of the "make it count" campaign and its closeness in timing to the sponsored tweets, consumers would not have already been aware of what the hashtag #makeitcount meant.

- Not all Twitter users would be aware of the footballers' and their teams' sponsorship deal with Nike.

THE ASA FINDS NIKE'S SPONSORED TWEETS BREACHED THE CAP CODE

In an instructive finding, the ASA announced:

> We considered there was nothing obvious in the tweets to indicate they were Nike marketing communications. In the absence of such an indication, for example #ad, we considered the tweets were not obviously identifiable as Nike marketing communications and therefore concluded they breached the Code. Citing: CAP Code (Edition 12) rules 2.1, 2.3 and 2.4 (Recognition of marketing communications)

In rendering its decision, the ASA provided an example that included a hashtag, #ad, within the body of the tweet as a way of making it "obviously identifiable" as an ad, echoing a recommendation of the FTC, which specifically suggested the inclusion of the hashtag "#ad" to make it clear that a tweet was part of an advertising campaign. See *The FTC's Revised Endorsement Guides: What People Are Asking.*

NIKE'S TWEETS ARE BANNED

Becoming the first brand to have its tweets banned in the United Kingdom, Nike was informed by the ASA that "the ads," i.e., sponsored tweets, must no longer appear. Nike was also warned by the ASA "to ensure that its advertising was obviously identifiable as such."

Today, Rooney's Twitter account contains a brief biography: "@NikeUK athlete," with a link to his Facebook page. He is also wearing a shirt with the Nike brand logo in his Twitter profile picture.

U.K. COMMITTEE ON ADVERTISING OFFERS ADDED GUIDANCE ON SOCIAL MEDIA MARKETING

The United Kingdom's Committee on Advertising Practice is the regulatory authority that creates the advertising codes that the ASA administers and enforces. In conjunction with the ASA decision relating to the Nike campaign, CAP offered its own analysis of the campaign and provided some additional guidance on the subject to marketers.

Supporting the ASA's analysis, CAP commented that the principle "marketing communications must be obviously identifiable as such" was "one of the most basic rules in the CAP Code." Noting that marketers were using "ever more innovative techniques," CAP offered how they might still remain compliant in plying their craft in innovative ways. "Consumer perception is key," CAP explained.

CAP noted that in traditional media, for example, advertising is generally easy to spot. It observed that in print media, express statements of sponsorship as required in a sponsored tweet were not required in print media because "most readers can instantly tell the difference between articles and ads," due to differences in the "style of presentation and the content of the ad," which, "taken together, are enough to make clear to readers that they are looking at an advertisement."

SAME RULES, DIFFERENT MEDIUM

In uncommon instances, however, even in traditional media, there are times when the style of presentation of commercial content heightens the risk of consumer confusion concerning the commercial nature of content, such as when commercial content is made to appear more like a news story than an ad. In such instances, according to CAP, an express statement of advertising might actually be required to meet the CAP Code's standard of being "obviously identifiable" as commercial from the perception of the consumer.

In citing this example, the ASA, like the FTC, demonstrates that the standard it is imposing in new media is really a continuation of the standard that has existed in traditional media and marketing compliance.

NO SPECIAL LANGUAGE FOR DISCLOSURE, BUT A #AS OR #SPON WOULD LIKELY DO IT!

Also like the FTC, CAP stated, "The Code is not prescriptive about the language used, it requires only that consumers recognise the advertisement for what it is." The FTC, for its part, has said that there is "no special language." Instead it notes, "The point is to give the readers the information." See *The FTC's Revised Endorsement Guides: What People Are Asking.*

Asking and answering the question "What could Nike have done to identify the advertisements more clearly?" CAP suggested: "Beyond clearer references to Nike itself, one option is to use #ad or #spon in the message, as recommended by IAB and ISBA guidelines." The FTC has suggested hashtags like "#ad" and "#paid." *Id.*

DISCLOSURE SYMBOLS WORK ONLY WHEN "WELL-ESTABLISHED IN CONSUMERS' MINDS"

Discussing the use of disclosure symbols that some media developers have begun to promote and use, CAP warned that such symbols could only be used once the symbol had become "well-established in consumers' minds."

The FTC, in contrast, has warned that a disclosure button "isn't likely to be sufficient." *Id.*

SNICKERS SHOWS THAT CELEBRITY-SPONSORED TWEETS CAN BE INNOVATIVE—AND COMPLIANT

In March 2012, before the Nike investigation, the ASA had conducted its first investigation of a Twitter ad campaign. In that investigation, the ASA cleared Snickers (owned by Mars Chocolate UK Ltd.) of any misconduct in a more detailed Twitter campaign than Nike's. Like Nike's campaign, the tweets sponsored by Snickers also involved two celebrities, one, a footballer, Rio Ferdinand,

and the other, a former glamour model, English media darling Katie Price. Both sent out a series of five tweets uncommon for their online personas. Ferdinand's tweets revolved around knitting and Price's around politics—each series ending in Snickers' popular catchphrase, "You're not you when you're hungry . . ." and the hashtags #hungry #spon.

As in the Nike investigation, the ASA found that the Snickers complaint also raised the question of whether the tweets were "obviously identifiable as a marketing communication" under CAP Code (twelfth edition) Rules 2.1, 2.3, and 2.4.

SNICKERS OFFERS TWO RESPONSES TO THE COMPLAINTS

Snickers explained that each celebrity had posted five tweets within the span of an hour. Snickers contended that only the final tweet made by each celebrity, which contained a mention and photo of the product, actually contained marketing content and, therefore, only the final tweet for each required a disclosure.

As a secondary explanation of its campaign, Snickers offered that the campaign:

> could be regarded as one marketing communication, rather than as five separate tweets, but that the circumstances meant it became a marketing communication only when the final tweets were posted. They said that would be a reasonable interpretation, in particular because the tweets occurred within close proximity to each other, and because in that context the first four of either series of tweets were random statements, again with no marketing content. Mars believed that, if that interpretation was adopted, the tweets became single marketing communications only when the final tweets were posted and therefore the nature of the "reveal" tweets again fulfilled the requirement that marketing communications were obviously identifiable as such.

THE ASA CONCLUDES ALL THE TWEETS WERE MARKETING—AND COMPLIANT

The ASA disagreed with Snickers' contention that the first four tweets became marketing communications "only when the fifth tweets were posted." The ASA viewed the first four tweets as "teasers," with the fifth tweet being the "reveal."

Nevertheless, the ASA found the tweets to be compliant as the "combination" of elements:

> was sufficient to make clear the tweets were advertising and that consumers would then understand each series of tweets was a marketing communication. In that particular context, and given the relevance of the first four tweets to the "You're not you when you're hungry . . ." strap line in the "reveal" tweets, we considered it was acceptable that the first four tweets were not individually labelled as being part of the overall marketing communications. We therefore concluded that the ads did not breach the Code.

This decision, when contrasted with the Nike decision, seems to make it clear that the ASA will not sanction innovation in social media marketing—but only noncompliance. As CAP explained, "Consumer perception is key."

BEWARE THE SPUR-OF-THE-MOMENT SPONSORED TWEET

Perhaps we can put this one under the "No Good Deed Goes Unpunished" category.

Gemma Collins, an English TV star with her own fashion line, went to the Toni and Guy salon to get her hair done. The salon decided to waive its fee for its celebrity patron. Collins was pleased with the salon's service and said as much to the staff there, who suggested that she tweet about it. "On the spur of the moment," it was decided that Gemma would send out a tweet expressing her endorsement of the salon and even offering visitors a 10 percent discount. The salon staff and Gemma believed that mention of a discount would make it clear that the tweets were marketing communications. Win-win for everybody! Unfortunately, not.

THE ASA UPHOLDS THE COMPLAINT

Using a similar pattern of analysis found in the Nike adjudication, the ASA stated:

> The ASA considered the average Twitter user would follow a number of people on the site and they would receive a number of tweets throughout the day, which they might scroll through quickly. We noted the Code did not just require ads to be identifiable as marketing communications but that they must be obviously identifiable as such.

The tweets appeared to have been written on a spontaneous visit to the salon and users could have interpreted them as referring to a preexisting 10% off sales promotion, which Gemma Collins had herself taken advantage of on her visit. The tweets did encourage users to quote "#gemma" but, in the context of the whole tweets, users could have overlooked the significance of that or not understood that it related directly to Miss Collins. In the absence of an identifier such as "#ad," we considered the tweets were not obviously identifiable as Toni and Guy marketing communications and therefore concluded they breached the Code. CAP Code (Edition 12) rules 2.1, 2.3 and 2.4

Though the ASA did not question the spur-of-the-moment nature of the tweeting, nor the effort made to alert viewers to the commercial nature of the tweeting, the ASA rested its decision squarely on the principle that ads must not simply be "identifiable as marketing communications but that they must be obviously identifiable as such." *CAP Code, Section 2.1.*

Although the investigations reviewed here were begun in response to complaints, the ASA has stated, "The ASA does not just wait for complaints—we proactively check to see that the Codes as well as our rulings are adhered to, for example by seeing if any necessary changes have been made to advertisements."

TAKEAWAYS

- The ASA Advertising Code does not just require ads or sponsored tweets to be "identifiable" as marketing communications; instead, under the Code, they "must be obviously identifiable as such." *CAP Code, Section 2.1.*

- Consumer perception is key.

- The inclusion of a brand link or a brand hashtag does not satisfy the "obviously identifiable" disclosure standard, nor does a coupon code.

- Awareness of the existence of a brand campaign or sponsorship cannot be assumed; it must be made "obviously identifiable."

- The use of certain hashtags, such as #ad or #spon, that make it obviously identifiable to the viewer that the content is commercial in nature is recommended by both the ASA in the United Kingdom and the FTC in the United States.

- Make sure that your compliance team is well versed in the latest social media marketing rules and vets your social media marketing campaign (however painful that thought might be!).

- Look to your ad agencies to help you with your social media marketing campaigns, but do not overlook a compliance review of the product.

- Avoid spur-of-the-moment social media marketing campaigns.

- Recognize that advertising authorities internationally are beginning to provide similar guidelines and solutions to social media marketing challenges.

- Always consider your social media marketing campaign from the viewer's perspective.

- When a sponsored celebrity is tweeting to millions of followers, consider that there are likely to be dramatic differences in the range of any ad viewer's perception and understanding; err on the side of caution.

- When in doubt, use the hashtag #ad or #spon—and even then, only if the addition of such disclosure clues removes your doubt concerning the appropriateness and compliance of your marketing campaign.

POSTSCRIPT ON NIKE BRAND AMBASSADOR WILSHERE

Shortly after being pushed into the spotlight for involvement in the Nike-sponsored tweet incident, footballer Jack Wilshere once again found himself in hot water because of a mistweet, actually two. This time, however, Wilshere was on his own when he received a formal warning from the Union of European Football Associations (UEFA), the governing body of football in Europe, for two messages on Twitter that suggested that he had made a bet on a teammate to score a point during a game. Though Wilshere was not playing in the game, having been out for the season because of an ankle injury, UEFA rules prohibit players from betting on any games in which their teams are involved.

Wilshere, according to a report in the *Guardian*, was quick to insist that he was merely joking about betting in his tweets, one of which said, "Frimmy nearly won me some money there!" But UEFA, according to the *Sun* (the U.K. daily tabloid that had tipped off UEFA to Wilshere's "betting" tweets), was less than amused, stating through a spokesperson that "[t]he player has been warned for being in breach of the principles of integrity of matches and competitions."

Under UEFA rules, sanctions can be substantial, including being banned from the sport.

The *Sun* noted that both tweets were deleted on the same day they had appeared. The *Sun* also reported that Wilshere closed his Twitter account in June 2012, the month in which the Nike story received intensive coverage. UEFA's warning to Wilshere regarding his soccer-related tweets was issued in July 2012.

TAKEAWAYS

- Never joke on Twitter about doing something that is illegal in real life.

- If your Twitter account does nothing but get you into hot water, it might be best to close it.

Best Practices for Compliant Social Media: Case Studies

SCOTT MONTY: DRIVING COMPLIANT SOCIAL MEDIA MARKETING

Few brand ambassadors are as closely identified with their brand as Scott Monty, or as he is better known, @ScottMonty. Monty recently stepped down from his post as head of social media for Ford Motor Company, where if he wasn't sharing an Instagram photo of himself via Twitter, you just might just have caught him blogging about social media marketing on his blog, http://scottmonty.com.

Prior to leaving his post, Scott Monty was kind enough to take some time to share a few key insights about compliant social media marketing, social media governance, crisis management, and some larger issues about social media for business, generally, that should be instructive for businesses, whether large or small.

> **Q. What's the best advice for businesses to stay on the right side of the law when using social media for marketing?**
>
> **A.** Get to know your legal team and bring them into the process early and often. It's better to make an ally out of your lawyers than to constantly be
>
> *(continued)*

working at odds, because their job is to protect the company from risk. Once you understand what their hot button issues are and what legal issues may affect the industry in which you do business, the easier it will be for you to work collaboratively.

Q. Who should be part of a company's social media governance team?

A. I suppose it depends on how seriously the company takes social media and how deeply it goes in the organization. Certainly communications, marketing, IT, customer service and legal are key members. HR could certainly be part of it as well since some of this may affect corporate culture, training, and employee issues.

Q. How does a global brand stay on top of changing social media and privacy laws?

A. Because social media touches so many areas of the business, it's important to know that social media specialists will never be able to understand the minutiae of each department's area of expertise. A global brand needs to rely on the lawyers in each region who are tasked with knowing and following privacy laws. We've found that if we raise our standards to the level of the most stringent country's laws, it covers us globally. But ultimately, we need the counsel of people who understand the nuances and specifics of regional disparities in the law.

Q. How can companies help their employees get social media right?

A. The first step is to have a well-crafted set of social media/digital communications guidelines or policy for employees (like, http://bit.ly/fordguidelines), and then to ensure a strong communication plan around it. Next, they can create a set of training modules to delve deeper into the area to help answer questions that may arise around specific situations or tools. Overall, having a staff available to give advice and counsel to employees is a good idea as well.

Q. What do you attribute Ford's social media success to?

A. Under our leadership, we have a culture of transparency and collaboration that fuels everything we do. In many ways, our executive team displays some of the key hallmarks of social media whether or not they participate on the platforms. And they encourage creativity and experimentation to help bring to life the passion that many of us share about Ford, recognizing that the power of a lot of what we do is in the hands of our employees.

Q. Has social media helped Ford sell cars? How?

A. It's difficult to ascribe specific sales to social media; we prefer to measure our results through longer-term and higher-funnel measures like awareness, consideration and intent, along with looking at reputational scores and sentiment. We try to measure consistently across a variety of media, including traditional earned media, to determine if we're successful. When you look at how people are perceiving Ford—from the beautiful design of our latest vehicles to the technology in them and the way we use cutting edge techniques to share our story and encourage others to do the same— it all has a halo effect that is pushing the needle in the right direction.

Q. Any tips on working with sponsored bloggers?

A. We typically don't pay bloggers for their work. We've actually created a set of rules for working with digital influencers that adhere to the WOMMA standards (http://bit.ly/fordbloggers). When we do pay travel expenses for bloggers to join us, we ask that they disclose that in their content, as the guidelines indicate.

Q. Best way to prevent a social media crisis?

A. There's no way to prevent a social media crisis; one can only be prepared for one. Part of that is having a strong understanding of crisis communications as it exists today, and how the digital and social channels can play a part in that. By being active on those channels on a regular basis, a company can build up goodwill and relationships that can pay off when a crisis hits, for it's likely the fans that will step up in defense of a brand if the need arises.

(continued)

> **Q. Best way to respond to a social media crisis?**
>
> **A.** The best way to respond is quickly, openly and on the same platform on which the crisis is evolving. Even if you don't have answers, it's important to let the public know that you're aware of the situation and working on it. And then when you are ready, it's critical to be as human as possible in your response. There's a great case study out there of how we did so in late 2008: http://bit.ly/rangerstation.

Ford's Social Media Policy: Five Core Principles

Ford's social media guidelines provide both detail and simplicity. At the center of its social media guidelines are five core principles for online social engagement:

1. Honesty about who you are

2. Clarity that your opinions are your own

3. Respect and humility in all communication

4. Good judgment in sharing only public information—including financial data

5. Awareness that what you say is permanent

Include these core principles in putting together your own social media policy, and you will have gone a long way in providing reliable guideposts for yourself and your employees in compliant social media.

"Times When an Official Response Is Needed": Crowdsourcing Brand Management

Although Ford empowers and encourages its employees to be "social," the company also informs its employees that there are times when an official company response is needed and encourages them to alert the company's communications or legal team when such instances are spotted.

Trouble moves at lightning speed on social media. By encouraging employees to alert the company's communications or legal team the moment a potential brand problem is spotted, the company taps into the power of its own workforce to keep customers happy and to keep the brand out of any hot water.

Compliant social media can be best served when employees are empowered, through proper training and social media guidelines, to be part of the brand management team. In this particular area, addressed by Ford, encouraging employees to direct hot potatoes to the communications or legal team is smart and efficient. It also, however, requires employees to have the confidence that their forwarding of such issues will be welcomed and that they will have a path to follow to actually communicate such alerts to the relevant team.

"When in Doubt, Ask"

Social media for business can be more than a bit complicated at times. Open internal communications with in-house communications specialists or corporate counsel is crucial for getting things right. Ford offers another social media marketing principle that social media marketers—or anyone messaging in social media for a business—should follow very closely: "When in doubt, ask." Encourage your employees to ask questions first—then tweet or post!

For Ford, this means encouraging employees to check with a member of the communications team or the legal office before posting. If your company is much smaller and doesn't have a communications or legal team, at least taking a moment to discuss the idea with others in the company when there is any question about the correctness of a post. And when in doubt, don't tweet; don't post. Period.

Ford's "Rules of Engagement with Online Influencers"

Ford is transparent in its engagement of social media influencers. The company candidly notes that it wants to give those active in social media a chance to drive its cars. However, although the company is eager to give social media influencers the opportunity to do a test-drive, the company is emphatic that it never instructs people on what to say. Articulating its astute understanding of the rules of social media engagement, Ford explains, "In social media, it must be your authentic opinion or it doesn't count." The company also insists on transparency: "We require anyone who we provide a vehicle or other experience to fully disclose that relationship."

In insisting on such transparency from the social media influencers it works with, Ford is fulfilling the FTC's mandate that it is the sponsoring company's responsibility to inform bloggers of their duty to disclose the material connection between them and a brand they may be blogging or tweeting about. *16 CFR Part 255, Guides Concerning the Use of Endorsements and Testimonials in Advertising*

Ford has even created a distinct online site for the issue of ethical influencer engagement, http://bit.ly/fordbloggers, complete with a set of social media blogger outreach guidelines:

1. Always request that our social media influencers be transparent and disclose their relationship, as well as anything they've received as a result of that relationship with Ford.

2. Insist on honesty of opinion. We want both positive and negative reviews of our vehicles.

3. Offer influencers engaging experiences that are worth talking about. We won't be cutting and pasting press releases into e-mails in hopes someone will post them.

4. Always carefully target our outreach to ensure that we aren't "spamming" anyone with unwanted messages.

5. Listen carefully to suggestions and concerns.

6. Compensate influencers for consulting or other duties they do for Ford. This compensation will solely be for their time as an advisor and will not include an expectation that they will write about the project—favorably or unfavorably.

7. Apologize quickly for any mistakes we make. No one is perfect and we are sure that we will make a misstep in our efforts to engage with the social web, but we will be sure to learn from our mistakes.

8. Share this policy with all influencers we work with, and guidelines, to provide information on how it handles blogger outreach.

The Word of Mouth Marketing Association

On the topic of dealing with social media influencers and social media marketing generally, Ford notes that it also follows the ethical guidelines hammered out by the Word of Mouth Marketing Association (WOMMA), http://womma.org/ethics/code. WOMMA, a nonprofit organization restricted to brand membership, is considered by many to be the leading nongovernmental authority on the subject of ethical social media marketing. Its online resources provide some practical guidance on the FTC's social media marketing rules.

DUNKIN' DONUTS: "A BRANDD BUILT FOR SOCIAL"

Few enterprises have succeeded with social media like Dunkin' Donuts. The brand boasts over 12 million Facebook fans and over 750,000 Twitter followers. A visit to either account shows a highly engaged community.

Dunkin' Donuts social media manager, Jessica Gioglio (@savvybostonian), explains part of the brand's success: "Dunkin' Donuts is a branDD (yes, that's how they spell it!) built for social." Gioglio remarks, "We don't run our social media program, our customers do. . . . They share special moments, like a Dunkin' Donuts run on their wedding day, or going to the beach and having an ice coffee." She went on to say, "We celebrate their loyalty."

No One Department "Owns" Social

In a trend being followed by larger, social media–savvy enterprises, Gioglio explains: "No one department owns 'social.' Embracing a cross-functional approach to social media, Dunkin' Donuts weaves into the task Interactive Marketing for contests, promotions, loyalty and mobile, Public Relations and Customer Service for content and community management, Media for advertising and strategic partnerships, and Legal for overall program counsel."

Get to Know Legal

"Ugh, talking to lawyers." I know, I know. But Gioglio has some sound advice on this point, echoed by her colleagues in other brands and industries: "Get to know your legal team and let them know what you're doing." This practice allows you to spot problems early and gives everyone added time to find solutions.

Have Regular Meetings—"Communication Is Key"

Gioglio also recommends holding regular meetings to review the brand's social media efforts, to look for trends, and to go over which social media marketing initiatives have been working and which have not. For Dunkin' Donuts, "regular" meetings mean biweekly meetings as well as program-specific meetings.

"Communication is key," she notes. During the process, Gioglio adds, "We take inspiration from our fans."

To drive home the importance of communication, Gioglio also recommends an "open door/phone/email policy and a no-question-is-too-silly" approach for members of the social media team. "And be super responsive," she emphasizes.

Evaluate New Platforms

The world of social media is always full of surprises. Seemingly overnight, new platforms, such as Instagram, Google+, and Pinterest take the public imagination by storm. Gioglio notes that Dunkin' Donuts doesn't shy away from innovation but is always evaluating new platforms.

Selecting Social Media Brand Ambassadors

Dunkin' Donuts has a simple criterion for selecting ambassadors: they must be passionate, social media savvy, and enthusiastic and have a "knowledge of brand touch points," Gioglio explains.

And an essential point for those who still may think that social media marketing can simply be relegated to doing in one's spare time, another important criterion for Dunkin' Donuts in selecting brand ambassadors is a "willingness to take on the time commitment required." Gioglio observes that "things happen very quickly in social media."

Brand ambassadors are aided in their social journeys by receiving specialized training sessions and regular communications.

Going "Glocal"

With a global presence, marked by over 50 regional and international Twitter accounts and growing, Dunkin' Donuts also has point people monitoring regional and international efforts. Gioglio explains that sensitivity to regional and cultural differences is all part of being social. To help in the process, she notes that the brand supports "go local" with geo-targeted Facebook posts that reflect differences in cities, states, regions, countries, and languages.

An important process in the success of going local when you are going global is to "leverage knowledgeable agency partners on the ground," she adds, a sentiment also echoed by many larger brands.

"DELL RINGS UP $6.5 MILLION IN SALES USING TWITTER"

I think of it as big ears. . . . We love to listen. We love to learn. We make our products and services better when we are connected with our customers.

—Michael Dell, Chairman and CEO of Dell

For most companies, getting the "C-suite" on board with social is one of the biggest challenges to social business. For Dell, getting employees to understand and be as "social" as their chairman and CEO, Michael Dell, may actually be the biggest challenge!

In 2009, "Dell Rings Up $6.5 Million in Sales Using Twitter" was a headline appearing in a Bloomberg news report and was repeated by scores of news outlets at the time. The story still gets cited in the world of social media marketing as a seminal example of "social business," the spreadsheet sense of social media marketing. The holy grail of "social" for business: #ROI – "Return on Investment."

For Michael Dell, however, whom you just may get to chat with on a Google+ hangout, social media is a "co-creation model where customers are giving us feedback and we're making products and services better as a result."

Dell Blogs Before Twitter—"Real People Are Here and We Are Listening."

Before Twitter was even a social network, however, Dell entered the world of social media with a simple message from its official corporate blog, *Direct2Dell*, that still speaks to the essence of successful social media marketing:

Real People Are Here and We Are Listening.

Though an early adopter in social, with a CEO who "gets" social and is social, Dell still works at improving social media expertise. As explained by Liz Bullock, director of social media and community at Dell, "We want to embed social in the fabric of our company. It's about socializing."

For a company that excels at social, the "secret" to compliant social media marketing success seems to be a combination of leadership and employee empowerment, empowerment through training. Said Bullock, "We believe our customer-connected employees are our rock stars."

Bullock continues, "Our mantra is: 'Listen, Learn, Engage and Act.'" For a company that has about 25,000 brand mentions a day, up from about 4,000 brand mentions a day four years ago, "listening" is social is no easy task. Says

Bullock, "We knew we needed to make social an enterprise venture. . . . We leveraged across the company. . . ."

Dell's Five Guiding Principles for Compliant Social Media Marketing

For companies engaging in social media on a large scale, the issue of social media marketing compliance is nothing short of scary. For Dell, compliant social media marketing has been fermented to five guiding principles:

- Protect confidential information.

- Be transparent.

- Follow the law.

- Be responsible.

- Have fun and connect.

There is sheer brilliance in the simplicity of Dell's social media marketing principles!

The Process of Embedding Social in Corporate Culture—"SMaC U"

Even with a CEO who is highly social, Dell does not leave social media adoption within the corporation to chance. For Dell, compliant social media marketing has become both a science and an art. To pass on its best practices, it has even created its own in-house Social Media and Community University, "SMaC U." I interviewed Ryan Garcia, legal director of social media and community at Dell, about the program.

> **Q. Can you tell me about Dell's Social Media and Community University program?**
>
> **A.** SMaC U is Dell's social media education and training program. It is open to all team members around the world. Any class can be taken by anyone in any order. Although we encourage everyone at Dell to take at least the class on our Social Media Principles if they participate in social

media, we require certification for team members whose job responsibilities include social media and community interaction or management.

The program currently consists of core classes (three), platform specific classes (about seven), skills classes (about eight), and a regular series of Power Hours which cover a variety of topics. All classes are taught live but we use tele-meeting software to allow global participation. The software has a chat window on screen so there's actually a great dialogue taking place during the class, makes for great sessions. Power Hours are recorded for later viewing.

We also have a Chatter group internally which is devoted to best practice sharing among Dell team members who have been trained. This provides ongoing peer-to-peer support and knowledge sharing, not only on best practices, successes, specific challenges, but also as a continuing education forum. Social media practitioners tend to be passionate about the topic so they also make great resources for continuing to learn about this emerging field.

We have an amazing group of trainers and SMaC ambassadors who teach the classes and the word of mouth has been fantastic. But we're also slowly converting content to online classes that scale better.

Q. What does the social media certification process involve?

A. While all classes are open to all team members, to become officially certified you must take a minimum of four classes. All three core curriculum classes must be taken. You must also take a class in a particular platform, preferably the platform for the community you'll be working with, such as Facebook or Twitter or LinkedIn. We also have a few special certification courses for executives and senior leaders, recognizing that we need to give them a higher level overview to see the issues their team will be addressing in a full certification course.

Q. What's been the impact of the program?

A. SMaC U has been an unprecedented success. When the classes first launched we had the lofty hopes that 1,000 people would take time out of their busy work schedules to take a class. We had 5,000 class participants

(continued)

that first year alone. That number is now over 40,000 with hundreds more taking classes every week.

But those are just numbers. To me, the greater impact for the program has been the incredible alignment we've seen across the company. Dell is active in a number of different segments, from consumer to large enterprise, and we cover a broad spectrum of offerings from computers to services. From our support team to salespeople to engineers and every other group you can imagine—they are all using social media in very different ways but they all have a fundamental understanding of our policies and principles and are using social media to deliver better business and customer value.

And legally speaking the program has been fantastic. The biggest complaint any in-house attorney will have is that they're constantly reactive with little chance to be proactive. SMaC U has given us the chance to be proactive about what our corporate policies are and ensure legal content and possible issues are incorporated into the training and education sessions for this emerging field. For example, classes include understanding of various social platforms' terms of service, something people tend to overlook. Therefore, our team members are aware of this consideration and either seek out legal counsel or act in accordance with the terms. I'm brought in on a number of social media legal issues, but I'd say 90 percent of the time the team member already knows most, if not all, of the legal answer thanks to the great job our trainers have done delivering the legal message in the courses. This lets me spend my time on more strategic efforts and staying ahead of emerging legal issues.

Q. How can others learn from Dell's in-house social media marketing training?

A. Start small then scale up. You can spend a lot of time designing a huge program that will encompass everything and everybody. But in the time it will take you to build that program you'll miss a lot of opportunities to get your message out. So start small and build the program. As you build the content you'll also find ways to tailor the content that makes sense for your organization.

Social media is becoming widely used in most people's lives. I think there is generally a thirst for understanding about how this development relates to employees in their professional lives. I think that is why we saw such a huge uptake on this front. The boundaries between professional and private and the public use of data raise a lot of questions and employees are keen to understand parameters and guideposts.

Q. Tips for companies struggling to create a social media policy?

A. You cannot start with a policy. Instead, start with your strategy. Once you figure out what it is you hope to accomplish in social media, then you can figure out how to set a policy that furthers those goals (and a training program to get you there).

Constantly revisit your policy. When something big happens, make sure your policy covers it. When nothing big happens, make sure your policy still reads on what your organization is doing.

Carefully consider the tone of your policy. Do you want to make it official and scare people into compliance? Do you want to make it conversational so team members are more likely to read it and remember it? Tone matters just as much as content. Possibly more.

And, we found our published policy is a great thing to have. The principles underpinning the policy make it more operational and digestible.

Q. How to begin to manage compliance/stay on top of evolving law when you cross so many national borders?

A. I don't think the way we handle legal issues is different for social media than for any other issue that faces an international company like Dell. We're already used to handling different marketing, employment, or sales laws in the different countries we operate in. What is different with social media is the content we create. When you ship a physical good, you can target it for a specific geography with its own set of laws. You can then impose limitations to make sure it stays there so you ensure compliance—that's harder to do with social media content. So we strive to enforce the strongest standard available on all content we create. For example, we use the FTC Endorsement Guidelines as a

(continued)

standard for disclosing our affiliation with content and third parties in every country, not just the U.S.. If a stronger standard is imposed in another country, we'll use that. What is important to us is that we not only follow the law but be completely transparent about our activities in this medium.

Q. How big is Dell's social media team? Grand tally on Dell's social media accounts?

A. We have a small core team that provides centralized resources like listening, governance, training and best practices. Beyond that core team we empower thousands of team members around the world to use social media in a way that aligns with Dell's principles and their specific business needs.

As for specific numbers, that changes daily. Currently there are more than 4,000 Dell certified social media and community professionals. We provide official links to our biggest accounts at dell.com/socialmedia but since we empower all of our employees to become certified there are numerous social media users who use their accounts as part of their job. We also constantly look at the best ways to provide information to our customers—sometimes that means providing a unique community (Alienware versus Large Enterprise, for example) and sometimes that means merging related communities to prevent fragmenting content and confusing customers.

Q. Any other insights you'd care to share?

A. I don't think I can overemphasize how valuable I believe our training program is for a large organization that is using social media in dozens, if not hundreds, of different ways. Our strategy, principles, policy (with its conversational tone) all work together but the training program delivers on the promise of the other three. Our team members are eager to learn about social media and our classes fill that need while empowering them to use social media in appropriate ways. I take no credit for the classes—it's an amazing team that has put them together and I'm happy to work with them to incorporate valuable legal lessons. But being proactive about emerging issues is a fantastic position.

I also think Dell has greatly benefited from looking at social media beyond traditional marketing activities. The vast majority of analysis and regulation about social media has been in the marketing arena, which makes sense because that's where you typically see the greatest overlap between corporations and consumers. But we're also seeing how the social media revolution is impacting all aspects of communication; that spills over into legal areas as well. So we're looking at social media issues beyond marketing—we look at support, product/service creation, employment, and a host of other areas. It's been amazing to see the benefits.

THE WALDORF ASTORIA: LAUNCHING AND MANAGING A LUXURY BRAND IN SOCIAL

The Waldorf Astoria in New York is synonymous with Old World luxury. In fact, it is, I was told, "*the* hotel that invented room service—literally."

Every U.S. president from Herbert Hoover on has stayed there, along with celebrities from all fields. Cole Porter and Frank Sinatra even called the place home for a period of time.

In this hotel that occupies a full city block, there are so many private entrances that it can easily and discreetly move in and out many high-profile guests at any given time. And talking about special guests, the hotel even has a person who only handles bookings dealing with members of the diplomatic corps, presidents (as in "of a country"), and members of royal families.

In a Tweet, the Waldorf Astoria Proves It's "Social"

Planning a Friday overnight stay in New York City, I happened to catch an online price break for a room at the iconic Waldorf Astoria. I booked it. Then I wondered if the blue-blooded Waldorf would be a "social" hotel. I turned to Twitter. Yep. There it was.

Ah, but would it truly be "social"? I would put it to the test, asking if, while I was a guest there, I might be able to speak to someone about the hotel's social media program.

The response was, "Of course!" Which is how, during my stay, I got to meet my charming guide, Meg Towner, the Waldorf's social media manager at the time.

Choose Carefully Your Social Media Manager

Meg Towner projects that genuine friendliness and smile that can't be faked. A smartly dressed, graceful young lady, she attentively awaited my arrival at the Peacock Alley Restaurant, one of three restaurants in the Waldorf Astoria—and our conference room for the interview.

The Disclosure

We were seated at a table for two next to the Steinway piano that Cole Porter used to have in his "home" at the hotel (he lived there in his later years). For a light lunch, Meg recommended sliders (at the Waldorf, "sliders" aren't your typical beef miniburgers; they are outrageously delicious lobster minisandwiches) and a Waldorf salad. We shared both. I must disclose that Meg treated me to the lunch and that my room was upgraded during my stay. (Disclosures serve a positive purpose—and in social media, they are required. Find a way to work them in.)

Old World Elegance Versus New Media Flashy

Meg explained that the Waldorf recognized a tension between its brand image of Old World elegance and the "flashiness" of social media. She candidly observed, "We knew we needed [to start using social platforms], but we weren't sure how to go about it."

There is great wisdom in this observation and cautious approach. Do note that it was not a question of understanding social media or its platforms, as Meg was practiced in both. Instead, it was a matter of considering how the use of social media would weave into benefiting the brand. It was also a matter of developing a plan and considering the implications of being active on social for a luxury brand with a unique high-society tradition.

Protect Your Brand Name as You Plan Your Entrance into Social

As the Waldorf Astoria weighed how it might best become part of the social media conversation, it took the precaution of preserving its brand name on the various social platforms about a full year before it started really using them. This is a sound approach, as too many brands find that they lost their brand name to squatters, or others who legitimately share the same name, as they debated joining the social media conversation, putting their brand names at risk of being hijacked—or, more properly, "brandjacked."

For those businesses with trademarked names, there are procedures that most social networks have in place for removing squatters or others who may simply share the same name, albeit unprotected by a trademark. For businesses without a trademarked name, however, the delay in preserving a brand name on a social network can leave the business without its primary name and without a method of getting it back. The penalty for this is a diluted brand name and diminished online "searchability," i.e., people being able to find you online when they look for you.

Social Media Marketing Assistance Becomes a Luxury Hotel Amenity

As Meg began to ply her social media sharing skills at the Waldorf, clients began to notice and enjoy the ease with which Meg navigated the social media networks. "I look over incoming events for the hotel and assess if they might benefit from social media sharing, and I'll ask them if they'd like us to help. We'll create a plan together," she said. She noted that clients have now begun to ask about the hotel's social media collaboration. So for the hotel that brought us room service and eggs Benedict, it seems that it may also have added another first to its list: social media collaboration as another luxury hotel amenity!

Meg explains that "live tweeting" has now become one of the amenities offered to guests for their special events, especially among charities. Meg cautions, though, that this amenity requires a good measure of discretion, transparency, and common sense. "We try to create an insider's view of what's happening during our special events, while following the guidelines our clients have given," she said. She notes that many of the hotel's clients are "just starting in social media." She adds, "We are not only their venue, but we are also their partner (in social media marketing)."

Knowing When to Tweet . . . and When Not To

"Privacy is of the utmost importance to many of our guests. You would never know the list of celebrities using our services. If someone famous decides to share on a social network that they're attending an event here, it is completely their decision," Meg explains. "We never call out someone on a social network who is staying here, unless they tweeted first; then we'll reply."

Keeping Compliant by Consulting with Legal

The Waldorf has given its social media manager direct access to the hotel's legal counsel, so that there is never a question from the social side about what might be proper or not. Meg notes that it's become a natural part of her post to regularly consult with the brand's attorney. She says that whenever she has a legal question, she generally sends an e-mail to the brand's counsel and that it is always responded to within 24 hours "at most."

This is an important point: not only must there be access to legal counsel for compliant social media marketing, but legal counsel must also prioritize timely responses, as anything beyond 24 hours in giving a response in social media likely means that an opportunity has already passed or a problem has already gotten much worse.

Set Listening Parameters

"Never more than four hours go by without checking our presence on our social media sites," Meg tells me. "That's the bare minimum, 24/7, seven days a week." With a smile, she explains that it means that she's up at least every four hours! She also notes that during the normal workday, the brand's presence and mentions of the brand are checked pretty constantly throughout the day and evening.

Better Safe Than Sorry: Being Creative on Pinterest

Asked about Pinterest, Meg was quick to answer: "We only post photos we have rights to!" So, yes, the Waldorf Astoria is on Pinterest, but due to copyright concerns, it will not be repining your pins—at least for the moment!

Meg explains that creating compliant content for Pinterest is a pretty easy task at the hotel, as it is full of eye-capturing images. "We have beehives on our roof (for the freshest honey), that people like to see. And our pastry chef is always calling me to take a picture of an incredible dessert." Event decorations also create constant image content as well.

Training, Collaboration, and Learning as You Go

Explaining the process of social media governance within the luxury hotel, Meg points out that she reports to the marketing director with whom she has established a great rapport and that she attends weekly meetings to go over upcoming events and to review past ones. She candidly notes that in social, it is "very much learn as you go." It is important to recognize that there is no way around this, given the dynamic nature of social media, social networks, and the technologies that bring them all together.

To stay on top of best practices in social media marketing, Meg explains that the hotel has given a wide ability to attend leading social media educational events so that she can keep learning from the best and brightest in the profession. She also mentioned that even within the hospitality industry, social media practitioners are quick to assist each other in sharing best practices.

She also has a keen understanding of the importance of her role for the hotel: "For many of our guests, I'm their first line of contact. They may send out a tweet months in advance of their staying with us to say that they're going to stay with us. We make it a point to share their excitement at coming to stay with us."

"So Is the Waldorf Astoria's Social Media Manager an Expert in Social Media?"

A trick question, I asked Meg, was whether she considered herself an expert in social media at this point. Her answer? "It's hard for anyone to call themselves an expert when the terrain is constantly changing." Well answered, Meg; well answered.

Leveraging Social with Tools

A couple of additional points from the interview: Meg's smartphone, of course, is her constant companion for monitoring social. She does use Hootsuite as the social networking platform, in part due to its ability to translate and due to its assigning options. She also noted that when she first started the post, she, together with other staff, had to evaluate when the period of greatest conversation on social took place so that brand and conversation monitoring and engagement could be best focused.

One of the greatest advantages of social for the Waldorf? "We're a huge hotel and we like to make to make our guests still feel like they are our only guest, and social media provides another touch point (to make this happen)," Meg said.

BEST PRACTICES IN COMPLIANT SOCIAL MEDIA MARKETING FROM THE WALDORF ASTORIA

Some excellent practices can be gleaned from the Waldorf Astoria's efforts.

- Define your purpose and strategy before diving into social.

- Preserve your brand name on the social platforms as soon as possible to protect your brand, even before you have put together your overall strategy. (Do you really want to go through the hassle, damage, and cost of removing a squatter?)

- Choose as a social media manager someone you have worked with and have been able to assess in terms of maturity, skill, and trust.

- Empower your people to engage. Don't set up silly roadblocks to communication. Find a community manager you trust, and *trust* the person.

- Keep your social media manager in the loop by including him or her in weekly manager and marketing meetings to discuss upcoming events and added opportunities to be "social."

- Provide your social media manager with direct, streamlined access to legal.

- Encourage the entire hospitality team to think of "social" when doing anything special, big or small (e.g., a spectacular cake that would make a great pin or Instagram share).

- Help your social media manager stay on top of best practices by being supportive of attendance at social media events, such as the #140 conferences and South by Southwest (SXSW).

- Recognize that social media marketing is a "learn-as-you-go" field, as the platforms are constantly changing and evolving. So learn as you go!

- Collaborate, even with your competitors, to home in on best practices.

- Let your brand mold all your social media conduct. (E.g., in the case of the Waldorf Astoria, privacy and discretion are of the utmost importance to its society clientele, which often includes celebrities and heads of state. Stay true to your brand.)

- Use social media to make each of your 2,000-plus guests feel like he or she is the only guest.

- Recognize the power of social media to connect and connect.

- Be agile when it comes to the allocation of social media resources. (E.g., in the case of the Waldorf Astoria, Meg and colleagues found that the highest social media communication points for guests tended to be later in the day and early evening when the hotel would be hosting various larger events. The hours of the social media manager were adjusted accordingly. Craft your plan and resources to the realities of your social experience.)

- Be mindful that "social" is 24/7, holidays included, and that there is an expectation that your brand will listen and respond in a timely fashion on its social networks. (For the Waldorf, this means scanning social media accounts at least once every 4 hours, at a minimum—24/7 . . . as in every 4 hours around the clock—that's right, around the clock!

- Your social media manager is your "customer quarterback," fielding questions and requests with no limit on the range of topics; make sure your entire organization understands this and equally understands the need to get answers back quickly or to grab the ball and run with it when tossed a task by the social media manager. There is no time for territorial squabbles: solve the problem; make the customer happy.

- Offer your in-house social media expertise as another amenity to guests, either by partnering with their own social media resources or by offering to promote and live-tweet events at the venue, particularly desired by organizations hosting charitable functions.

COLE HAAN'S PINTEREST CONTEST GETS "PINNED" BY THE FTC

Essentially the problem centered on lack of transparency on the pin boards the contestants created—it was not apparent that the pin boards were part of a contest.

The Law: Prohibition of Unfair or Deceptive Acts, *Section 5, 15 USC 45*

Section 5 of the Federal Trade Commission Act, *15 USC 45*, prohibits "unfair or deceptive acts or practices in or affecting commerce."

"Deceptive acts," under the law, include an "omission" or "practice" that "misleads or is likely to mislead the consumer."

The Contest: #WanderingSole—$1,000 Prize for the Most Creative Pinterest Board

Pinterest is a social platform that describes itself as a "visual discovery tool." As you likely already know from previous chapters, users create collections of images, known as "boards," showcasing various interests or subject matters, and the posted images are known as "pins." The boards and pins are searchable.

Putting Pinterest to use to promote its shoes, fashion retailer Cole Haan announced a contest that invited Pinterest users to create a "Wandering Sole" Pinterest board using five shoe images from Cole Haan's own "Wandering Sole" Pinterest board. Contest participants were instructed to include the hashtag #WanderingSole and to also include five images of the contestant's "favorite places to wander."

The Problem: Inadequate Disclosure of a Material Connection Between the Contestants and Cole Haan

In a public correspondence to Cole Haan, in March 2014, the FTC set forth its view that "the pins featuring Cole Haan products were endorsements of the Cole Haan products, and the fact that the pins were incentivized by the opportunity to win a $1,000 shopping spree would not reasonably be expected by consumers who saw the pins."

Citing Section 5 of the FTC Act, the FTC noted that when a "material connection" exists between a marketer and endorser and their relationship is "not otherwise apparent from the context" of an endorsement communication, such as the posting of product images to a social site, there must be a disclosure of that relationship between the marketer and endorser.

In this instance, the FTC concluded, "[E]ntry into a contest to receive a significant prize in exchange for endorsing a product through social media constitutes a material connection that would not reasonably be expected by viewers of the endorsement." By not requiring contestants to make it clear that they were posting the Cole Haan images as part of a contest, the retailer had, according to the FTC, run afoul of the requirement of disclosing "material connections" when endorsements are made.

The FTC also concluded that requiring contestants to use the hashtag #WanderingSole was insufficient to adequately alert viewers to "the financial incentive—a material connection—between contestants and Cole Haan."

The Penalty: A Warning and Expectation of Compliance

Despite its very public expression of concern to Cole Haan, the FTC concluded that it would not "recommend enforcement action at this time." Instead, the FTC cautioned that it expected the retailer to "take reasonable steps to monitor social media influencers' compliance with the obligation to disclose material connections when endorsing its products."

In determining not to pursue an enforcement action, the FTC offered three mitigating factors:

1. The FTC had not "previously publicly addressed whether entry into a contest is a form of material connection, nor have we explicitly addressed whether a pin on Pinterest may constitute an endorsement."

2. The contest ran for a short time and drew a relatively small number of contestants.

3. After the start of its investigation, Cole Haan "adopted a social media policy that adequately addresses our concerns."

Lessons Learned

This very public investigation, at the expense of Cole Haan, a highly regarded, major retailer (*disclosure:* my shoemaker of choice!), provides businesses with some very important lessons:

1. Regulators are watching for your regulatory compliance when you run a social media campaign, regardless of the social platform.

2. Entry into a contest to receive "a significant prize" in exchange for endorsing a product through social media "constitutes a material connection that would not reasonably be expected by viewers of the endorsement," and as such, a disclosure of the connection must be made.

3. The FTC did not define its phrase "a significant price," and businesses would be well advised to err on the side of disclosure in running social media contests. Elsewhere the FTC has not established monetary limits in the arena of endorsement disclosure obligations.

4. The FTC did not elaborate on what would constitute an adequate disclosure of the "material connection" between the retailer and contestant, though it did conclude that the hashtag #WanderingSole was an inadequate disclosure. Elsewhere the FTC has said that, in certain instances, including the hashtag #Ad or #Sponsored in a tweet on Twitter might be sufficient disclosure of a sponsored tweet. Adding the hashtag #Contest might bring a contest-related endorsement closer to compliance, though the FTC has left this uncertain.

5. If you are using Pinterest as a platform for a contest, you must instruct your contestants to label both their pins and boards, used in connection with the contest, as being part of a contest.

6. Take "reasonable steps to monitor social media influencers' compliance with the obligation to disclose material connections when endorsing" your business's products. It is not enough that businesses inform their contestants to disclose their connection with the business; the business sponsoring the contest must undertake some monitoring of its contestants to ensure that they are following through with their obligation to disclose their material connection.

7. Always err on the side of transparency and explicit disclosure in running a social media contest.

8. Adopt a social media policy that addresses the FTC's concerns about how to conduct a contest using social media.

Conclusion:
The Future of Social Media Law
for Business

THE GOOD

The evolution of social media law is playing out in a very public way, with regulatory agencies and legislative bodies inviting public comment to help them craft policies that will promote business innovation while protecting consumers. Whatever the regulatory bodies that regulate your business might be, chances are they have made and will continue to make announcements about public hearings to address compliance issues relating to new technologies and social platforms. This is particularly true within the United States and European Union.

Big data? The Internet of things? Native advertising? Wearable technologies? Each has prompted public hearings with public comment from the regulatory bodies we look to for guidance in our conduct.

Globally, the laws that are developing in the social space are expanding familiar themes and following similar courses across national boundaries, tending to apply long-established business rules concerning consumer protection and truth in advertising to the new technologies and social platforms. While the technologies and platforms have become far more complicated than ever before, the guiding principles of acting within these spaces have remained anchored in familiar principles of fair conduct and responsibilities relating to the protection and privacy of consumer data. The application of these steady principles to mind-boggling technologies presents much of the challenge, as businesses come to recognize that while social platforms and technologies may change, the principles and rules that govern basic business conduct rarely do.

THE BAD

"The bad," not surprisingly, is simply the other side of the coin: everyone is having trouble figuring out how to apply time-tested business and marketing practices to social platforms and technologies that are evolving at a dizzying pace. Not long ago, one of the biggest challenges in the social space was achieving compliance with disclosures in the shrinking space of "mobile" screens. The confined space, then, was the comparatively small screen (compared with the screen of a computer desktop or laptop) of a smartphone. Now, however, we are facing the challenges posed by the digital display of a fitness band or a smart watch or a smart appliance in a smart home or smart office.

Indeed, the human body itself is already becoming the newest platform for your business, service, advertising, and data collection. "Connected things" that are wearable on your person and made to generate and share data are already giving way to designs of items such as contact lenses that are equipped with camera lenses or augmented reality overlays.

Each technological advance should give device and platform developers, as well as the marketers and businesses that tap into them, pause to ask: "How will we protect the data we are helping to generate or share or store?" "How will engage our community in some way with these new technologies and platforms, whether through advertising or interactive communication, while still remaining compliant with familiar consumer protection obligations in unfamiliar places?"

WHEN YOU HEAR "TECH," THINK "SOCIAL"—AND THINK "COMPLIANCE"

As we look to the future of social media marketing law, we must think "technology" and "technological advances." It is not enough that your sneakers can keep track of your jogging path, distance, and time, as compared with the same data from your friends; wearable technology will now track your heartbeat and even your mood.

Stop in to a café to grab a drink to refresh yourself? Your "fitness" band may also automatically tell you, depending on the customizations you have selected and geotagging of your location, what the stock prices are for the café shop brand you are visiting, and even whether your vital statistics suggest that you perhaps should not be making any investment decisions at this time based on your mood. Such a scenario is not something far-fetched; it is at our doorstep—or rather, at the next stop on your next run.

It is the social aspect of technological advances that makes marketers salivate, as every tweet and post is another potentially infectious ripple in the "Internet of everything," where every "thing" has the potential to broadcast consumer preferences and product or service testimonials in ways that tie back to people, making them the sort of testimonials we tend to deem the most trustworthy. And the data emanating from our wearable technology, smart appliances, and connected homes add to the "volume, variety, and velocity" of "big data," that hard-to-comprehend, but now filterable, mammoth amount of information swirling about in the Internet, ready for scores of business to tap into.

So for every technological advance, consider how your business will leverage it not only for your fundamental business purpose but for the "social" business and data intelligence opportunity it creates as well. And then ask, how are we applying our compliance obligations? If you don't know the answer, find and talk to someone who does.

INNOVATION COMES WITH RISK

In this rapid evolution and intermingling of technology and social and business, there is danger for businesses that dare to innovate and to be first, especially when the nature of the beast is such that regulators are frequently forced to regulate after, not before, a new technology is launched, often using the conduct of early adopters to define the permissible boundaries of new technologies or practices.

In a world where the ability to create a wearable device that tracks and transmits potentially very sensitive data is pretty accessible to even the smallest of startups, the likelihood of serious missteps is high. The race to "be first" should not come at the expense of due diligence and compliance with existing regulatory obligations.

WHAT IS A BUSINESS TO DO WHEN TECHNOLOGY OUTPACES THE LAW?

The challenge of staying within the law when using technologies and social platforms that have not yet been vetted by regulators is a challenge that some businesses will accept to be the disruptive force within their industry that reaps the rewards of innovation and of being first. To those who dare, paying strict attention to the regulatory guidance that does exist within their industry and applying it as best as possibly can be done is a course that should be rigorously followed.

When those within the pharmaceutical industry were clamoring for social media guidance from the Food and Drug Administration (FDA), particularly with respect to mobile platforms, the FDA consistently responded by saying that pharmaceuticals should look to existing rules and regulations for guidance. Many wondered how "existing rules" could possibly be used to give good guidance when they were written before the birth of mobile and social. Yet until the FDA issued its draft social media guidance in 2014, the mantra of "follow existing guidelines" was the best guidance the industry could use for compliant social media conduct. That mantra remains the best guidance many will find as technology continues to outpace the evolution of law.

Don't Think You Don't Have to Be Compliant If You Can't Be

"What?"

Simply put, if you can't figure out a way to fulfill your compliance obligations because of the limitations of a new technology or platform, you shouldn't use that technology or platform. There is, generally speaking, no exception in the law that gives you a pass on compliance simply because a technology or social platform is new.

HOW TO STAY ON TOP OF SOCIAL MEDIA LAW AS A BUSINESSPERSON WITH TOO FEW HOURS IN THE DAY

How can a nonlawyer be expected to stay on top of the law within the social space when even lawyers are having trouble staying on top of it? Be social—and listen carefully in the social space.

If you follow your business field within the social space, it will be difficult not to learn of regulatory changes that affect you and your business as they relate to social media marketing. Find your regulatory agency on Twitter and Facebook and periodically check the sites. These organizations are pretty much all being social at this point and tend to flag issues relating to social media from their social accounts.

Finally, be social in the traditional sense. Talk with others in your field about their use of social media and their understanding of best practices. Have someone from your enterprise attend social media conferences to stay on top of best practices—and instruct the person not to skip out on the compliance-related sessions!

And when a question of law remains, reach out to an attorney from your jurisdiction; look for one who has a ready understanding, as best one can, of social media law. Good luck!

SHARE YOUR THOUGHTS!

Social medial law is a work in progress. A new area of law has been born. Regulatory rules are being written and rewritten with each new advance in technology.

As social media law advances, this book may be updated to address those advances. I welcome you to share with me your thoughts and suggestions—and if I happen to use something you have shared, I will be glad to credit you in the next edition!

Please feel free to tweet me at @GlenGilmore, or e-mail me at GlenGilmore @GlenGilmore.com.

And for updates on social media law, please follow my blog at http://SocialMediaLawToday.com or join me on Twitter at @GlenGilmore, @SocialMediaLaw1, @FinancialSM, @HealthcareSMM, and @EUSocialMedia.

References

CHAPTER 1

Grant Thornton, "Social Media and Its Associated Risks," http://www.grantthornton.com/portal/site/gtcom/menuitem.91c078ed5c0ef4ca80cd8710033841ca/?vgnextoid=324b4c0939f73310VgnVCM1000003a8314acRCRD&vgnextfmt=default&vgnextrefresh=1

"More Than 75 Percent of Businesses Use Social Media, Nearly Half Do Not Have Social Networking Policies," http://www.businesswire.com/news/home/20110714005259/en/75-Percent-Businesses-Social-Media-Social-Networking

"Study: 60 Percent of Companies Using Social Media Have No Plan," http://fuelingnewbusiness.com/2010/06/24/study-60-percent-of-companies-using-social-media-have-no-plan/

"Social Media for Managing Relationships with a Large Customer—BAE Systems and the Dept. of Defence," http://www.youtube.com/watch?v=Utqabc8iwrc

"NLRB Report on Employer Social Media Policies," http://www.nlrb.gov/news/acting-general-counsel-releases-report-employer-social-media-policies

U.S. Department of Labor, Wage and Hour Division (WHD), Overtime Pay, http://www.dol.gov/whd/overtime_pay.htm

"Worldwide Study Shows Global Business Anti-Social in a Social Media Age," http://www.satmetrix.com/company/press-and-news/pr-archive/pr20120517/

"NLRB Launches Webpage Describing Protected Concerted Activity," http://www.nlrb.gov/news/nlrb-launches-webpage-describing-protected-concerted-activity

National Labor Relations Act, *29 U.S.C. §§ 151-169*

Lafayette Park Hotel, 326 NLRB 824, 825 (1998), enfd., 203 F.3d 52 (D.C. Cir. 1999)

Lutheran Heritage Village–Livonia, 343 NLRB 646, 647 (2004) (NLRB two-step inquiry)

University Medical Center, 335 NLRB 1318, 1320-1322 (2001), enf. Denied in pertinent part 335 F.3d 1079 (D.C. Cir. 2003) ("Ambiguity and the absence of limiting language or context fatal")

Tradesmen International, 338 NLRB 460, 460-462 (2002) (Surviving NLRA scrutiny by limiting scope through examples)

Republic Aviation Corp. v. NLRB, 324 U.S. 793, 803 n.10 (1945)

REFERENCES

Fair Labor Standards Act (FLSA), *29 U.S.C. 8, § 207*

"New York Times Further Restricts Free Access," http://online.wsj.com/article/SB1000142405270
23047244045772933370568332422.html

CHAPTER 2

"When Social Media Gets You Fired: Francesca's CFO Is Out," http://www.latimes.com/business/
money/la-fi-mo-social-media-francescas-20120514,0,2912412.story

"Francesca's Fires CFO Gene Morphis Over Social Media Use," http://bloom.bg/JARfDZ

"Francesca's Fires CFO Gene Morphis Over Social Media Use," http://buswk.co/IRgpgi

Fair Credit Reporting Act (FCRA), *15 U.S.C. § 1681 et seq.*

"The FTC's Revised Endorsement Guides: What People Are Asking," http://business.ftc.gov/
documents/bus71-ftcs-revised-endorsement-guideswhat-people-are-asking

"FTC Correspondence to Social Intelligence Corp.," http://privacyblog.littler.com/uploads/file/
FederalTradeCommissionLetterReSocialIntelligenceCorporation.pdf

"How Social Media Can Help You Land That New Job," http://mashable.com/2012/04/06/social
-media-job-infographic/

"Employer Access to Social Media Usernames and Passwords," http://www.ncsl.org/issues-research/
telecom/employer-access-to-social-media-passwords.aspx

"April 14, 2011 ACLU Letter to Maryland Dept. of Corrections," http://www.aclu-md.org/
uploaded_files/0000/0040/11.pdf

"Protecting Your Passwords and Your Privacy," https://www.facebook.com/notes/facebook-and
-privacy/protecting-your-passwords-and-your-privacy/326598317390057

"How to Tweet Your Way Out of a Job," http://wp.me/pbOIs-Xv

"Twitter Gets You Fired in 140 Characters or Less," http://on.msnbc.com/LvuLn9

"Study Finds One Third of Employers Have Disciplined Employees Using Social Media," http://
www.socialbusinessnews.com/study-finds-one-third-of-employers-have-disciplined-employees
-using-social-media-2

"Jobvite 2012 Social Recruiting Survey," http://web.jobvite.com/2012-social-recruiting-survey
.html?utm_source=M-D-SRSurvey12-blog

"17 People Who Were Fired for Using Facebook," http://www.businessinsider.com/facebook-fired
-2011-5?utm_source=twbutton&utm_medium=social&utm_campaign=warroom

"FCRA & Mobile Apps: A Word of Warning," http://business.ftc.gov/blog/2012/02/fcra-mobile
-apps-word-warning

USA vs. Spokeo, Inc. Consent Order, http://www.ftc.gov/os/caselist/1023163/120612spokeoorder.pdf.

"Spokeo to Pay $800,000 to Settle FTC Charges Company Allegedly Marketed Information to
Employers and Recruiters in Violation of FCRA," http://www.ftc.gov/opa/2012/06/spokeo.shtm

FTC, "Fair Credit Reporting," http://www.ftc.gov/opa/reporter/finance/creditreporting.shtml

Fair Credit Reporting Act (FCRA), *15 U.S.C. § 1681 et seq.*

CHAPTER 3

"Transparency for Copyright Removals in Search," http://googleblog.blogspot.com/2012/05/
transparency-for-copyright-removals-in.html#!/2012/05/transparency-for-copyright-removals-in
.html

REFERENCES

"Twitter Transparency Report," http://blog.twitter.com/2012/07/twitter-transparency-report.html

"The Twitter Rules," https://support.twitter.com/articles/18311-the-twitter-rules#

"Facebook Confirms It Shut Down the Cool Hunter's Facebook Page over Copyright Infringement," http://tnw.to/f5kn

"The Cool Hunter—When Facebook Disables Your Fan Page," http://www.thecoolhunter.net/article/detail/2126/when-facebook-disables-your-fan-page

YouTube Copyright Center, http://www.youtube.com/yt/copyright/what-is-copyright.html

The Digital Millennium Copyright Act of 1998, http://www.copyright.gov/legislation/dmca.pdf

"Injuries as Debris Flies into Daytona Stands During Fiery NASCAR Crash, *CNN.com*, http://www.cnn.com/2013/02/23/us/florida-daytona-crash/index.html

"NASCAR Blocks Eyewitness Video of Daytona Crash, but YouTube Reverses the Takedown," http://vrge.co/YtwZIC

"NASCAR Crash: What Happened to Fan's Video?#comments," http://www.washingtonpost.com/blogs/erik-wemple/wp/2013/02/23/nascar-crash-what-happened-to-fans-video/

17 USC § 107— Limitations on exclusive rights: Fair use

Circular 9, U.S. Copyright Office, Work-Made-for-Hire Under the 1976 Copyright Act

CHAPTER 4

"FTC Closing Letter to Ann Taylor Stores," http://www.ftc.gov/os/closings/100420anntaylorclosingletter.pdf

Section 5 of the Federal Trade Commission Act, *15 U.S.C. § 45*

"Social Studies: Applying the FTC's Revised Endorsement Guides in New Marketing Media," http://business.ftc.gov/documents/social-studies-applying-ftcs-revised-endorsement-guides-new-marketing-media

"FTC Publishes Final Guides Governing Endorsements, Testimonials," http://www.ftc.gov/opa/2009/10/endortest.shtm

"Ann Taylor Investigation Shows FTC Keeping Close Eye on Blogging," http://adage.com/u/GjWiI1b

"Sears Settles FTC Charges Regarding Tracking Software," http://ftc.gov/opa/2009/06/sears.shtm

"MySpace Settles FTC Charges That It Misled Millions of Users About Sharing Personal Information with Advertisers," http://ftc.gov/opa/2012/05/myspace.shtm

"Public Relations Firm to Settle FTC Charges That It Advertised Clients' Gaming Apps Through Misleading Online Endorsements," http://ftc.gov/opa/2010/08/reverb.shtm

In the Matter of Reverb Communications, Inc., et al., FTC File No. 092 3199

"FTC Settling Case over 'Fake' iTunes Reviews," http://news.cnet.com/8301-13578_3-20014887-38.htm

"Firm to Pay FTC $250,000 to Settle Charges That It Used Misleading Online 'Consumer' and 'Independent' Reviews," http://ftc.gov/opa/2011/03/legacy.shtm

CHAPTER 5

"FTC Staff Revises Online Advertising Disclosure Guidelines," http://www.ftc.gov/opa/2013/03/dotcom.shtm

FTC, "How to Make Effective Disclosures in Digital Advertising," http://www.ftc.gov/os/2013/03/130312dotcomdisclosures.pdf

REFERENCES

"FTC Reboots .com Disclosures: Four Key Points and One Possible Way to Bypass the Issue Altogether," http://business.ftc.gov/blog/2013/03/ftc-reboots-com-disclosures-four-key-points-and-one-possible-way-bypass-issue-altogethe

The FTC Act, *15 U.S.C. § 57a(a)(1)(B)*

CHAPTER 6

"10 Companies That Hit the Bullseye with Online Contests," http://mashable.com/2012/01/09/online-contests/

"With Pinterest-Fueled Photo Contest, Panasonic Wades into New Social Waters," http://adage.com/article/digital/panasonic-social-waters-pinterest-photo-contest/235502/

31 U.S.C. §§ 5361–5366, Unlawful Internet Gambling Enforcement Act of 2006

"CAN-SPAM Act: A Compliance Guide for Business," http://business.ftc.gov/documents/bus61-can-spam-act-compliance-guide-business

"How to Run a Legitimate Contest, Sweepstake, or Giveaway," http://www.sba.gov/community/blogs/community-blogs/business-law-advisor/how-use-contests-sweepstakes-and-giveaways-mark

"Prize Offers: You Don't Have to Pay to Play!" http://www.ftc.gov/bcp/edu/pubs/consumer/telemarketing/tel17.shtm

"California Department of Consumer Affairs: Rules for Operation of Contests and Sweepstakes," http://www.dca.ca.gov/publications/legal_guides/u-3.shtml (Business and Professions Code sections 17539-17539.3, 17539.35)

"Contests/Sweepstakes/Gifts/Prizes," http://consumerwiki.dca.ca.gov/wiki/index.php/CONTESTS/SWEEPSTAKES/GIFTS/PRIZES

Rhode Island, Title 11, Chapter 50 of the Rhode Island General Laws, 1956, Reenactment of 1994, http://sos.ri.gov/documents/business/misc/GamesofChance.pdf

"How to Ensure Facebook Doesn't Tear Down Your Wall," http://bit.ly/pR0W1c

"Busting Common Misconceptions About Contests, Sweepstakes and Giveaways on Facebook," http://www.bulbstorm.com/media/Facebook-Promotion-Myths-Whitepaper.pdf?utm_source=Landingpage-FBM1&utm_medium=Whitepaper&utm_campaign=Q311-FBmyths

"SAS Up for Grabs," http://www.youtube.com/watch?v=r2zzZsoPrtM&feature=player_embedded

Direct Marketing Association, "Sweepstakes Do's and Don'ts for Marketers: A 'Plain Language' Guide to the Deceptive Mail Prevention and Enforcement Act of 1999," http://www.dmaresponsibility.org/Sweepstakes/

"Internet Rallies to Send Pitbull to the Most Remote Walmart in America," http://gawker.com/5922523/internet-rallies-to-send-pitbull-to-the-most-remote-walmart-in-america

"Pitbull Heading to Walmart in Alaska After Internet Prank, http://articles.nydailynews.com/2012-07-18/news/32734315_1_armando-christian-perez-pitbull-kodiak

"Horace Mann School for the Deaf in Allston Gets a Personal Gift from Taylor Swift," http://www.boston.com/names/2012/10/01/horace-mann-school-for-the-deaf-allston-gets-personal-gift-from-taylor-swift/GDs3zPxWK5XO2msI1JxirJ/story.html?comments=all

"Twitter Guidelines for Contests on Twitter," https://support.twitter.com/groups/31-twitter-basics/topics/114-guidelines-best-practices/articles/68877-guidelines-for-contests-on-twitter#

REFERENCES

"The Twitter Rules," https://support.twitter.com/articles/18311-the-twitter-rules#

"Google+ Pages Contest and Promotion Policies," http://www.google.com/intl/en/+/policy/pagescontestpolicy.html

"LinkedIn Promotions Guidelines," http://developer.linkedin.com/linkedin-certified-developer-program-terms-and-promotions-guidelines

"Pinterest Acceptable Use Policy," http://pinterest.com/about/use/

"Pinterest Terms of Service," http://pinterest.com/about/terms/

"Tumblr Contest, Sweepstakes, and Giveaway Guidelines," http://www.tumblr.com/policy/en/contest_guidelines

"YouTube's Contest Policies and Guidelines," http://support.google.com/youtube/bin/answer.py?hl=en&answer=1620498

"YouTube Partner Program," http://www.youtube.com/yt/creators/partner.html

"Section 74.06 of the Competition Act," http://www.competitionbureau.gc.ca/eic/site/cb-bc.nsf/eng/01279.html

"All Ontario Guide for Business: Promotional Contests," http://allontario.ca/2012/08/misleading-advertising-and-labelling/

At Risk, volume 20, issue 1, British Columbia, Spring/Summer 2012, http://www.fin.gov.bc.ca/PT/rmb/ref/AtRiskSpringSummer2012.pdf

"Resort Company Penalized for Running Misleading Contests," http://www.competitionbureau.gc.ca/eic/site/cb-bc.nsf/eng/03157.html

CHAPTER 7

"Facebook Wins an $873 Million Judgment Against Spammers That It Will Never Collect," http://techcrunch.com/2008/11/24/facebook-wins-an-873-million-judgment-against-spammers-that-it-will-never-collect/

"Marketing Tactics: Facebook Wins $873 Million Judgment in Spam Case," http://www.insidefacebook.com/2008/11/24/marketing-tactics-facebook-wins-873-million-judgment-in-spam-case/

Order Granting 13 Facebook, Inc.'s Application for Default Judgment by Court Against Adam Guerbuez and Atlantis Blue Capital. Signed by Judge Jeremy Fogel on 11/21/08. *(jflc2, Court Staff) (Filed on 11/21/2008)*, http://docs.justia.com/cases/federal/district-courts/california/candce/5:2008cv03889/206207/25/

"MySpace Wins $234 Million in Anti-spam Case," *Los Angeles Times*, http://articles.latimes.com/2008/may/14/business/fi-myspace14

"Facebook Files Federal Suit Against 'Spam King' Sanford Wallace," http://www.insidefacebook.com/2009/02/27/facebook-files-federal-suit-against-spam-king-sanford-wallace/

"Facebook Security's Notes, Spam Updates (MaxBounty)," http://www.facebook.com/note.php?note_id=442722120765

FCC, "Spam: Unwanted Text Messages and Email," http://www.fcc.gov/guides/spam-unwanted-text-messages-and-email

"CAN-SPAM Act: A Compliance Guide for Business," http://business.ftc.gov/documents/bus61-can-spam-act-compliance-guide-business

REFERENCES

MySpace, Inc. v. Wallace, 498 F. Supp. 2d 1293 (C.D. Cal. 2007)

Facebook, Inc. v. MaxBounty, Inc., Case No. CV-10-4712-JF (Order Denying Motion to Dismiss, September 14, 2011)

15 U.S.C. 7701, et seq., "Controlling the Assault of Non-Solicited Pornography and Marketing"

Canada's Anti-Spam Legislation, http://fightspam.gc.ca/eic/site/030.nsf/eng/home

Canadian Radio-Television and Telecommunications Commission Act, the Competition Act, the Personal Information Protection and Electronic Documents Act and the Telecommunications Act *S.C. 2010, c. 23 http://lois-laws.justice.gc.ca/eng/AnnualStatutes/2010_23/FullText.html*

EU - Unsolicited communications - Fighting Spam, http://ec.europa.eu/information_society/policy/ecomm/todays_framework/privacy_protection/spam/index_en.htm

UK Information Commissioner's Office, http://ico.gov.uk/

ICO, "Marketing Texts," http://www.ico.gov.uk/for_the_public/topic_specific_guides/marketing/texts.aspx

"Fine Threatened Over Mobile Spam Deluge," http://www.bbc.co.uk/news/technology-19788367

"ICO Blog: Illegal Marketing Clampdown Begins as Spam Texters Set for Six Figure Fine," http://www.ico.gov.uk/news/blog/2012/illegal-marketing-clampdown-begins-as-spam-texters-set-for-six-figure-fine.aspx

"The Twitter Rules," https://support.twitter.com/articles/18311-the-twitter-rules#

FCC, "Spam: Unwanted Text Messages and Email," http://www.fcc.gov/guides/spam-unwanted-text-messages-and-email

"Addressing Spam on Pinterest," https://pinterest.zendesk.com/entries/21307138-addressing-spam-on-pinterest

"Instagram Community Guidelines," http://help.instagram.com/customer/portal/articles/262387-community-guidelines

CHAPTER 8

"Privacy and Data Management on Mobile Devices," http://pewinternet.org/Reports/2012/Mobile-Privacy.aspx

"FTC Publishes Guide to Help Mobile App Developers Observe Truth-in-Advertising, Privacy Principles," http://www.ftc.gov/opa/2012/09/mobileapps.shtm

"Remarks of Commissioner Julie Brill Before the Executive Committee of the CTIA—The Wireless Association," http://www.ftc.gov/speeches/brill/110607ctiaremarks.pdf

"FTC Issues Final Commission Report on Protecting Consumer Privacy," http://www.ftc.gov/opa/2012/03/privacyframework.shtm

"Apple's App Store Downloads Top 15 Billion," http://www.apple.com/pr/library/2011/07/07Apples-App-Store-Downloads-Top-15-Billion.html

FTC, "Marketing Your Mobile App: Get It Right from the Start," http://business.ftc.gov/documents/bus81-marketing-your-mobile-app

CHAPTER 9

"Judge in US Defamation Rules Blogger Not Journalist," http://reut.rs/v7X0su

Electronic Communications Privacy Act of 1986 (ECPA), U.S. Department of Justice, http://www.it.ojp.gov/default.aspx?area=privacy&page=1285

REFERENCES

"The Legal Magic Bullet That Protects Twitter and Yelp," http://paidcontent.org/2011/03/05/419
-the-legal-magic-bullet-that-protects-twitter-and-yelp/

"Section 230 of the Communications Decency Act," *Citizen Media Law Project*, http://
wwwcitmedialaw.org/section-230

Reno v. American Civil Liberties Union, 521 U.S. 844 (1997)

18 U.S.C. § 2510-22, Electronic Communications Privacy Act of 1986

47 USC § 230, Communications Decency Act (Protection for private blocking and screening of
offensive material)

"Investigative Blogger Must Pay $2.5 Million," *Courthouse News Service*, http://www.courthousenews
.com/2012/03/29/45154.htm

"Judge Clarifies That Bloggers Can Be Journalists (Just Not One in Particular)," http://
mediadecoder.blogs.nytimes.com/2012/04/02/judge-clarifies-that-bloggers-can-be-journalists
-just-not-one-in-particular/?pagewanted=print

Time, Inc. v. Hill, 385 US 374 (1967)

New York Times Co. v. Sullivan, 376 U.S. 254 (1964)

"Number of States with Shield Law Climbs to 40," http://www.rcfp.org/browse-media-law-resources/
news-media-law/news-media-law-summer-2011/number-states-shield-law-climbs

Battaglieri v. Mackinac Center for Public Policy, 680 N.W.2d 915, 919 (Mich. Ct. App. 2004)

"Blogger Giving Advice Resists State's: Get a License," http://www.nytimes.com/2012/08/07/us/
nutrition-blogger-fights-north-carolina-licensing-rebuke.html?_r=1

"Setting the Record Straight," http://www.ncbdn.org/file_a_complaint/recent_press_inquiry/

Privacy, 48 Calif. L. Rev. 383 (1960) - California Law Review

"Java Judge Orders Google and Oracle to Reveal Paid Bloggers," Wired Enterprise, *Wired.com*, http://
www.wired.com/wiredenterprise/2012/08/google-v-oracle-paid-bloggers/

"Oracle v. Google Trial: Evidence of Willful Infringement Outweighs Claims of Approved Use,"
http://www.fosspatents.com/2012/04/oracle-v-google-trial-evidence-of.html

"Google, Oracle Must Disclose Payoffs to Bloggers, Journalists," Intellectual Property, *Technologist*,
http://shar.es/vyVmU

Cal. Civ. Code § 3344 : California Code — Section 3344

"California Facebook Settlement Protects Right of Publicity," http://blogs.findlaw.com/california_
case_law/2012/06/california-facebook-settlement-protects-right-of-publicity.html

17 U.S.C. Sec. 512

CHAPTER 10

http://www. defense.gov/socialmedia

http://www.defense.gov/home/features/2009/0709_socialmedia/

"DoD Social Media Policy," http://www.dtic.mil/whs/directives/corres/pdf/DTM-09-026.pdf

"Social Media @ DoD," http://www.defense.gov/home/features/2009/0709_socialmedia/

http://www.osc.gov/haFederalFurtherRestrisctionandActivities.htm

10 U.S.C. § 933 : US Code — Section 933: Art. 133. Conduct unbecoming an officer and a
gentleman"

Uniform Code of Military Justice, *10 U.S.C.A. § 801 et seq.,* http://www.au.af.mil/au/awc/awcgate/
ucmj.htm

REFERENCES

"Defense Department to Announce Balanced Social Media Policy," http://www.defense.gov/news/
newsarticle.aspx?id=55948

"Marine Discharged for Obama Facebook Comments," http://online.wsj.com/article/SB100014240
52702304811304577366121551396072.html

10 U.S.C. § 933 : US Code — Section 933: Art. 134

"Frequently Asked Questions Regarding Social Media and the Hatch Act," http://www.osc.gov/
documents/hatchact/federal/Social%20Media%20and%20the%20Hatch%20Act%202012.pdf

U.S. Office of Special Council, The Hatch Act, http://www.osc.gov/hatchact.htm

The Hatch Act, 5 U.S.C. § 1501 et seq

CHAPTER 11

"What Happens to Your Facebook Account When You Die?" *Lawyers.com Blog*, http://blogs.lawyers
.com/2012/02/what-happens-to-facebook-account-when-you-die/

James Pitkin, "Access Denied: A Beaverton Woman's Fight for Her Dead Son's Website Ends in a
First-of-a-Kind Lawsuit Against Facebook.com," *Willamette Week*, April 18, 2007, http://www
.wweek.com/portland/article-6889-access_denied.html

Electronic Communications Privacy Act of 1986 *(ECPA Pub. L. 99-508, Oct. 21, 1986, 100 Stat.
1848, 18 U.S.C. § 2510-2522*

Stored Communications Act, *18 U.S.C. §§ 2701-12*

"Who Owns Your Social Media Accounts?" http://econsultancy.com/blog/10046-who-owns-your-social
-media-accounts?utm_campaign=blogtweets&utm_medium=socialnetwork&utm_source=twitter

"Lawsuit May Determine Who Owns a Twitter Account," http://nyti.ms/uEWPRD

CHAPTER 12

International Chamber of Commerce's Commission on Marketing and Advertising, http://www
.iccwbo.org/advocacy-codes-and-rules/areas-of-work/marketing-and-advertising/

Advertising and Marketing Communication Practice Consolidated ICC Code

"Advertising and Marketing Community in China Adopts ICC-Based Code," http://bit.ly/Nj94w6

"ICC Regulator FAQ," http://codescentre.com/index.php/toolkit/faq-s?view=category&id=95

China Responsible Marketing Code, http://info.wfa.be/ICAP-WFA/China_Responsible_
Marketing_Principles.pdf

ICC Commission on Marketing and Advertising, http://www.iccwbo.org/advocacy-codes-and-rules/
areas-of-work/marketing-and-advertising/

"New Code for Marketing Communications in the Fast-Evolving Media Era to Be Adopted by
European Advertising Self-Regulatory Bodies," http://www.easa-alliance.org/News/Press-releases/
page.aspx/47?xf_itemId=27&xf_catId=2

"Self-Regulation in Europe," http://www.easa-alliance.org/About-SR/Self-regulation-in-Europe/
page.aspx/124

The International Council on Advertising Self-Regulation, http://www.google.com/url?sa=t&rct=
j&q=&esrc=s&frm=1&source=web&cd=2&ved=0CD8QFjAB&url=http%3A%2F%2Fwww
.easa-alliance.org%2Fbinarydata.aspx%3Ftype%3Ddoc%2FICAS_memberleaflet_oct11
.pdf%2Fdownload&ei=5BELUPC7Lqnd6wHnyeWUCg&usg=AFQjCNHupO9pjRAx5X
Lo6wWRdc_YZyYL1Q&sig2=qMryobomFYbjOCSzucXtrg

REFERENCES

EASA, "Cross-Border Complaints," http://www.easa-alliance.org/Complaints-compliance/
Cross-Border-Complaints/page.aspx/247

"Issue Brief—Digital Marketing Communications," http://www.easa-alliance.org/Issues/Digital
-Media/page.aspx/97

CHAPTER 13

"About the IAB," http://www.iabeurope.eu/About.aspx

ASA Advertising Codes, http://www.asa.org.uk/Advertising-Codes.aspx

"Monitoring Compliance," http://www.asa.org.uk/ASA-action/Monitoring-compliance.aspx

"ASA Adjudications," http://www.asa.org.uk/ASA-action/Adjudications.aspx

"Brands, Here's How to #makeitcount on Twitter and Not Fall Foul of the ASA like Wayne Rooney
and Nike," http://premgyani.visibli.com/share/HOQbkH

"Nike Given Red Card for Rooney Tweets," News, *Marketing Week*, http://www.marketingweek
.co.uk/news/nike-given-red-card-for-rooney-tweets/4002286.article

"Nike Twitter Campaign Banned in UK for Lack of Transparency," http://mashable
.com/2012/06/20/nike-twitter-banned/

"Nike Becomes First UK Company to Have Twitter Campaign Banned," http://gu.com/p/
38exv/tw

"ASA Adjudication on Nike (UK) Ltd," http://www.asa.org.uk/ASA-action/Adjudications/2012/6/
Nike-(UK)-Ltd/SHP_ADJ_183247.aspx

"TOWIE Star Criticised by ASA for Tweet," http://gu.com/p/39vzz/tw

IAB Europe EU Framework for Online Behavioural Advertising, http://www.iabeurope.eu/
media/94528/2012-06-08_iab_europe_oba_framework.pdf

ASA Council, http://www.asa.org.uk/About-ASA/ASA-Council.aspx

UK Committee on Advertising Practice, http://www.cap.org.uk/About-Us.aspx

UK Committee on Advertising (Non-Broadcast), http://www.cap.org.uk/About-Us/CAP-Non
-broadcast.aspx

"Arsenal's Jack Wilshere Warned by Uefa over Twitter Betting Comment," http://gu.com/p/38qmh/
tw

"Jack Wilshere Betting Row: Wilshere Rapped for Arsenal Wager Boast," *The Sun*, http://www
.thesun.co.uk/sol/homepage/sport/football/4420291/Jack-Wilshere-betting-row-Wilshere
-rapped-for-Arsenal-wager-boast.html

"£65m Deal Makes Wayne Rooney 'World's Highest Paid Player,'" http://www.metro.co.uk/
sport/844898-65m-deal-makes-wayne-rooney-worlds-highest-paid-player

The UK Code of Non-broadcast Advertising, Sales Promotion and Direct Marketing (CAP Code),
http://www.cap.org.uk/The-Codes/CAP-Code.aspx

"The FTC's Revised Endorsement Guides: What People Are Asking," http://business.ftc.gov/
documents/bus71-ftcs-revised-endorsement-guideswhat-people-are-asking/

"ASA Adjudication on Mars Chocolate UK Ltd," http://www.asa.org.uk/ASA-action/
Adjudications/2012/3/Mars-Chocolate-UK-Ltd/SHP_ADJ_185389.aspx

"ASA Adjudication on Toni and Guy (Lakeside) Ltd," http://www.asa.org.uk/ASA-action/
Adjudications/2012/7/Toni-and-Guy-(Lakeside)-Ltd/SHP_ADJ_193054.aspx

REFERENCES

CHAPTER 14

"Dell Rings Up $6.5 Million in Sales Using Twitter (Update2)," *Bloomberg*, http://www.bloomberg
.com/apps/news?pid=newsarchive&sid=akXzD_6YNHCk

"Interview with Michael Dell," *Discovery*, http://dsc.discovery.com/tv-shows/curiosity/
videos/m-dell-how-has-social-media-helped-businesses-communicate-with-consumers.htm

"FTC Closing Letter in the Matter of Cole Haan," *FTC File No. 142-3041, March 20, 2014,* http://
www.ftc.gov/system/files/documents/closing_letters/cole-haan-inc./140320colehaanclosingletter
.pdf

Federal Trade Commission Act, *Section 5: Unfair or Deceptive Acts or Practices,* http://www
.federalreserve.gov/boarddocs/supmanual/cch/ftca.pdf

CONCLUSION

"FTC to Examine Effects of Big Data on Low Income and Underserved Consumers at September
Workshop," http://www.ftc.gov/news-events/press-releases/2014/04/ftc-examine-effects-big
-data-low-income-underserved-consumers

"What You Should Know About the EU's 'Internet of Things' Privacy Framework," http://
socialmediavoice.com/2011/04/what-you-should-know-about-eus-new.html?spref=tw

"Looking for Guidance, Pharma Left Waiting," http://adage.com/article/news/drug-makers-wait
-fda-ruling-social-media-dtc-ads/149214/

"FTC: .com Disclosures: How to Make Effective Disclosures in Digital Advertising," http://www.ftc
.gov/sites/default/files/attachments/press-releases/ftc-staff-revises-online-advertising-disclosure
-guidelines/130312dotcomdisclosures.pdf

"FDA Issues First Draft of Social Media Guidelines," *PR Week,* http://www.prweekus.com/article/
fda-issues-first-draft-social-media-guidelines/1280679

"Over 17 Million Selfies Uploaded to Social Media Every Week," http://www.dailymail.co.uk/femail/
article-2536597/Were-selfie-obsessed-Over-17-million-self-portraits-uploaded-social-media
-week-55s-taking-aged-18-24.html

"Google Eyes a Creepier Glass—a Camera-Bearing Contact Lens," http://readwr.it/r1hi

"Obama Takes 'Selfie' at Mandela's Funeral Service," *Washington Times*, http://wtim.es/1i2yEi2

"Can You Tweet from Your Fridge?" http://on.wsj.com/N585uc

Index

INDEX

Glen Gilmore, Esq.

G len Gilmore is a social media marketing strategist, educator, and attorney who has been recognized among the "Top 50 Social Media Power Influencers" two years in a row by Forbes, the "Top 100 Thought Leaders" in the fields of content marketing and the Internet of Things by Onalytica, and a "Twitter powerhouse" by the Huffington Post. He is one of the top twenty people most retweeted by digital marketers in North America.

A contributing author to *Strategic Digital Marketing*, Gilmore has provided customized social media training to members of the Fortune 500, including Johnson and Johnson and FedEx, as well as to nonprofit and business enterprises of various sizes.

Gilmore develops and teaches executive MBA courses in digital and social media marketing at Rutgers University, where he has also presented executive courses in brand management and crisis communications, optimizing emerging tech and trends in digital marketing and compliance, as well as social media law and governance.

His comments on digital marketing, social media, and emerging digital trends have been quoted in the Associated Press, Reuters, ABC News, CNN, MSNBC, Bloomberg, Politico, *Fortune*, and *USA Today*, among others.

Dubbed a "man of action" by *TIME* magazine, Gilmore is a former two-term mayor of Hamilton, New Jersey's eighth-largest city. During his tenure as mayor, Gilmore served as the chair of the New Jersey League of Municipalities Economic Development Task Force and as a member of the board of directors of Robert Wood Johnson University Hospital. He has helped develop and deliver crisis leadership training funded by the U.S. Department of Homeland Security, through Texas A&M University. A former judicial law clerk and municipal prosecutor, he is a member of the American Bar Association.

A part-time restaurateur (his wife is the full-time restaurateur), he wrestles firsthand with the challenges and opportunities of using social media for a small business.

You may find him on Twitter at @GlenGilmore, where he has over 260,000 followers, as well as at @SocialMediaLaw1, @HealthcareSMM, @FinancialSM, @CrisisSocMedia, @NYSocialMedia, @UKSocialMedia, and @EUSocialMedia.